edicated January 14th. 1912.

MW01125937

"Every Christian congregation has a history and a story to tell. In *A Light on the Hill*, Caleb Morell tells the story of Capitol Hill Baptist Church in Washington, DC. You can take for granted that any church located in the heart of the federal government of America's capital city is going to have a particularly interesting story. But this is no ordinary history. It is one of the most compelling histories of a church that I have ever read. It is really well done and tells the incredible story of a congregation that started with a vision of ministry to the nation's capital but now reaches to the ends of the earth with its witness and influence. This is an honest and moving story of faithful believers who, in season and out of season, kept a congregation alive. Above all, it is a story of God's faithfulness to Christ's church."

R. Albert Mohler, Jr., President, The Southern Baptist Theological Seminary

"This beautifully written, well-researched book tells the story of a faithful, Bible-believing, gospel-preaching church in our nation's capital. It provides a fascinating and instructive picture of God's providence in the life of a congregation. Those who are called to shepherd the flock will find meaningful encouragement, useful perspective, and sobering warning in this history of the Capitol Hill Baptist Church in Washington, DC. Christ loves his bride, and histories of his people gathered into congregations afford us the opportunity to reflect on God's faithfulness to use his ordinary means of grace to accomplish his purposes and build up the church. I sat in the pews of this church when I was a teenager serving as a US Senate page. More recently, I have followed the ministry of this congregation for the last thirty years because it is pastored by my dear friend Mark Dever. But I had no idea that the history of this church was so interesting and important. Caleb Morell has now remedied that, and delightfully so. I'm so thankful for his diligence in mining the past and presenting it in such an enjoyable and edifying way."

Ligon Duncan, Chancellor and CEO, Reformed Theological Seminary

"Many books on American religious history offer surprisingly little information about the everyday life of churches, the institutions that define Christian faith for the average believer. Caleb Morell's *A Light on the Hill* offers a major corrective to this deficiency with a riveting account of how one evangelical congregation changed and matured over time. Not only does Morell brilliantly tell the story of Capitol Hill Baptist Church, but he also places the church and its people in a rich cultural and theological context."

Thomas S. Kidd, Yeats Endowed Chair of Baptist Studies, Midwestern Baptist Theological Seminary

"I love the church, I love churches, and I love books about churches. I've always loved reading biographies of specific churches, and this is among the best I've ever read. Based on years of archival research, and with a good flare for the dramatic, Morell tells the fascinating 150-year story of Capitol Hill Baptist Church in Washington, DC. Morell's approach is edifying without being pedantic, honest without being censorious, and rich in detail without getting lost in the weeds. The result is a book that deserves a wider audience than local church histories usually enjoy."

> **Kevin DeYoung,** Senior Pastor, Christ Covenant Church, Matthews, North Carolina; Associate Professor of Systematic Theology, Reformed Theological Seminary, Charlotte

"Through meticulous research and the lives of vivid characters, Caleb Morell tells the story of one of the most significant evangelical churches in America. He relates times of grim struggle as well as joyous success—because both shed light on the broader history of Washington, DC, and American Protestantism and both offer thought-provoking lessons for Christians today."

> **Molly Worthen,** Associate Professor of History, University of North Carolina at Chapel Hill

"The summer after September 11, 2001, I headed to Washington, DC, to help Congress bolster homeland security. I didn't know what I wanted to do with my career. A ministry recommended that I check out Capitol Hill Baptist Church. My life and ministry have never been the same. In the more than twenty years since that summer, I have never known a more influential church. I have met leaders around the world who were raised up and sent out by this congregation. Thanks to Caleb Morell we now have a history of God's remarkable work among the saints on Capitol Hill. What an engaging and often inspiring story."

> **Collin Hansen,** Vice President for Content and Editor in Chief, The Gospel Coalition; Host, *Gospelbound* podcast

"The history of Washington's Capitol Hill Baptist Church is an instance of luminous particularity—in this case how the story of a singular church sheds light on the entire landscape of evangelical Christianity in America. From the aftermath of the Civil War to the era of Donald Trump, this one strategically located church has borne witness to the faithfulness of God and continues to do so still. Well researched and well written, this is an irrepressible story and a great read!"

> **Timothy George,** Distinguished Professor of Divinity, Beeson Divinity School, Samford University; General Editor, Reformation Commentary on Scripture

"The history of American Christianity is in many ways the history of local churches. The community of disciples now called Capitol Hill Baptist Church has long been a local church that gathers in one of the most significant and strategic locales in the United States. In *A Light on the Hill*, Caleb Morell offers a model for writing local church history. Morell's book is well researched but sympathetic and edifying. He contextualizes the church's history but acknowledges throughout that God is the one who has worked in and through the church. He draws upon the stories of key members (some quite famous!) and signals events (both good and bad) to illumine the church's unique story. And he reminds readers that decline never has to mean demise. The Lord delights in revitalizing local churches, through godly leaders committed to scriptural means, for his glory and the sake of the kingdom. Highly recommended."

Nathan A. Finn, Professor of Faith and Culture and Executive Director of the Institute for Transformational Leadership, North Greenville University

"Alongside the United States Capitol, the Supreme Court, and the Library of Congress, Capitol Hill hosts another crucial institution—Capitol Hill Baptist Church. Founded in 1867, the church has taken a stand for the historic Christian gospel and for a polity rooted in the Bible, making it a model for others. This carefully researched volume shows how that has been achieved."

David Bebbington, Emeritus Professor of History, University of Stirling

A Light on the Hill

A Light on the Hill

*The Surprising Story of How a Local
Church in the Nation's Capital
Influenced Evangelicalism*

Caleb Morell

Foreword by Mark Dever

WHEATON, ILLINOIS

A Light on the Hill: The Surprising Story of How a Local Church in the Nation's Capital Influenced Evangelicalism

© 2025 by Caleb Morell

Published by Crossway
       1300 Crescent Street
       Wheaton, Illinois 60187

All rights reserved. No part of this publication may be reproduced, stored in a retrieval system, or transmitted in any form by any means, electronic, mechanical, photocopy, recording, or otherwise, without the prior permission of the publisher, except as provided for by USA copyright law. Crossway® is a registered trademark in the United States of America.

Cover design and illustration: Jordan Singer

First printing 2025

Printed in the United States of America

Scripture quotations are from the ESV® Bible (The Holy Bible, English Standard Version®), © 2001 by Crossway, a publishing ministry of Good News Publishers. Used by permission. All rights reserved. The ESV text may not be quoted in any publication made available to the public by a Creative Commons license. The ESV may not be translated in whole or in part into any other language.

All emphases in Scripture quotations have been added by the author.

Hardcover ISBN: 978-1-4335-9289-8
ePub ISBN: 978-1-4335-9291-1
PDF ISBN: 978-1-4335-9290-4

Library of Congress Cataloging-in-Publication Data

Names: Morell, Caleb, 1992- author.
Title: A light on the hill : the surprising story of how a local church in the nation's capital influenced evangelicalism / Caleb Morell ; foreword by Mark Dever.
Description: Wheaton, Illinois : Crossway, 2025. | Includes bibliographical references and index.
Identifiers: LCCN 2024011449 (print) | LCCN 2024011450 (ebook) | ISBN 9781433592898 (hardcover) | ISBN 9781433592904 (epdf) | ISBN 9781433592911 (epub)
Subjects: LCSH: Evangelicalism—Washingon DC—History. | Capitol Hill Baptist Church (Washington, D.C.)—History.
Classification: LCC BV3775.W3 M67 2025 (print) | LCC BV3775.W3 (ebook) | DDC 286/.1753—dc23/eng/20240925
LC record available at https://lccn.loc.gov/2024011449
LC ebook record available at https://lccn.loc.gov/2024011450

Crossway is a publishing ministry of Good News Publishers.

SH			34	33	32	31	30	29	28	27	26	25
15	14	13	12	11	10	9	8	7	6	5	4	3	2	1

For the members of Capitol Hill Baptist Church, past, present, and future.
May you continue to shine as lights in the world (Phil. 2:15).

Contents

List of Illustrations   *xiii*

Foreword by Mark Dever   *xix*

Introduction: A Light on the Hill   *1*

1   "What Shall the Harvest Be?": 1867–1878   *7*

2   "A Helper of the Downtrodden and Lowly": 1878–1882   *33*

3   "With Conscience Void of Offence toward God and Man":
1882–1884   *53*

4   "We Do Our Own Thinking in This Church": 1885–1889   *69*

5   "We Have a Leader of National Reputation": 1890–1895   *81*

6   "The Future Is Bright with Promise": 1896–1912   *105*

7   "War, Fuel Famine, and Influenza Epidemics": 1913–1918   *119*

8   "No Modernism Will Be Tolerated at All in This Church":
1919–1943   *137*

9   "Holding Forth the Word of Life": 1944–1955   *155*

10   "A Beachhead for Evangelical Christianity": 1956–1960   *181*

11   "Jesus Doesn't Need a Parking Lot": 1961–1980   *193*

12   "When a Christian Leader Falls": 1981–1993   *227*

13   "Preach, Pray, Love, and Stay": 1994–2000   *251*

14   "Doing Nothing and Church Planting": 2001–Present   *269*

Conclusion   *297*

Afterword   *301*
Acknowledgments   *305*
Illustration Credits   *309*
General Index   *315*
Scripture Index   *325*

Illustrations

Figures

1.1   Thomas Ustick Walter (1804–1887)   *11*

1.2   E Street Baptist Church, Washington, DC   *13*

1.3   Amos Kendall (1789–1869)   *15*

1.4   Joseph W. Parker (1805–1887)   *18*

1.5   An artist's sketch of Capitol Hill in 1872   *21*

1.6   Celestia A. Ferris (1844–1924)   *22*

1.7   Metropolitan Baptist Church's first building   *26*

1.8   Tombstone of Abraham and Celestia Ferris   *31*

2.1   Parker Hall, the main building of Wayland Seminary   *36*

2.2   Tombstone of Joseph W. Parker   *50*

3.1   Lester Edwin Forrest Spofford (1843–1887)   *56*

3.2   Letter of Resignation of W. M. Ingersoll   *61*

3.3   New building of Grace Baptist Church, built by East Capitol Street Baptist Church   *64*

4.1   William H. Young (1853–1915)   *71*

4.2   Sketch of proposed new church building at corner of 6th and A Streets NE   *75*

4.3   The 1876 and 1888 church buildings, side-by-side   *76*

5.1   General Green Clay Smith (1826–1895)   *83*

5.2   Church directory, Metropolitan Baptist Church, 1895   *86*

5.3   Children's Sunday school class in front of Metropolitan's new building   *90*

5.4   Warren C. Brundage's life insurance policy application   *93*

5.5   Metropolitan's membership and Sunday school scholars   *94*

5.6   Women's Sunday school class in 1945   *99*

5.7   Front cover of the *Metropolitan Messenger* in 1910   *101*

6.1   Liston D. Bass (1854–1930) in a 1908 newspaper   *108*

6.2   John Compton Ball (1863–1950)   *111*

6.3   John Compton Ball's preaching license   *112*

6.4   Newly constructed Metropolitan Baptist Church in 1912   *115*

6.5   Metropolitan Baptist cornerstone-laying ceremony   *116*

7.1   Stephen T. Early (1889–1951)   *121*

7.2   Interior of Metropolitan's sanctuary decorated for Palm Sunday   *124*

7.3   Interior of sanctuary with folding chairs in the west hall for Palm Sunday   *124*

7.4   Billy Sunday's outdoor tabernacle   *127*

7.5   John Compton Ball greeting Thomas Joseph Early Jr.   *133*

8.1   Newspaper clipping featuring Amy Lee Stockton
       (1892–1988)   *138*

8.2   Metropolitan's *Evening Star* advertisement for T. T. Shields,
       W. B. Riley, and J. Frank Norris   *141*

8.3   John Compton Ball in the pulpit   *148*

8.4   John Compton Ball in the pulpit on Easter Sunday   *149*

8.5   Symbolic burning of Metropolitan's mortgage   *150*

8.6   Service commemorating John Compton Ball's retirement   *151*

8.7   Walter Brooks greets John Compton Ball   *152*

9.1   Billy Graham (1918–2018) preaching at
       the Capitol building   *156*

9.2   Metropolitan's choir director and a church member in
       military uniform   *157*

9.3   Agnes Shankle and students from her Sunday school class   *158*

9.4   K. Owen White and John Compton Ball at portrait
       unveiling   *160*

9.5   K. Owen White with John Compton Ball and
       Agnes Shankle   *163*

9.6   Metropolitan's choir   *165*

9.7   K. Owen White officiating a baptismal celebration   *168*

9.8   K. Owen White and missionaries with President Truman at
       the White House   *169*

9.9   *Evening Star* newspaper clipping picturing Billy Graham,
       J. Walter Carpenter, and Cliff Barrows   *173*

9.10   Crowds listening to Billy Graham speaking on
       the steps of the Capitol   *175*

9.11   Advertisement for Metropolitan Baptist Church's
       radio ministry   *177*

9.12   Agnes Shankle's Sunday school class   *179*

10.1   Announcement of Walter Pegg's sermon series in
       the church bulletin   *184*

10.2   Carl F. H. Henry (1913–2003)   *186*

10.3   Revision of church roll, December 1956   *189*

11.1   Protesters blocking construction crews   *195*

11.2   Mary's Blue Room   *197*

11.3   Metropolitan's first parking lot   *199*

11.4   Jeanette Devlin directing the children's choir   *202*

11.5   J. Walter Carpenter discusses school integration in
       the *Metropolitan Messenger*   *204*

11.6   Sketch of the Johenning Baptist Center's new building   *207*

11.7   Front cover of the *Metropolitan Messenger* in 1961   *213*

11.8   John R. Stuckey officiating at the Lord's Supper on
       New Year's Eve   *218*

11.9   Margaret Roy, Luella Dicks, and Jessie Reichard   *222*

11.10 Wade Freeman pictured at the church's centennial
       celebration   *224*

12.1   Walt Tomme Jr.   *233*

12.2   Bill, the young man and deacon who stayed and
       fought for the church   *237*

12.3   Harry Kilbride (1934–2022)   *239*

12.4   Harry Kilbride's book *When a Christian Leader Falls*   *247*

13.1   Roger Nicole, R. Albert Mohler Jr., Timothy George, and Harold J. Purdy   *259*

13.2   Mark Dever on his balcony   *260*

14.1   Card advertising the fall 2001 CHBC sermons   *276*

14.2   CHBC net membership increases and decreases 2001–2019   *279*

14.3   T4G 2011 speakers   *290*

Tables

4.1   Protracted meetings at Metropolitan Baptist Church, 1884–1888   *77*

4.2   Measures of effectiveness of protracted meetings, Metropolitan Baptist Church, 1884–1888   *78*

14.1   CHBC membership and budget, 1999–2005   *280*

Foreword

NOT LONG AGO, I asked the author, "Who will buy a book on the history of a church?" He replied, "I'm not sure. Maybe people who like biographies? I'm telling the story of a life, the life of a congregation."

As I thought about it, that answer sounded better and better. And then I read the manuscript, and I found it surprisingly compelling! People I'd never heard of sprang to life! The author has researched thoroughly and written elegantly. He has selected stories to typify themes in one decade after another. Individual characters come alive—the one-armed Antietam vet, the widow foundress of the church, the scamming pastor, the female evangelist, the pastor whose mind was changed by Martin Luther King Jr.'s "Letter from Birmingham Jail." I could go on and on.

The reader will be glad to know that this is not a mere chronicle—that is, a verbal timeline along the lines of "this happened in 1894, and then this in 1895; in March this occurred, and then this other person died in July." Caleb Morell has masterfully given us an overview of a congregation's life—a moving, multigenerational picture. He has succeeded in telling one story, stretched over 150 years.

My interest in this church (and churches generally) is not unique. Pastors who've labored here before me have done many of the same things that I've attempted. There really is nothing new under the sun—everything from membership classes and purges to expositional preaching and prayer meetings—all these were being done before I became pastor or was even born! The compelling figures are numerous— Joseph Parker, the abolitionist pastor who argued with Lincoln in person; Agnes Shankle, the faithful member who stood up to the pulpit search committee and perhaps, thereby, saved the congregation from liberal compromise; K. Owen White, the reforming expositor who later gained fame for a question he asked Senator John F. Kennedy when he ran for president. So packed with characters is this story that not all of these tasty details could be included. But there are so many more stories and so many interesting characters.

My own connection with this congregation not only increases my interest but also gives me a particular, strange sensation in the last couple of chapters. If the Lord tarries, I am helped to see how little of me (or anyone) is left on the pages of a book that recounts thirty years of my life and ministry in a congregation.

I pray that God will use the story—humbling to me, helpful to you—of this one local church to encourage you to persevere in faithfulness and to consider how you can stir up others to such love and good deeds as we read about in these pages. And I pray that he will, in his grace, keep this light on the Hill shining brightly until Christ returns.

Mark Dever
SENIOR PASTOR
CAPITOL HILL BAPTIST CHURCH
WASHINGTON, DC
JANUARY 2024

Introduction

A Light on the Hill

*Through the years of its history Metropolitan has been known
as a Bible-believing, Gospel-preaching church. It has not been
afraid to raise its voice in defense and proclamation of the truth!*

K. OWEN WHITE, SEPTEMBER 14, 1947[1]

THIS IS NOT THE STORY of an extraordinary church. No sitting US
president has ever attended its services. Little attention has ever been
paid to it by press or academy. Even to this day, passersby and tourists
visiting the national capital hardly take notice of the large brick building at the corner of Sixth and A Streets NE.

True, the church has had its share of colorful members and pastors: the abolitionist and educator Joseph W. Parker, the congressman
and governor turned pastor and temperance advocate Green Clay
Smith, early leaders of the conservative resurgence of the Southern
Baptist Convention like K. Owen White and Carl F. H. Henry, and
the pioneer of church health and Baptist ecclesiology Mark Dever.

---

1   K. Owen White, "Pastor's Paragraphs," Metropolitan Baptist Church Bulletin, September 14, 1947,
    MS 1792, box 9a, folder 6, Capitol Hill Baptist Church Archives, Washington, DC (hereafter,
    CHBC Archives).

Capitol Hill Baptist Church has truly enjoyed an abundance of gifted preachers and larger-than-life characters. As church clerk Francis McLean commented in 1892, "If we've been spoiled with anything it has been by good preaching."[2]

But this is not fundamentally a story about any of them. Ultimately, this story is about God and how he delights to do extraordinary things through ordinary people and ordinary churches.

Jesus's promise that the gates of hell would not prevail against his church (Matt. 16:18) was not given to any particular church but to the church universal. No local church is promised that it will remain until Christ's return. Rather, from the days of the apostles, new churches have been birthed and rebirthed, died and disappeared to this day. But though not given to any particular church, Jesus's promise to the church universal will not be fulfilled apart from the local church as members faithfully pass the torch of the gospel from one generation to the next.

Oftentimes, however, our zeal for gospel advance exceeds our wisdom and our trust in God's ordinary means. Like the Israelites of old, we are more impressed with the height of Saul than the heart of David. So we overestimate what we can do in the short term and underestimate what God can do in the long run. We settle for new programs rather than investing in people. And we operate in fear rather than by faith in God's promises. In a dizzying world of distractions and new methods, where do we look for models of quiet faithfulness that endures?

From Celestia A. Ferris's first prayer meeting in November 1867 onward, the story of Capitol Hill Baptist Church reminds us that the work of God has been carried on by ordinary people who lived hidden lives and who rest in unvisited tombs. Some, such as Celestia's husband, Abraham Ferris, did not even live to see the church planted in 1878. But they believed that the local church was a cause worth giving their lives for, even if they did not see the results in their own

---

2   Francis McLean, "The Reunion," February 29, 1892, MS 1322, box 5, folder 22, CHBC Archives.

lifetimes. And it is only because of their quiet faithfulness that the church is what it is today. As Francis McLean wrote in 1886, "We are working partly for those who come after us."[3] Or as Matt Schmucker told his wife at one of the church's lowest moments in 1992, "We're here for the people who will come."[4]

In our age of megachurches and celebrity pastors who burn hot and fast and rarely last, the idea of unpaid lay members spending their lives for local churches sounds absurd. But the fruit speaks for itself, and 150 years later, the gospel is still being proclaimed from the pulpit of Capitol Hill Baptist Church. This book probes the factors and conditions that contribute to gospel faithfulness. How does a church preserve the gospel? What factors contribute to church health? How does a healthy church steward success and grow without becoming unhealthy?

The relevance of these questions is nowhere more clearly indicated than in the alarming rate that churches are closing their doors around our nation and cities today. In their 2023 book *The Great Dechurching*, Jim Davis, Michael Graham, and Ryan Burge describe a religious shift in the last twenty-five years greater than at any other time in American history, as more people have left the church than all those who became Christians during the First and Second Great Awakenings and the Billy Graham crusades combined.[5] Many of these empty pews indicate churches that abandoned the gospel and ceased to be churches long before their buildings were converted to condominiums. Others left the city due to rising rates of crime and have yet to return to their neighborhoods of origin. To this day, few of Washington's oldest churches remain centered on the gospel and present in their neighborhoods.

3   Clerk's Annual Report, December 31, 1886, MS 1583b, box 6, folder 5, CHBC Archives.
4   Matt Schmucker, interview with the author, September 7, 2022, part 1, Washington, DC.
5   Jim Davis and Michael Graham with Ryan P. Burge, *The Great Dechurching: Who's Leaving, Why Are They Going, and What Will It Take to Bring Them Back?* (Grand Rapids, MI: Zondervan Reflective, 2023), 5.

Though hardly the oldest Baptist church in Washington, DC, Capitol Hill Baptist Church has not moved on from the gospel nor moved on from its location. Ultimately, the church stayed centered on the gospel and present in the place God planted it because of the ordinary people who worked, prayed, sowed, and stayed. This book is an attempt to tell their story: the story of the church that stayed.

This is not a story of a perfect church. It contains as many warnings as it does positive examples. There were fights, splits, conflicts, and dissensions. There were contentious members' meetings filled with vitriol and spite. There were as many nights of tearful sowing as there were days of joyful reaping. But throughout seasons of plenty and seasons of scarcity, the light of the gospel has continued to shine on Capitol Hill.

Early in the life of Capitol Hill Baptist Church, the bulletins often contained this prayer: "May the Metropolitan Baptist Church continue to be 'A Light Set on a Hill.'"[6] The prayer combines the two images from Jesus's words in Matthew 5:14: "You are the light of the world. A city set on a hill cannot be hidden." From its earliest days, Capitol Hill Baptist Church understood itself to be a light on the Hill. Not *the light* but *a light*. As the church's music director wrote in 1963, "Therefore we will look to the future and work in the present and those future generations shall look back on us and say, 'Yes, the light still burned brightly on Capitol Hill.'"[7]

This book tells the story of how Capitol Hill Baptist Church has navigated the past century and a half as an evangelical witness in Washington. Through wars and pandemics, racial unrest and church splits, God has kept the light of the gospel shining on Capitol Hill. Along the way, we are introduced to the ordinary people who made

---

6   Fortieth Anniversary Celebration of Gilbert A. Clark's Class, March 4, 1938, MS 1360, box 5, folder 25, CHBC Archives.

7   John D. Cochran, "85 Years on Capitol Hill," February 24, 1963, MS 1371, box 5, folder 27, CHBC Archives.

history, as Capitol Hill Baptist Church was transformed from a small congregation in sleepy East Washington to a thriving congregation just blocks away from the center of world power.

Capitol Hill Baptist Church has been known by three names throughout its history. It was formed in 1878 as Metropolitan Baptist Church. In 1963, the church added "Capitol Hill," and for thirty years it was known as Capitol Hill Metropolitan Baptist Church (or CHMBC). In 1995, the name changed again, this time dropping "Metropolitan," to its present name (or CHBC). All three names are used throughout, alternating use based on time period.

Throughout you will meet the warring factions that split during the Civil War and the pastor who reunited them. You will meet the washerwoman, Celestia Ferris, who started the prayer meeting and Sunday school that later covenanted as a church. You will hear how a church split nearly destroyed the church just six years into its existence—and meet the remarkable pastor who saved it. You will learn about the church's involvement in the fundamentalist movement, participation in World War I, and response to the Spanish flu. You will discover how Capitol Hill Baptist became a bastion for neo-evangelicalism after World War II, organizing Billy Graham's 1952 crusade in Washington and becoming the home church to Carl F. H. Henry, the founding editor of *Christianity Today*. You will hear about the church's attempts to grapple with racial unrest during the Civil Rights Movement and its commitment to remaining a city church while other churches were relocating to the suburbs. Finally, you will discover the challenges Mark Dever faced when arriving in 1994 as a freshly minted PhD from Cambridge University. Behind all of these events and figures, however, is the eternal God and Lord of history who is writing the story of this church, and of every church, into a tapestry of grace that will stretch through eternity.

Is the light of the gospel still shining in your church? What will it take for the torch of the gospel to be passed to another generation?

It will take ordinary men and women who share the conviction of missionary Jim Elliot, whose immortal words are etched into a pillar on the edge of CHBC's property: "He is no fool who gives what he cannot keep to gain what he cannot lose."[8] It will take patience, perseverance, and—above all—prayer so that if the Lord tarries, it will yet be said, "The light still burns brightly on Capitol Hill."

---

8   Quoted in Elisabeth Elliot, *Through Gates of Splendor* (Wheaton, IL: Tyndale, 1981), 172.

1

"What Shall the Harvest Be?"

1867–1878

THE SNOWFALL WAS LIGHT on that Monday evening in November 1867. Hundreds of granite and marble gas street lights populated the emerging neighborhood of Capitol Hill with their oversized bronze and glass lanterns, illuminating the gently falling snow with a warm, white light. As the snow, interspersed with smoke, shone in the moonlight, a handful of warmly dressed figures could be seen making their way to a small, two-story frame house at 214 A Street NE—the home of a newly married couple, Abraham and Celestia Ferris.[1]

There was nothing ostentatious about the house. Built in 1857, the dwelling predated the late Victorian brick homes that would come to populate the Capitol Hill neighborhood. Yet from its perch on a berm atop a low brick wall, the home gave off an artificial appearance of grandeur as it peered over A Street. Its three bedrooms, each warmed by separate

---

1 Many of the details surrounding this first prayer meeting come from the anonymous manuscript Historical Sketch of Metropolitan Baptist Church, n.d., MS 1344, box 5, folder 23, Capitol Hill Baptist Church Archives, Wasington, DC (hereafter, CHBC Archives). Based on a cross comparison with the church minutes that ordered a history to be drawn up, the document appears to date to approximately December 21, 1887. Cf. Metropolitan Baptist Church Minutes, December 21, 1887, MS 1602, p. 130, box 6, folder 7, CHBC Archives.

fireplaces, made for a typically modest Civil War-era home. The front door opened to a cozy drawing room, with a brick fireplace on the right, around which the Ferrises and their eight guests gathered.

Another newly married couple, Bentley and Francis Murray, attended the gathering that evening. Originally from New York, Bentley Murray had come to Washington in 1863 seeking a political job in the Lincoln administration.[2] A third pair of newlyweds, Mr. and Mrs. Forrest Spofford, were present, having married just three months earlier.[3]

Also present were John and Fannie Skirving, the oldest couple in the group. John Skirving Jr. had come to Washington in the 1850s with his father, who had been an associate of the nationally famous Thomas Ustick Walter, the chief architect for the US Capitol dome. As the Skirvings walked from their residence at 108 Eleventh Street SE along East Capitol Street toward the Ferrises' home, John and his family enjoyed an unobstructed view of the newly completed Capitol dome, the project that had originally brought their family to Washington.

Not to be left out, Celestia's sixty-year-old mother, Anna, and older sister Camilla likewise made the familiar trek to the Ferrises' home that evening. The group of friends had been called together by Celestia, but the cause for their gathering was near and dear to the hearts of each one. They had gathered to pray for a Baptist church to be established on Capitol Hill.

This prayer was no small request. At that time, no Baptist church— or church of any denomination—could be found east of First Street or north of Pennsylvania Avenue.[4] Other than the Murrays, who were members of Second Baptist Church in Navy Yard, the families were all members of E Street Baptist Church, which met just over a mile away on the 600th block of E Street NW.

2 *Laws of the State of New York* (Albany: Weare C. Little, 1862), 832. Cf. "Murray, Bentley P.," Seward Family Digital Archive, accessed October 5, 2021, https://sewardproject.org/node/76431.

3 For additional biographical details, see Patricia F. Staley, *Norwich and the Civil War* (Charleston, SC: History Press, 2015), 92.

4 St. Joseph's Roman Catholic Church was organized in 1868 at the corner of C Street and Second Street.

Celestia, who was twenty-three at the time, had moved from upstate New York to Washington with her family in 1849. Her mother immediately joined E Street Baptist Church, followed by Celestia, who joined by baptism at age fourteen on June 6, 1858.[5] Alongside her sisters Camilla and Emily, Celestia was active in the Sunday school work at E Street, as well as the Woman's Foreign Missionary Society, supporting missionary work internationally and locally.[6]

A Nation at War and a Church Divided

But as Celestia was coming of age, the nation was coming apart.[7] At twelve, Celestia would have listened with horror to stories of murder and intrigue in "bleeding Kansas." At fifteen, she would have watched fear overtake the capital in October of 1859 in the wake of John Brown's raid on Harper's Ferry only sixty miles away. At sixteen, she would have witnessed tensions rise in the city leading up to the presidential election of 1860 and heard reports of a mob attacking a local Republican office on the night of Lincoln's election. Weeks later, she would have heard shouts of jubilation a few days before Christmas at the announcement of the secession of South Carolina. Walking the streets of Washington, she would have overheard scarcely veiled talk of treasonous plots coming from saloons, cafes, and open carriages.

Then the war came. As the Mason–Dixon line divided the country, sectarian strife enveloped Washington's churches, with some churches supporting the Union, some supporting the Confederacy, and others seeking to remain neutral. Celestia's own church—E Street Baptist Church—was not spared from strife, a fact that no one knew better than Thomas Ustick Walter.

5   List of Members of E Street, 1858, 23. Records housed at Restoration Church, 3850 Nebraska Avenue NW, Washington, DC.

6   Celestia Ferris's name appears alongside her sister Emily's regularly in the minutes of the Woman's Foreign Missionary Society of the E Street Baptist Church (1874–1886), preserved at Restoration Church, Washington, DC.

7   The following anecdotes are summarized from accounts reproduced by Margaret Leech, *Reveille in Washington: 1860–1865* (New York: NYRB Classics, 2011), 16–27.

Walter had come to Washington in 1851 as the chief architect of the US Capitol expansion, including the erection of its magnificent dome. He was a world-famous architect, professor, and inventor. He was also a devout Baptist. Walter's religious sentiments were decidedly conservative. He considered the Calvinistic Philadelphia Baptist Confession of Faith (1742)—the American version of the Second London Baptist Confession—the true standard of doctrine ("the faith once delivered to the saints").[8] He opposed innovations in settled ecclesiological practices, even minute details such as the manner of dispensing communion or the posture of the pastor when baptizing.[9] In the worship gathering, he hoped for simplicity and reverence. In preaching, he longed for clarity on doctrine, the simple (though not simplistic) recounting of the gospel, and the plain exposition of Scripture.[10] As he wrote to his wife after one disappointing church service, "I want that instruction to be in accordance with the Bible, but I fear that the days of such teaching are passed."[11]

In politics, as in religion, Walter favored the old ways. Although he was a native of Philadelphia and not a Southerner, he was a slaveholder. While he disdained abolitionists, he reserved his greatest ire for so-called Black Republicans like Abraham Lincoln and Charles Sumner, who in his view were entirely to blame for bringing "these horrid evils upon us."[12] When it came to abolitionism, Walter did not mince words:

Abolitionism I hate with a perfect hatred, and believe both [Abolition and Unitarianism] to be <u>unreasonable, impolite, contemptible</u>

---

8 Thomas Ustick Walter to George W. Anderson, February 16, 1864, Thomas Ustick Walter Collection, Athenaeum of Philadelphia.
9 Thomas Ustick Walter to Rev. Warren Randolph, October 2, 1865, Thomas Ustick Walter Collection.
10 Thomas Ustick Walter to Amanda Walter, April 24, 1865, Thomas Ustick Walter Collection.
11 Thomas Ustick Walter to Amanda Walter, April 21, 1865, Thomas Ustick Walter Collection.
12 Thomas Ustick Walter to George W. Anderson, February 1, 1861, Thomas Ustick Walter Collection.

and <u>wicked</u> in the highest degree, and I have no doubt that the day is not far distant when both will be rooted out of every hole and corner of our land: they both feed on the same pabulum and both must fall before a pure gospel.[13]

To what extent Walter's anti-abolition views were representative of the sentiments of the members of E Street Baptist Church, which Walter joined with his family on moving to Washington, is impossible to say. Nevertheless, Walter soon began teaching a weekly Sunday School class at E Street, which may very well have been attended by Celestia Ferris.

Figure 1.1. In addition to architecture, Thomas Ustick Walter (1804–1887) taught Sunday school classes at E Street Baptist Church in Washington, DC, where he was a member.

13 Thomas Ustick Walter to J. D. King, May 25, 1859, Thomas Ustick Walter Collection (emphasis in original).

Everything changed with the onset of the Civil War. On Saturday, April 13, 1861, news reached Washington that the federal garrison at Fort Sumter had come under fire by Confederate forces. The *Evening Star*—Washington's evening paper—was the first to break the news: "War commenced. Conflict at Charleston. Immense excitement. Bombardment of Fort Sumter."[14] No papers were printed on Sunday. Washingtonians were completely in the dark as the fog of war descended on the nation.

The *Evening Star* described in detail the panic that engulfed Washington from Saturday night into Sunday as residents surrounded newspaper offices for "any news from Charleston." "On Saturday afternoon the pressure upon the Star office was the most intense we have experienced," they wrote. Not only was the interior of the office jammed but also the street in front of the office for some distance was blocked in all directions by the anxious crowd. Those who obtained papers were unable to exit because of the crowd. Fast as the presses worked, they were entirely unable to supply the demand or to thin the crowd of news seekers. Late Saturday evening, the *Evening Star* received news of the surrender of the Union forces at Fort Sumter. The news, the paper later recounted, "was really so unpalatable, that it was at first utterly discredited."[15] But once verified, disbelief gave way to white-hot rage and a thirst for revenge.

As churches gathered for worship the next day, pastors had a choice to make: How would each pray for the divided nation? Joseph Spencer Kennard was only a few years into his pastorate of E Street. As he stepped into the pulpit for his customary pastoral prayer that Sunday, he invoked divine blessing in support of the Federal government, omitting to pray for Jefferson Davis and the Confederate States of America. The deliberate and public display of his political sympathies did not go unnoticed by the congregation. As soon as the prayer concluded, the Southerners in the congregation rose in unison and, after a strained moment of silence, walked out.[16]

---

14   "The Latest News," *Evening Star*, April 13, 1861, 3.
15   "The War News in Washington," *Evening Star*, April 15, 1861, 3.
16   Joseph Spencer Kennard, *Psychic Power in Preaching* (Philadelphia: G. W. Jacobs, 1901), xv–xviii.

Meanwhile, chaos reigned outside the church. Rumors of an imminent Confederate invasion of the capital prompted thousands of Northerners to flee further north. As Thomas Ustick Walter wrote to John Skirving, "Things are in an awful condition here—so terrible that I consider it my duty to get my family off as soon as possible."[17] Telegraph lines to the North and South were cut, leaving Washington in complete darkness. From banks to mercantile shops, the sound of hammers could be heard as owners fitted doors with iron bars and covered windows, preparing for an imminent siege. Meanwhile, local militia were called out and stationed in the Capitol building, the Treasury, and the White House. "This place is done," Walter wrote. "War is upon us."[18]

Figure 1.2. The congregation of Third Baptist Church, founded in 1842, changed its name to E Street Baptist Church in August 1846 after completing its building at 602 E Street Southeast.

As war descended on Washington, divisions deepened at E Street Baptist Church. A *New York Times* article claimed that the church

17 Thomas Ustick Walter to John Skirving, April 20, 1861, Thomas Ustick Walter Collection.
18 Thomas Ustick Walter to Robert Walter, April 20, 1861, Thomas Ustick Walter Collection.

was under the sway of "those who believed in the divine nature of the peculiar institution," namely, slavery.[19] False rumors spread that E Street's former pastor and current president of Columbian College, George Whitefield Samson, was a Confederate sympathizer.[20] But the real crux of the matter came down to questions of church membership and control over the church's Sunday school.

Over the previous months, a proxy war had started over control of the church's Sunday school, with the majority—including Celestia Ferris and Thomas Ustick Walter—deciding that nonmembers would not be permitted to teach or hold the office of Sunday school superintendent.[21] Seeing that they had lost, the minority sought to disband the church and divide up its assets, but when this too failed, Kennard resigned, taking forty-one members to constitute a new congregation: Calvary Baptist Church.[22]

When he resigned, Kennard took with him the chief agitator against E Street's strict practices of membership: Amos Kendall. Kendall, who had served as postmaster general under President Andrew Jackson, made a fortune investing in the company of Samuel Morse, the inventor of the telegraph. Kendall had attended E Street since 1847 and supported the church financially, but he refused to join as a member as a matter of principle. "Your creeds require men to believe undoubtedly altogether too much," he explained to one pastor, "and make religion consist more in *professions of faith* than in the active performance of Christian duties."[23]

Thomas Ustick Walter did not shrink from laying blame over the split at E Street squarely on the shoulders of Kendall. "My impression

---

19 "Religious Emeute at Washington," *New York Times,* May 12, 1862.

20 Thomas Ustick Walter to Amanda Walter, July 8, 1861, Thomas Ustick Walter Collection.

21 Minutes of E Street Baptist Church (1857–1871), February 18, 1862, 79–80, Restoration Church, Washington, DC.

22 Minutes of E Street Baptist Church (1857–1871), May 12, 1862, 100–101.

23 Amos Kendall, *Autobiography of Amos Kendall* (Boston: Lee and Shepard, 1872), 656 (emphasis in original).

is that all these reports originate in that quarter," he wrote to his wife on July 8, 1861. "I would as soon have a family of wild buffaloes after me, as to have that Kendall tribe at my heels."[24]

Figure 1.3. Amos Kendall (1789–1869), postmaster general under President Andrew Jackson, pictured during or shortly after the Civil War.

Frustrated by his lack of control over E Street as a nonmember, Kendall agreed to financially support the newly formed Calvary Baptist Church, personally bankrolling its building but only on the condition that he, as a nonmember, would be in control of the church.

24 Thomas Ustick Walter to Amanda Walter, July 8, 1861, Thomas Ustick Walter Collection.

He accomplished this in two ways. First, Kendall ensured that the church's *constitution* made provision for nonmembers (such as himself) to vote in church elections and business meetings. Second, he retained personal control over the church *deed*, meaning that if the church at any point failed to keep the terms of their agreement, it would forfeit the property.[25] Control of the building would belong to him and his descendants in perpetuity. In this way, Kendall would keep the church under his thumb, as he had failed to do with E Street. Such was the nature of church life in the nation's capital.

Meanwhile back at E Street, Walter's own family was imploding. His oldest and youngest sons enlisted in the Union Army. But his second son and namesake, Thomas Ustick Walter Jr., enlisted in the Confederate Army of Northern Virginia. Walter's unbearable pain over the possibility of his sons meeting on the battlefield only increased with Thomas Jr.'s parting words. Thomas Jr. told his father that if he met his brothers on the "field of blood," he would know "neither kith nor kin."[26]

The war, and the possibility of losing his sons, rocked Walter to his core. Even though he had previously defended that "peculiar institution," he now prayed for its end: "Let slavery go—the quicker the better!"[27] Whereas before the war he had been content to blame both sides ("Northern fanaticism and southern fire-eating has brought it all about"), he now leveled his denunciations squarely at Southern secessionists.[28]

Alone in Washington, with his wife in Philadelphia and his sons fighting for opposing sides, Walter continued his work of constructing

25 Carl W. Tiller and Olive Marie Tiller, *At Calvary: A History of the First 125 Years of Calvary Baptist Church, Washington D.C., 1862–1987* (Manassas, VA: Trinity Rivers, 1994), 8, 11; Kendall, *Autobiography*, 663-64.

26 Thomas Ustick Walter to Thomas Ustick Walter Jr., August 12, 1862, Thomas Ustick Walter Collection.

27 Thomas Ustick Walter to Thomas Ustick Walter Jr., August 12, 1862, Thomas Ustick Walter Collection.

28 Thomas Ustick Walter to Horace Walter, May 2, 1861, Thomas Ustick Walter Collection.

the Capitol dome. But the project had lost its luster. He could no longer gaze at the colossal cast-iron structure without thinking of the cast-iron cannon balls tearing limb from limb on countless battle-fields. Even Walter's crowning achievement, the raising of the Statue of Freedom on top of the dome on December 2, 1863, seemed like a twisted farce. The Lady's sheathed sword and calm repose atop the nation's motto, *E Pluribus Unum* ("Out of many, one"), all seemed to mock Walter's pain and the plight of the nation. How could a divided country, divided families, and divided churches ever hope to be reconciled again?[29]

Reconciled at Last

In January 1865, an old man bearing a striking resemblance to Gen. Robert E. Lee arrived in Washington, DC. In fact, just days after Lee's surrender at Appomattox, the citizens of Richmond frequently mistook Joseph W. Parker for Lee. But Parker was a pastor, not a general. He had recently retired from Shawmut Avenue Baptist Church in Boston and moved to Washington to coordinate the efforts of the New England Freedmen's Aid Society in establishing schools and colleges for African Americans in the South.[30] Though his primary objective was training Black teachers and starting schools, Parker did more than anyone to bring unity to the fragmented Baptists of Washington, and his work started with none other than Amos Kendall.[31]

29 Thomas Ustick Walter to Mary Ann Elizabeth King, August 2, 1862, Thomas Ustick Walter Collection. For a description of the Statue of Freedom, see *Art in the United States Capitol* (Washington, DC: United States Government Printing Office, 1976), 354.

30 "Address to the Public by the Committee on Correspondence of the Educational Commission," *The Liberator*, March 7, 1862, 3. Cf. New England Freedmen's Aid Society Records, 1862–1878, box 1, folder 21, vol. 1, Educational Commission Records, 1862–1874, Massachusetts Histori-cal Society; James M. McPherson, *Struggle for Equality: Abolitionists and the Negro in the Civil War and Reconstruction* (Princeton, NJ: Princeton University Press, 1964), 170; James Melvin Washington, *Frustrated Fellowship: The Black Baptist Quest for Social Power* (Macon, GA: Mercer University Press, 2004), 66.

31 Joseph Whiting Parker Memoirs, 1880, MS 14909, pp. 160, 124, 246, Special Collections, University of Virginia Library, Charlottesville.

Figure 1.4. Joseph W. Parker (1805–1887) pastored two of Boston's most prominent churches before resigning to coordinate the work of the New England Freedmen's Aid Society among former slaves during the Civil War.

On his first Sunday in Washington, Parker walked three blocks from his hotel on Pennsylvania Avenue to the old law school building of Columbian College at Fifth and D Streets NW for the worship service of Calvary Baptist Church. Instantly recognized, he was prevailed upon to preach the following Sunday. Afterwards, the church's benefactor, Amos Kendall, invited Parker to dine, but the pastor declined. The next Sunday, Parker preached again and, for a second time, declined Kendall's invitation to dinner. Only after preaching a third time and receiving still another invitation to dine with Kendall did Parker finally accept. After supper, when left alone with Kendall, Parker began to inquire of him if he regarded himself as a Christian, to which Kendall replied that he "hoped he was."[32]

"Have you ever declared yourself as on the Lord's side?" Parker pressed.

"No," Kendall answered, understanding that Parker was referring to baptism.

"Then you are reckoned with his enemies," Parker charged the affronted Kendall. "Wicked men use your name and point to your life as an argument against the church, saying there is no necessity of maintaining the institutions of the Christian religion," said Parker, gaining momentum as he spoke. "They say, 'Mr. Kendall is a good man. But he is no Christian. So why should I join a church?' Because the better the men, the stronger the testimony against the church."

Kendall was perplexed but still defensive. "But what can I do?" he protested. "I can't accept the creed of any church."

"Do you regard baptism as a rite by which men declare themselves as friends of Christ, as separating themselves from the world?" Parker asked.

"Most certainly I do," Kendall answered. "The ordinance of baptism makes this declaration of loyalty to Christ and of faith in and submission to him."

"Then if you are willing to take your place as his disciple," Parker explained patiently, "and declare yourself as his disciple, I should baptize you. Obey; do what you know as duty and the way will open before you."[33] With this, Parker bade the flustered Kendall goodnight, leaving him to ponder the state of his soul.

To everyone's surprise, just a few weeks later at Calvary's weekly prayer meeting, Kendall stood and declared his intention to join the church by baptism.[34] He explained his reasons, using almost verbatim the words Parker had spoken to him weeks earlier: "Though for many years I have endeavored to live the life of an upright man, yet, by not

32 Parker Memoirs, 144. The following exchange is taken verbatim from Parker's memoirs.
33 Parker Memoirs, 144–45.
34 Kendall, *Autobiography*, 658–59.

attaching myself to the church, I feel that my life was a standing opposition to Christianity."[35]

So on Sunday, April 2, 1865—a week before Lee's surrender in
Virginia—Kendall was baptized into church membership of Calvary.
As a sign of good will, the baptismal pool at E Street Baptist Church
was graciously offered to Calvary for the occasion.[36] "The next news
from Washington," Parker wrote, "was that he [Kendall] had been
baptized and united with the church. As he moved forward his difficulties with creeds disappeared and his happiness increased."[37] Alongside
sectional strife, church membership had played no small part in the
conflict at E Street. But all of Amos Kendall's concerns seemed to have
been alleviated by his encounter with Joseph W. Parker.

The battle between E Street and Calvary Baptist Church had ended,
just in time for the end of the Civil War. A month later, Thomas Ustick
Walter concluded his work on the US Capitol dome, returning from
fractious Washington back to the City of Brotherly Love. Even as E
Street and Calvary found a way to settle their differences, somehow
Walter's family was reunited as his son Thomas voluntarily took the oath
of allegiance to the federal government and was restored to his family.[38]

The war had taken its toll on the country, on its churches, and on
Walter. Gone were the 620,000 brave men who fought "kith and kin" on
endless fields of blood. Gone were the scattered members of the churches

---

35 Kendall, *Autobiography*, 660. In a letter to Rev. A. B. Earle dated March 31, 1865, Kendall used
    similar wording to describe his reasons for being baptized and joining the church at last: "The
    impulse which decided me to unite with them was, in part, a belief that I could do more good
    in the church than out of it, and in part, that my position was in effect a *standing argument with
    the world against Christianity*. I felt that I was looked upon and spoken of as a good man, but
    not a Christian; involving the plain inference, that to be a good man it was not necessary to be
    a Christian." Absalom Backas Earle, *Bringing in Sheaves* (Boston: James H. Earle, 1869), 105
    (emphasis in original).

36 Tiller and Tiller, *At Calvary*, 7.

37 Parker Memoirs, 145.

38 "Thomas has returned to loyalty to the government; he has taken the oath of allegiance, and has
    written me a very good letter. While he stands true to his country I am willing to let the past alone."
    Thomas Ustick Walter to J. D. King, February 16, 1864, Thomas Ustick Walter Collection.

of the once-populous metropolis turned overnight into a military encampment. And gone were the proslavery sentiments of millions who, like Walter, once held the institution as a matter of political and scriptural necessity. But out of the ashes of death, a new day was dawning.

As Lady Freedom sheathed her sword on the pinnacle of Walter's Capitol dome, her gaze settled on a part of the city destined to emerge from the rubbles of war: the long-overlooked neighborhood known as Capitol Hill.

Figure 1.5. An artist's sketch of Capitol Hill in 1872 depicts pre-Civil War era townhouses at 7th and Maryland Avenue NE in Washington. The empty lots, newly constructed gas streetlamps, and worn picket fence give a sense of what Capitol Hill looked like.

A Sunday School Started

By the time Robert E. Lee surrendered the Army of Northern Virginia on April 9, 1865, Celestia Anne *Hunt* (as she was then known) was two weeks from turning twenty-one. As Union troops repopulated the war-weary city, one man caught her attention as they attended services at E Street Baptist Church: a handsome corporal from New Jersey named Abraham Ferris.

As a soldier in Company K of the Seventh New Jersey in the Army of the Potomac, Ferris witnessed the worst of the war, including the

Peninsula Campaign and the Battle of Gettysburg. He distinguished himself at the Battle of Williamsburg in 1862 by saving his captain's life. While the captain was searching for wounded men in the woods during a lull in the battle, a Confederate soldier appeared and shot him just below the ear, nearly severing his tongue. Ferris gave chase, killed the rebel soldier, and carried the wounded captain back to safety.[39]

Ferris began attending services at E Street Baptist Church after an injury forced him to transfer to the Veteran Reserve Corps. Not long after, he was converted and, on July 29, 1866, was baptized into membership of E Street Baptist Church.[40] Less than a year later, on April 23, 1867, Abraham and Celestia were wed.[41] Soon after settling into their home at 214 A Street NE, the Ferrises called their friends together on a crisp November night in 1867 to pray for a Baptist church to be established on Capitol Hill.

Figure 1.6. The only surviving picture of Celestia A. Ferris (1844–1924), founder of the prayer meeting and Sunday school that led to the formation of Metropolitan Baptist Church.

39 This story is recounted in John Hayward, *Give It to Them, Jersey Blues! A History of the 7th Regiment, New Jersey Volunteers in the Civil War* (Hightstown, NJ: Longstreet House, 1998), 34–35.
40 Minutes of E Street Baptist Church (1857–1871), July 29, 1866, 193, Restoration Church.
41 Marriage Records, film no. 002079252, District of Columbia Marriages, Clerk of the Superior Court, Records Office, Washington, DC.

Although Celestia Ferris and her band of friends did not know all the difficulties facing the Baptists of Washington, they prayed to an all-knowing God who did. And as they prayed, he answered—in ways that will only be fully comprehended in eternity. For four years, they continued to pray, until by 1871 their group had grown large enough to open a Sunday school on Capitol Hill. They called it the Capitol Hill Baptist Sunday School. Each Sunday afternoon, the Ferrises, Murrays, Spoffords, and Skirvings sang hymns, read the Bible, and memorized Scripture with neighborhood children. They did not have their own building yet, so they rented a one-story, wooden school building at the corner of Seventh and A Streets NE.[42]

In the nineteenth century, Sunday schools did not exist to provide childcare during services but to evangelize and catechize those who would not otherwise be afforded religious upbringing. Many of the children attending the "Sabbath school" worked during the week and lacked elementary education. Many could not even read. They were the children of immigrants, freed slaves, or poor Whites who lived in squalid conditions, "Alley Dwellings," as they were known, often with one leaky latrine servicing up to thirty families.[43]

Sunday school workers like Celestia Ferris went to such decrepit places to, in their words, "compel the people to come in that the Lord's house might be filled."[44] They hoped to provide children with educational opportunities and religious instruction not otherwise available at home. They hoped to divert children from the sin of "Sabbath-breaking" which, in their minds, would taint the city and the nation.[45] But most

---

42 According to church clerk Francis McLean, this school building successively housed three churches: "Metropolitan Presbyterian, the Metropolitan Baptist and the Grace M.E. Church South." Francis McLean, "The Reunion," February 29, 1892, MS 1322, box 5, folder 22, CHBC Archives.

43 James Borchert, *Alley Life in Washington: Family, Community, Religion, and Folklife in the City, 1850–1970* (Champaign, IL: University of Illinois Press, 1982).

44 "Metropolitan Baptists Celebrate Anniversary," *Washington Herald*, March 1, 1908, 4.

45 Anne M. Boylan, *Sunday School: The Formation of an American Institution, 1790–1880* (New Haven, CT: Yale University Press, 1988), 6–7.

of all, they hoped and prayed that the seeds sown into the hearts of these young people would eventually yield fervent and faithful church members.[46] As Francis McLean would later recall in 1891, "Thus from the starting point, step by step, have all these interests grown, and all are indebted to the Sunday-school."[47]

The work was an instant success. By 1874, the Sunday school workers were ready to purchase property and formally incorporate as an association, which they called the Metropolitan Baptist Association. In their constitution, adopted on June 12, 1874, the forty-four members stated that their aim was the "organization and establishment of a Baptist Church in the Eastern section of the city."[48] Their progress toward that goal took a significant step forward with the purchase of a vacant plot of land at the corner of Sixth and A Street NE on November 7, 1874.[49] The trustees chose the lot because it was one of the highest points of elevation on Capitol Hill.[50]

---

46 As Boylan writes, by 1880 the American Sunday school had become "the primary recruiting ground for church members." Boylan, *Sunday School*, 166.

47 Francis McLean, "Our Sunday-School," *The Metropolitan Baptist*, April 1891, 3, Kiplinger Research Library, Washington, DC.

48 Constitution of the Metropolitan Baptist Association, June 12, 1874, MS 1600, p. 1, box 6, folder 6, CHBC Archives.

49 Proceedings of Board of Trustees, Metropolitan Baptist Association, May 25, 1874, MS 651, box 2, folder 1, CHBC Archives. The trustees purchased the lot from Robert Prout for $1,000. An elderly Episcopalian minister, Prout was the son of the famous landowner William Prout, who had been one of nineteen landowners who signed the 1791 agreement with President George Washington to convey portions of their land to the US government to create a permanent seat of government. Prout, a Baltimore merchant and land speculator, had in turn purchased the land, along with five hundred acres, from Jonathan Slater on March 11, 1791, just days before the location of the federal city was announced, for £20 per acre. Before selling the land to Prout, Slater had used the land for tobacco farming, erecting a plantation on the site where he lived with four "free white females" and twenty-nine slaves, which may have made him the largest slaveholder in the District. "Agreement of the Proprietors of the Federal District, 30 March 1791," in *The Papers of George Washington: Presidential Series*, vol. 8, *22 March 1791–22 September 1791*, ed. Mark A. Mastromarino (Charlottesville: University of Virginia Press, 1999), 24–26, 30; "From George Washington to Thomas Jefferson, 31 March 1791," Founders Online, National Archives, https://founders.archives.gov/; Bob Arnebeck, *Through a Fiery Trial* (Lanham, MD: Madison Books, 1994), 45.

50 "The congregation own the lot on the corner of 6th and A streets, which is said to be the highest point on Capitol Hill." "In the Churches," *Evening Star*, March 3, 1894.

With property in hand, the association began constructing a one-room, brick Sunday school building. To keep the cost low, they agreed to provide the materials themselves. Celestia Ferris even suggested that each child bring any bricks they could find to the construction site. Enthused by her instructions and no doubt eager to please their teacher, two of the girls visited a brickyard in the southeast section of the city and asked for a few bricks. When the owner of the brickyard asked their reason, they explained that they were helping to build a church and that their Sunday school teacher had instructed them to collect bricks. Impressed by their importunity, the owner promised to see what he could do.

In short order, a large stack of brand-new bricks appeared on the church property, courtesy of the brickyard owner. Encouraged by their success, the two girls proceeded to visit two other brickyards, telling them what the first man had done. As a result, two more loads of bricks appeared overnight at the corner of Sixth and A Street NE, one from each of the brickyard owners.

Through the ingenuity and resourcefulness of the children, the only bricks purchased for the erection of the building were the ones used on the front of the building. The rest were collected by children. As Celestia Ferris and others had prayed for the Sunday school children to become "living stones" (1 Pet. 2:5), the very bricks through which the chapel was constructed were the result of prayer.[51]

On February 6, 1876, nine years after their first prayer meeting, the new chapel was dedicated.[52] The trustees congratulated the association on the completion of the chapel, writing that "there is every encouragement to go forward in the good work for which it was organized."[53] With an association formed, property acquired, and a building erected, Celestia Ferris and her band of friends were finally ready to begin holding Sunday services on Capitol Hill.

---

51 This story is recounted in many sources but done so with greatest detail in Historical Sketch of Metropolitan Baptist Church, n.d., CHBC Archives.

52 The date comes from a list of donations on February 6, 1876, under "Dedication," Constitution of the Metropolitan Baptist Association, 32.

53 Constitution of the Metropolitan Baptist Association, 32.

Figure 1.7. The earliest known phtograph of Metropolitan Baptist Church's first building, built in 1876 and demolished in 1911 to construct the present building.

A Church Formed

Between 1876 and 1878, the Metropolitan Baptist Association began hosting a weekly prayer meeting on Wednesday evenings and, soon after that, a Sunday evening prayer service.[54] At last the Baptists of Capitol Hill felt ready: they had a suitable building, manageable debt, and favorable prospects for growth. But they still needed the financial support and the encouragement of other Baptist churches in Washington.

Financial support proved exceptionally difficult to acquire. In 1878 the United States was in its fifth year of an economic recession. The "Panic of 1873" had settled into the "Long Depression," with unemployment peaking in 1878 at an estimated rate of over 10 percent.[55] For many DC churches, it was difficult enough to maintain their own churches, much less contribute to a new one. Thus, the revered Baptist

---

54 Constitution of the Metropolitan Baptist Association, 29.
55 John D. Buenker and Joseph Buenker, *Encyclopedia of the Gilded Age and Progressive Era* (New York: Routledge, 2021), 32.

statesman and deacon at E Street, Andrew Rothwell, argued that the organization of a Baptist church on Capitol Hill should be delayed to "a not distant future day" when "they have cleared their property from debt."[56]

When a group of representatives from Capitol Hill met with Calvary Baptist and E Street on January 3, 1878, most of the questions revolved around "financial prospects and numerical strength."[57] Even beyond contributing to the work financially, Calvary and E Street knew that by encouraging the formation of this new church, they would be losing members who would be diverting their time, attention, and resources elsewhere.

Despite the recession, everyone chipped in to help get the work off the ground. Former rivals—like Calvary and E Street—locked arms together to plant a church on Capitol Hill. Calvary Baptist Church gave $200, Second Baptist $100, and E Street $75. Joseph Parker contributed $25 of his personal funds toward the new venture, and Calvary Baptist also donated old hymn books.[58]

Finally, on February 4, 1878, a group of pastors and representatives of the Baptist churches of Washington, DC, convened at the small brick chapel on Capitol Hill to discuss the prospect of giving recognition to a new church. The chair called the meeting to order by asking those gathered to open Philip Bliss and Ira Sankey's *Gospel Hymns and Sacred Songs*[59] to sing Emily S. Oakey's hymn, "What Shall the Harvest Be?" Though only a few years old, the song was already a favorite among Baptists. Many knew it by heart.

Reflecting on Jesus's parable of the sower, the hymn describes various seasons of sowing—in "weakness and might," with an "aching heart," and with "teardrops"—before concluding with confidence:

---

56 Metropolitan Baptist Church Minutes, February 4, 1878, 4.
57 Metropolitan Baptist Church Minutes, January 3, 1878, 2.
58 Constitution of the Metropolitan Baptist Association, 12, 42.
59 Philip P. Bliss and Ira D. Sankey, *Gospel Hymns and Sacred Songs* (Cincinnati, OH: John Church / Biglow & Main, 1875).

Sown in the darkness or sown in the light,
Sown in our weakness or sown in our might,
Gathered in time or eternity,
Sure, ah! sure, will the harvest be.[60]

With their rich bass and tenor voices reverberating throughout the brick chapel, the pastors and delegates reminded each other of the common mission and purpose that had brought them together that evening. Despite the years of infighting, the church splits, and the war that had rent the nation apart, they were still united by one Spirit in a common mission: gospel sowing and harvest gathering.

That evening the Baptists of Washington came together to lend their support for the first time since the war to establishing a new church in the nation's capital. By passing the following resolution, these once alienated churches were doing more than planting a church. They were planting a flag for Christ in the very heart of the nation:

Resolved, That we tender to the brethren and sisters composing the Metropolitan Association an expression of our fraternal sympathy in their efforts to establish a Gospel church in this section of the city; and reposing confidence in their discretion, wisdom and piety, we recommit to them the matter of organizing said church and the time such organization shall be made.[61]

The jubilant Baptists of Capitol Hill wasted no time in communicating the good news to the rest of their band, urging all interested parties to bring "their letters" to a meeting to be held on Sunday February 27, 1878, where they would formally covenant as a church.[62]

60 Emily S. Oakey, "What Shall the Harvest Be?" (1870).
61 Metropolitan Baptist Church Minutes, February 4, 1878, 4.
62 Metropolitan Baptist Church Minutes, February 13, 1878, 5.

At long last, the church was born. On Sunday, February 27, 1878, at 7:30 p.m., dozens gathered in the chapel at the corner of Sixth and A to covenant together and form the Metropolitan Baptist Church.[63] After a reading of Scripture and prayer, the business began. Letters from various Baptist churches were read one by one, indicating the name and city of the church each person was coming from, as well as the date of the letter. The plurality of letters came from Second Baptist Church in Navy Yard (thirteen in total).[64] Ten came from E Street Baptist Church.[65] Also represented were members joining from Calvary Baptist Church and First Baptist Church, with the four remaining constituent members joining from churches outside of the District.[66]

After the reading of the letters, the members rose to covenant with each other before the Lord:

> Having been led, as we believe, by the Spirit of God to receive the Lord Jesus Christ as our Saviour, and on the profession of our faith, having been baptized in the name of the Father, and of the Son, and of the Holy Ghost, we do now, in the presence of God, angels, and this assembly, most solemnly and joyfully enter into covenant with one another, as one body in Christ.[67]

63 Metropolitan Baptist Church Minutes, February 27, 1878, 5.

64 Metropolitan Baptist Church Minutes, February 27, 1878, 6. These members included Nathan Ellsworth, Martha R. Ellsworth, Anna M. Fenton, Ellen Fitzhugh, John Kingdon, Alverda L. Kingdon, Marion J. N. McLean, Bentley P. Murray, Fannie J. Murray, Charles S. Patten, James Wilker, George W. Williamson, Theodosia E. Williamson.

65 Coming from E Street Baptist Church were Lucy H. Diver, Thurston Lowell, Camilla Lowell, Emma Patten, John Skirving, Fannie Skirving, Carrie F. Skirving, Anna W. Skirving, L. E. Forrest Spofford, Sarah M. Spofford. Metropolitan Baptist Church Minutes, February 28, 1878, 6.

66 Coming from Calvary Baptist Church were Mary A. Pearce and Sarah Pearce; from First Baptist Church, Oliver and Martha Longan. Harriet Detterer and Susan F. Moore brought letters from Tenth Baptist Church in Philadelphia; Mary J. Mount came from Central Baptist Church, Trenton, NJ; and Mary A. P. Taylor brought a letter from Hightstown Baptist Church in Hightstown, NJ. Metropolitan Baptist Church Minutes, February 28, 1878, 6.

67 Metropolitan Baptist Church Minutes, February 28, 1878, 6–7.

Prayer was then offered, and all united in singing "Blest Be the Tie That Binds." A more fitting hymn could hardly be imagined:

> We share our mutual woes,
> our mutual burdens bear,
> and often for each other flows
> the sympathizing tear.
>
> When we are called to part,
> it gives us inward pain;
> but we shall still be joined in heart,
> and hope to meet again.[68]

As they sang to one another, they knew they were making a promise—a covenant. They knew they lacked the ability to keep that covenant by their own power, so they prayed, asking God for grace and aid in time of need.

Tragically, Celestia's husband Abraham did not live to see that day. He died less than a year before, on July 28, 1877, at the age of forty-four from lingering Civil War wounds. He was buried in Arlington Cemetery, leaving her as a thirty-three-year-old widow and mother of three young children. With memories of her recently departed husband swirling through her mind, Celestia joined the newly formed church in singing those words,

> When we are called to part,
> it gives us inward pain;
> but we shall still be joined in heart,
> and hope to meet again.

---

68 John Fawcett, "Blest Be the Tie That Binds" (1782). The congregation closed its quarterly members' meeting on January 21, 1880, by singing this same hymn. Metropolitan Baptist Church Minutes, January 21, 1880, 50.

Figure 1.8.   Tombstone of Abraham and Celestia Ferris in Arlington Cemetery, Virginia. The inscription indicates that Abraham was a corporal in Company K of the 7th New Jersey in the Army of the Potomac.

The name Celestia Ferris only appears occasionally in the minutes of the church, of which she remained a faithful member until her death on December 1, 1924, at age eighty.[69] She lived what George Eliot has called "a hidden life," spending her days performing "unhistoric acts" and being buried in an unvisited tomb in Arlington.[70] Her name, however, has not been forgotten, and her legacy continues in the lives impacted through the ministry of the church she started.

The band of friends had come a long way since that first night of prayer in 1867. Without prayer, what would have happened? Would

69 "Mrs. C. A. Ferris, 80, Church Leader, Dies," *Evening Star* December 3, 1924, 7.

70 George Eliot, *Middlemarch* (New York: Penguin Books, 1994), 838.

it have lasted? Would it still be bearing fruit today, apart from the prayerful initiative of twenty-three-year-old Celestia Ferris? Prayer had birthed a Sunday school, which had grown into a church. But they still had a long way to go to become a beacon of light on the Hill. Their greatest and most pressing need was for a regular pastor. And for that, the hopes of the happy band lay once again in the hands of the inestimable Joseph W. Parker.

2

"A Helper of the Downtrodden and Lowly"

1878–1882

ALTHOUGH METROPOLITAN was officially a church, plenty of work remained to be done. There was wood to split in order to keep the terra-cotta-lined wood stove heated during the cold winter months, grass to cut outside the chapel, fences to move and paint, and sidewalk repairs to attend to. On the south and west edges, a chipped picket fence marked off the bounds of the church property from the lots owned by its neighbors, including a coal yard on the adjacent lot. On the north end of the lot, the uneven grading of Sixth Street and A Street NE made for an unattractive corner, necessitating the placement of wooden steps as a temporary solution to the "vanished and vanishing sidewalk." Even more inconveniently, the building was not yet connected to the District's sewage system, forcing attendees to avail themselves of an outdoor privy.[1]

Despite these external concerns, the church's greatest need was for a "permanent pastor." Between 1877 and 1878, the church had hired

---

1 Reports of Board of Trustees, October 21, 1878, MS 654, box 2, folder 2, Capitol Hill Baptist Church Archives, Washington, DC (hereafter, CHBC Archives).

Stephen H. Mirick to preach and lead services until "such time as it may be deemed advisable to call a regular Pastor."[2] With Mirick's health worsening and the church's financial position strengthening, the members felt ready to call a pastor who could "devote his whole time to the work before us."[3] For that, the fledgling congregation on Capitol Hill turned once again to Joseph W. Parker.

Joseph W. Parker

In 1878 Joseph Whiting Parker (1805–1887) was not just one of the most seasoned and experienced Baptist pastors in DC but one of the most respected pastors in the country. His varied responsibilities had included lengthy pastorates at two of Boston's most prominent churches: First Baptist Church of Cambridge and Shawmut Avenue Baptist Church. During the Civil War he had gained notoriety for coordinating the efforts of the New England Freedman's Aid Society by organizing schools for former slaves across the South.[4] No stranger to

2   Metropolitan Baptist Church Minutes, March 8, 1878, MS 1602, p. 10, box 6, folder 7, CHBC Archives. According to William Cathcart, Mirick was "quite active in promoting Sunday-school interests and in supplying churches destitute of pastors." William Cathcart, *The Baptist Encyclopaedia* (Philadelphia: L. H. Everts, 1883), 801. Before helping Metropolitan, Mirick had served as president of the Albemarle Female Institute in Charlottesville, Virginia (where the Baptist missionary Lottie Moon studied); pastor of First Baptist Church in Camden, New Jersey; and professor of Greek at Lewisburg College (now Bucknell University). Neil A. Benfer, "A History of First Baptist Church, 735 Park Street, Charlottesville, Viginia," MS 99 (unpublished manuscript, n.d.), pp. 4–10, Albemarle Charlottesville Historical Society, Charlottesville, Viginia; *Manual of the First Baptist Church of Lewisburg: Containing a Historical Account of the Church, Declaration of Faith, Covenant, Rules of Order* (Lewisburg, PA: First Baptist Church of Lewisburg, 1859), iii.
3   Metropolitan Baptist Church Minutes, December 18, 1878, 36.
4   Joseph Whiting Parker Memoirs, 1880, MS 14909, p. 246, Special Collections, University of Virginia Library, Charlottesville. Parker's unpublished memoirs were transcribed by his great-grandson and were held by Virginia Parker in Phillipsburg, New Jersey. In 1962, James M. McPherson, while a graduate student at Johns Hopkins University, made use of Parker's memoirs for his dissertation "The Abolitionists and the Negro During the Civil War and Reconstruction" (PhD diss., Johns Hopkins University, 1962), which was published as James M. McPherson, *The Struggle for Equality: Abolitionists and the Negro in the Civil War and Reconstruction* (Princeton, NJ: Princeton University Press, 2014), 170n36. Later the transcription of Parker's memoirs was deposited with the Special Collections of the University of Virginia. James M. McPherson, personal correspondence with author, January 15, 2021.

Washington, Parker met repeatedly with president Abraham Lincoln, successfully convincing the president to move the location of the trial of one of his parishioners to Boston.[5] Between 1861 and 1864, Parker gave himself tirelessly to the work of educating freed people, visiting each of the Atlantic States many times, training teachers, preachers, and organizing schools in many towns and cities.[6]

Wherever possible, Parker sought to reclaim church buildings, which had often been confiscated by Union generals for military use. One day, Parker presented his credentials to a military surgeon who was using a church edifice for a military hospital, ordering him to vacate the property so that it could be used by an African American congregation. When the frustrated surgeon snarled, "Why you are a sort of pope, aren't you?" Parker replied, "Yes. A Christian minister and military pope. Go!"[7]

During his frequent visits to the nation's capital, Parker took special interest in the state of African American churches. He played an instrumental role in forming Berean Baptist Church and Wayland Seminary—the training college for African Americans that Booker T. Washington later attended—which named its main building Parker Hall in his honor.[8]

Supporting Black churches and educating the formerly enslaved had become a passion of Parker's through his firsthand encounters with slavery as a twenty-four-year-old. Before confronting slavery's horrors, Parker's views were typical for a Northerner and a Protestant, regarding the institution as "a necessary evil." Gradually, Parker's views changed.

5 Parker Memoirs, 143-145. Matthew Martens discusses Parker's role in the famous "Smith Case" in detail in Matthew T. Martens, *Reforming Criminal Justice: A Christian Proposal* (Wheaton, IL: Crossway, 2023), 71–72, 89–90.

6 Cathcart, *The Baptist Encyclopaedia*, 892.

7 Parker Memoirs, 127–28. Parker's unusual role in confiscating buildings for the use of the freedmen is discussed in James Melvin Washington, *Frustrated Fellowship: The Black Baptist Quest for Social Power* (Macon, GA: Mercer University Press, 2004), 66.

8 Albert Witherspoon Pegues, *Our Baptist Ministers and Schools* (Springfield, MA: Willey, 1892), 562. Pegues describes Parker as one of four "chief patrons" of the seminary that trained hundreds of African American teachers and pastors. Parker also moderated the interracial council that gave recognition to Berean Baptist Church on May 16, 1877. Minutes of the Berean Baptist Church, May 16, 1877, 3–4, The People's Archive, Washington, DC.

Figure 2.1. Parker Hall, the main building of Wayland Seminary (now defunct), then located at Meridian Hill in Washington, DC. In 1899 Wayland merged with another school to become Virginia Union University in Richmond.

In 1829, Parker moved to Charlotte County, Virginia, where he lived on a 1,790-acre slave plantation called Homewood and taught the children of the plantation's owner and operator, Nicholas Sterling Edmunds (1776–1864).[9] With the encouragement of Edmunds, Parker began visiting slave cabins to "talk of Jesus Christ" and the good news of salvation.[10] "Some of them were converted," Parker wrote. "I was most deeply interested in their spiritual welfare."[11] From 1829 to 1831, Parker witnessed extraordinary fruit. In addition to the slaves, nearly sixty or seventy of his students were converted, including five of Edmunds's children. One day, the normally reserved Edmunds fell around Parker's neck, embracing him, and saying, "All that makes me so happy in my family I owe to you!"[12] Parker was happy in his

9   Parker Memoirs, 11. For more details into Nicholas Edmunds and his plantation, see the Edmunds family papers, 1826–1950, MS 1Ed596a, Virginia Historical Society, Richmond, VA.
10   Parker Memoirs, 14.
11   Parker Memoirs, 14.
12   Parker Memoirs, 13.

work, convinced by the fruit of his evangelism that he ought to pursue pastoral ministry.

Then, almost overnight, everything changed. On August 21, 1831, just a hundred miles from Edmunds's plantation, Nat Turner led a slave rebellion that shook the nation. When the carnage ended two days later, dozens of White Virginians and over a hundred slaves were dead. Across the Southern states, legislators responded by passing the most restrictive laws against African Americans to date. According to a law passed that same year in Virginia, any White person who "assemble[d] with negroes for the purpose of instructing them to read or write" or "associate[d] with them in an unlawful assembly" could be sentenced up to six months' imprisonment.[13] Suddenly, the very things Parker had been doing among the slaves on Edmunds's plantation became illegal.

Days later, over breakfast, Edmunds looked up at Parker and told him plainly, "I think you should not religiously instruct the negroes anymore."

Surprised, Parker asked why, pointing to the example of one slave who had recently been converted. "Don't you think John is a Christian? Is he a worse slave than before?"

"I believe John is a true Christian," Edmunds responded. "If my hope of heaven were half as bright as my confidence that John is fit for it, I should be a much happier man than I am."

"Is John not as good and faithful a servant as he was before his conversion?" Parker pressed.

"Entirely faithful and I could trust him with anything. But he feels himself," Edmunds paused, searching for the right words. "He feels himself a man accountable to God. You see when Isaac was buried the other day, I saw him standing on the pile of earth they had thrown out and heard him exhorting his fellow servants to prepare to meet their God in the judgment. You see, John feels he is a man accountable to

---

13 *The Code of Virginia* (Richmond: William F. Ritchie, 1849), 748 (§ 54.198.32). For further discussion see Randolph Ferguson Scully, *Religion and the Making of Nat Turner's Virginia: Baptist Community and Conflict, 1740–1840* (Charlottesville, VA: University of Virginia Press, 2008).

God, and, what God requires of a man, and a master may require of his slave may be very different things and opposite. So you must stop instructing my slaves."

Feeling his blood rising, Parker went on the offensive. "Do you believe that Jesus Christ has given us a system of religion which has bidden us to preach to every creature which is dangerous for all to be instructed in?"

"We can't philosophize on that subject," said Edmunds, waiving his hand dismissively. "But suppose you go down to the negro quarter tonight and read that part of the sermon on the mount which says, 'Therefore, whatsoever ye would have men do to you, do ye even so to them,' and you explain it and talk to them of all the excellence of this precept, and so on. Have I a single negro on the plantation so dull that he will not stop and say, 'If you please, Mar, does Mars Nick treat us as he would have us treat him?' You must answer them. Now if you say 'Yes,' they know you lie and you can do them no good. But if you say, 'No,' you damage my character among them. I tell you sir, we can do nothing toward giving Christian light and instruction. We are bound to keep them as dark as possible. You must desist from teaching them at all."

At this, Parker's heart stirred, "My dear sir, can you stand the full blaze of the light of salvation through Jesus Christ and rejoice for yourself and your family, while you shut it entirely from those absolutely dependent on you? For while you remember that the soul of the master and slave are regarded of equal value by him who died to save them, and before whom both are soon to appear in the day of judgment!"

At this Edmunds burst into tears. "Mr. Parker, for God's sake, don't name the day of judgment in connection with slavery! But you must desist from teaching my slaves."[14]

As Parker puzzled over Edmunds's instructions and whether to comply, he came to see the system of slavery clearly for what it was. "Slavery

14 Conversation recounted in Parker Memoirs, 15–16.

seemed to me," Parker wrote, "An outrage upon the rights of man."[15] Not long after, without warning, Parker was informed that he must leave Edmunds's house and never return. Packing his belongings and tearfully leaving the children and the slaves he had grown to love, Parker set out for the North, not to return to the plantation again until after the Civil War.[16]

Nearly fifty years later in 1878, having completed theological studies at Newton Theological Institution in Massachusetts, pastored two prominent churches in Boston, led the efforts of the New England Freedmen's Aid Society to former slaves, and brokered peace between Washington's fractious churches, Parker was enjoying his semiretirement on a farm in Maryland while serving as an interim pastor at E Street Baptist Church.[17] Having spent the previous half-century in ceaseless labor, seventy-three-year-old Parker's intention was to never become a pastor again.[18] He was happy on his farm spending each morning among the shrubs and trees with hoe and knife, busy in work, thought, and prayer.[19] A year earlier he had reluctantly agreed to preach at E Street on an interim basis and had been encouraged by the fruit. "The seed fell onto good soil," he wrote, and the church grew spiritually and numerically. "In no one of my favored pastorates was I happier or more thoroughly appreciated. This seemed now to be a home for me for the rest of my working life."[20]

Everything changed on a snowy December evening in 1878 when representatives of Metropolitan Baptist Church came knocking on his door. Let in by a housekeeper, they found the "venerable pulpit orator" in the living room, resting his leg from a recent fall on the ice.[21]

15 Parker Memoirs, 18.
16 Parker Memoirs, 228.
17 William Allen Wilbur, "Temple Baptist Church, Washington D.C., Through Ninety Years" (unpublished manuscript, October 9, 1932), 14, Restoration Baptist Church Archives, Washington, DC.
18 Parker Memoirs, 304.
19 Parker Memoirs, 110.
20 Parker Memoirs, 306–7.
21 Parker Memoirs, 307–8.

Though Parker had long desired to see a Baptist church established on the Hill, and even personally contributed funds toward the chapel in 1874, he had never seriously contemplated becoming its pastor.[22] After all, Metropolitan had little to offer Parker in terms of worldly goods or comfort. "They were few and poor," Parker later explained, "had a small chapel in an undesirable location, and could pay but little salary." In short, there was every reason, humanly speaking, for saying no.[23]

Nevertheless, to everyone's surprise, Parker accepted the call. As Parker wrote in his memoirs, "When I entered the ministry, I had promised to go wherever he wanted me, even if it was central Africa."[24] Consequently, Parker accepted the call to Metropolitan not because of what it offered him but because of what he offered it. "It seemed to me a church should be formed as the Metropolitan had been," Parker explained, not "out of division and quarrel" but "legitimately formed." Parker feared that unless he accepted the position, it was unlikely that the church, like a tender sapling, would find a pastor and that perhaps it would not even survive.[25]

On January 30, 1879, Parker notified Metropolitan that after careful consideration, he would accept their call. "Though the relation and work of Preacher and Pastor are not new to me," Parker wrote, "yet I begin with you feeling a deep sense of our dependence on God." Having begun in prayer, Parker was eager that the church continue to be sustained—not by the name of its pastor—but by the prayers of its people. "I shall expect from you an earnest cooperation and unceasing prayer for direction and aid in our work," he exhorted them.[26]

Parker was the man who had reconciled E Street and Calvary in 1865. Now it was Parker who would help Metropolitan in its time of need.

---

22 Report of the Treasurer, Metropolitan Baptist Association, July 15, 1874, MS 1600, p. 22, box 6, folder 6, CHBC Archives.
23 Parker Memoirs, 307–8.
24 Parker Memoirs, 105.
25 Parker Memoirs, 307–8.
26 Joseph W. Parker to Metropolitan Baptist Church, January 30, 1879, MS 1080, box 5, folder 3, CHBC Archives.

Putting What Remained into Order

Parker's pulpit ministry began on April 1, 1879.[27] He had determined not to make salary an issue and accepted the paltry $800 a year he was offered, cutting his already meagre salary from E Street in half.[28] At the time, Metropolitan had a membership of forty-five. Parker later wrote that if he had known how "depressed" its condition was financially, he could not possibly have accepted the invitation.[29] Nevertheless, despite receiving numerous offers to pastor elsewhere with far more lucrative salaries, he kept his course and continued to pastor Metropolitan for nearly three years.[30]

Parker's early preaching at Metropolitan was "thoroughly didactic."[31] His method of preparing sermons was to decide on a text and theme for the coming week on Sunday night before going to bed. On Monday morning, he would not leave his study until he had planned the structure of the sermon and written the introduction. In that way, he could go about his business during the week with the "sermon brewing all the while and illustrations coming to me." Both morning and evening sermons would be written and revised before Friday at noon. In that way he was "never overwhelmed and nervous on Saturday if an unexpected event occurred." On Saturday night he would review his sermon points so that "all is right in my mind," because, as he wrote, "from the first I resolved not to read my sermons" but to preach them.[32]

For his part, Parker especially relished the "advantage of short range shot" he enjoyed as a preacher in the Capitol city. Rebukes issued toward public injustices or corrupt officials delivered in a sermon on a Sunday quickly found their intended target, regardless of political

27 Metropolitan Baptist Church Minutes, April 1, 1879, 39; Parker Memoirs, 308.
28 Parker Memoirs, 309.
29 Parker Memoirs, 308.
30 Parker Memoirs, 310.
31 Parker Memoirs, 309.
32 Parker Memoirs, 33–34.

office or whether they attended services. As Parker wrote, "I endeavor to improve and sometimes bring down the game at which I fire."[33]

Parker wasted no time putting what remained into order. Of first priority was the creation of the church's governing documents: its statement of faith, church covenant, and rules of church order and discipline. Together, these three documents were referred to as the "Church Manual of the Metropolitan Baptist Church."[34] Far from being a mundane matter, these documents were the result of three months' labor by a church committee before they were presented to the church for approval.

For their statement of faith, the church adopted J. Newton Brown's version of the New Hampshire Confession of Faith (1833), the most widely used confession among Baptists.[35] As they explained to the Columbia Association of Baptist Churches in 1879, their goal was not ingenuity but continuity, not innovation but preservation of the doctrines that distinguished the people called Baptists.[36]

When it came to the church covenant, however, the members of Metropolitan decided to draft their own document. Though the covenant would later be revised to its present form, the terms of the original covenant would ever set a high bar for future generations.[37] In their covenant, the members promised "to exercise a Christian care and watchfulness over each other." They covenanted to "admonish one another in the spirit of meekness," to "not forsake the assembling of ourselves together," and to "uphold the public worship of God and the ordinances of His house." The covenant included duties to non-members as they pledged to "strive to promote every good work for the

---

33 Parker Memoirs, 225.

34 Metropolitan Baptist Church Minutes, March 15, 1878, 15.

35 William Joseph McGlothlin, *Baptist Confessions of Faith* (Philadelphia, PA: American Baptist Publication Society, 1911), 299–301.

36 F. McLean to the Columbia Association of Baptist Churches, November 13, 1879. A copy of this letter is transcribed in the Metropolitan Baptist Church Minutes, December 31, 1879, 46–47.

37 For an overview of how the church covenant changed over the course of the church's history, see Mark Dever, "History of Our Church Covenant," Capitol Hill Baptist, accessed November 15, 2021, https://www.capitolhillbaptist.org/.

elevation of mankind." In a city fraught with political disagreements and strong opinions, the covenant gave special attention to maintaining unity in the church, as members agreed to "earnestly endeavor to avoid doing, or giving utterance to anything which may grieve or offend any from the least to the greatest of those for whom Christ died." Finally, the covenant concluded with the benediction of Hebrews 13:20–21:

And may the God of peace, who brought again from the dead our Lord Jesus Christ, that Great Shepherd of the sheep, through the blood of the everlasting Covenant, make us perfect in every good work, to do His will; working in us that which is well-pleasing in his sight, through Jesus Christ, to whom be glory forever and ever.[38]

As for church officers, Metropolitan adopted the fourfold model of pastor, deacons, trustees, and treasurer.[39] As was common in nineteenth-century Baptist polity, the board of deacons exercised "spiritual oversight of the church" while the board of trustees oversaw the practical needs of the church.[40] In addition to assisting the pastor in the administration of ordinances, deacons provided "general oversight of the church," including visiting the sick and advising the pastor.[41] In contrast, the board of trustees was charged with holding in trust and maintaining the physical church property.[42] It was not until 1998 that the church changed its constitution to have a plurality of elders.

38 Metropolitan Baptist Church Minutes, March 15, 1878, 18–19.
39 "Rules of Church Order and Discipline," art. 4, sec. 1: "The officers of the church shall consist of a Pastor, Clerk, Treasurer and two Deacons." Metropolitan Baptist Church Minutes, March 15, 1878, 20.
40 Metropolitan Baptist Church Minutes, April 20, 1887, 124.
41 "Rules of Church Order and Discipline," art. 5, sec. 2, Metropolitan Baptist Church Minutes, March 15, 1878, 21.
42 Metropolitan Baptist Church Minutes, March 9, 1878, 11. While these responsibilities, biblically speaking, lay under the purview of the deacons, as Edward T. Hiscox explains, this diaconal role was delegated to trustees for "expediency" and "to meet any requirements of civil law." Edward T. Hiscox, *The Baptist Church Directory* (New York: Sheldon, 1859), 26, 27.

In their rules for church order and discipline, Metropolitan likewise drew on a variety of sources to create an original document.[43] The manual explained, "Candidates for admission by baptism" were not to "appear before the church to relate their religious experience until the Pastor and Deacons shall be satisfied that their conversion is genuine and that they understand and adopt the views of doctrine and practice held by this church." After being examined by the pastor and deacons, baptismal candidates would appear before a church meeting to be voted into membership, pursuant to baptism.[44]

When it came to the practice of church discipline, the church manual was especially strict. Following the steps laid out in Matthew 18:15–20, the manual laid the burden of reconciliation on the member sinned against. If sinned against by another member, the agrieved party was "to seek an opportunity to converse privately with the offender, with a view to the reconcilement of the difficulty." Additional people were only to be made aware of the offense if the initial attempt at reconciliation failed. Only if additional attempts by multiple members failed to "reconcile the offender," then "it shall be the duty of the offended to lay the matter before the church." Such actions, the manual explained, should never be taken lightly and never without the "previous knowledge of the Pastor and Deacons."

If a member continued in sin, ignoring the warnings of the entire church, then the church was obligated to respond by excluding them from membership, cutting them off "from the membership and communion of the church." Causes of church discipline, the manual explained, included outward violations of God's moral law, habitual absences from the church's public worship, advocating doctrines contrary to the statement of faith, and producing discord in the body. More than mere words, these reflected the actual

43 Metropolitan Baptist Church Minutes, March 15, 1878, 20–25.
44 "Rules of Church Order and Discipline," art. 1, sec. 2., Metropolitan Baptist Church Minutes, March 15, 1878, 20.

practices of the Metropolitan Baptist Church during the ensuing months and years.[45]

Church Discipline and Racial Reconciliation

On December 17, 1879, Joseph Parker brought the name of one of the church's own trustees, Charles L. Patten, before the church for discipline. As the heavyhearted pastor explained, Patten had "separated from his wife" in order to be with another woman and fellow member, Alma C. Smith. This shocking revelation led the church to form a committee, composed of the pastor and deacons, to meet with Patten to find out why he had separated from his wife. For months, Parker and the deacons patiently and prayerfully sought to meet with Patten and Smith in order to convince them of their sin.[46]

After working for over six months, however, on July 14, 1880, the deacons reported to the church that despite numerous meetings, Patten and Smith remained unrepentant.[47] Following remarks by Parker and others, the church adopted a resolution excluding them from membership.[48] As church clerk Francis McLean put it in his annual letter for 1880, the "right hand of fellowship [was] withdrawn."[49]

Discipline was not always dramatic, but it was never hasty. On October 18, 1882, sister Lucretia E. Douglas was excluded from membership for long-standing nonattendance. For nearly three years, the pastor and deacons had met with Douglas and engaged in "considerable conversation" regarding her spiritual and practical needs, to no avail.[50] Finally, the congregation voted to exclude her from membership, as "she has not attended any of the meetings of this church for two years past and

---

45 "Rules of Church Order and Discipline," art. 7, sec. 1, Metropolitan Baptist Church Minutes, March 15, 1878, 22–23. Cf. discussion of Metropolitan Baptist Church's disciplinary practices in Mark Dever, *Nine Marks of a Healthy Church*, 4th ed. (Wheaton, IL: Crossway, 2021), 161–65.

46 Metropolitan Baptist Church Minutes, January 20, 1880, 48–49.

47 Metropolitan Baptist Church Minutes, July 14, 1880, 55.

48 Metropolitan Baptist Church Minutes, May 5, 1880, 54

49 Clerk's Annual Report, January 1, 1881, MS 1579, box 6, folder 5, CHBC Archives.

50 Metropolitan Baptist Church Minutes, October 18, 1882, 55.

has offered no excuse nor explanation."[51] Nor was this an unusual case. According to a report by the pastor and deacons in 1889, the most common reason for excluding someone from membership was "lack of interest, non-attendance, and failure to contribute to the support of the gospel, with evidence inconsistent with Christian calling."[52]

The goal of church discipline, however, was never permanent separation but eventual reconciliation, and the church occasionally saw excommunicated members restored to full membership. On October 17, 1881, Parker called for a special members' meeting from the pulpit, to take place immediately following the close of the morning service.[53] After prayer, he presented the case of W. H. Pearce, a newly married usher in the church and the son of a member. At the meeting, Parker brought the motion that Pearce be excluded immediately for "notorious and flagrant immorality."[54] After remarks by the pastor and deacons, the church voted to immediately discontinue Pearce's connection with the church.[55]

By God's grace, however, that was not the end of the story. Just over a month later, on December 1, 1881, Pearce appeared at a meeting of the church requesting their forgiveness. On motion, Pearce was unanimously voted back into membership.[56] Far from being treated as a second-class member by the church after his restoration to membership, Pearce was reappointed to his position as an usher at the next members' meeting.[57] Thus, church discipline or exclusion was never an end in itself. The goal of church discipline was to protect the purity of the church in order to enable the members to abide by the covenant that

51 Metropolitan Baptist Church Minutes, October 18, 1882, 66.
52 Report of Board of Pastor and Deacons, July 17, 1889, MS 2, box 1, folder 1, CHBC Archives.
53 Metropolitan Baptist Church Minutes, October 17, 1881, 61.
54 "Rules of Church Order and Discipline," art. 7, sec. 2, Metropolitan Baptist Church Minutes, March 15, 1878, 23.
55 As the membership book notes, "Connection with church discontinued Oct. 17/81." Membership Book, October 17, 1881, MS 1538, p. 5, box 6, folder 1, CHBC Archives.
56 Metropolitan Baptist Church Minutes, December 1, 1881, 62. As the membership book reports, "Restored to membership." Membership Book, December 1, 1881, 5.
57 Metropolitan Baptist Church Minutes, December 1, 1881, 63.

bound them together in membership: to "walk together in brotherly love," to "exercise a Christian care and watchfulness over each other," and, by God's strength, "to walk in newness of life."[58]

Under Parker's leadership, Metropolitan grew from fifty members in 1879 to seventy-four in 1880 to ninety-eight in 1882. When the church added two more members to its rolls to make it an even hundred, a local Baptist paper praised Metropolitan as a "Model Church." "There are but three persons in it who do not contribute to its support," the article explained, "and those three are themselves so poor as to need and receive aid from the church." In other words, every member was a contributing member, except the three who found themselves in need of benevolence. "This is as it should be," the article continued. "The moment we really become too poor to assist in the propagation of the Gospel, that moment do we become a real and deserving object of charity."[59]

The congregation loved their pastor, and he loved them. "Our pastor is earnest, zealous and untiring in his efforts for us," the church clerk wrote in 1883.[60] At one quarterly meeting, the church abruptly went into "executive session," sending Parker from the chair into a separate room without explanation. As it turned out, the congregation simply wished to surprise Parker by voting to raise his salary. When a deacon was sent to retrieve the "exiled pastor," and Parker was told the reason for being sent out, he responded by paraphrasing Robert Burton, "'What can't be cured must be endured' with a self-willed people."[61]

When Metropolitan applied and joined the Columbia Association of Baptist Churches in 1879, it was joining an exclusively White association.[62]

---

58 Metropolitan Baptist Church Minutes, March 15, 1878, 18–19.
59 "A Model Church," *The Baptist Beacon*, April 1, 1882, Library of Congress Special Collections, Washington, DC.
60 Francis McLean to the Columbia Association of Baptist Churches, November 15, 1883, MS 901, box 3, folder 1, CHBC Archives.
61 Metropolitan Baptist Church Minutes, January 21, 1880, 49; Robert Burton, *The Anatomy of Melancholy* (London: Thomas Tegg, 1845), 402.
62 Francis McLean to the Columbia Association of Baptist Churches, November 13, 1879, Metropolitan Baptist Church Minutes, November 20, 1879, 46–47.

Through the church's influence, that began to change. On November 18, 1879, Stephen H. Mirick, Metropolitan's original interim pastor, wrote to the association of the need to "gather our forces," uniting "with our own brethren of the same household," including "our colored brethren." As Mirick explained, "They form a large portion of our denomination, being gathered into more than thirty Churches." Mirick urged the Columbia Association to open its doors to Black churches rather than remain segmented. As Mirick insisted, "The great body of them would welcome any cordial effort on our part to counsel and help."[63]

The next year, on November 17, 1880, at the annual meeting of the Columbia Association presided over by Parker, two Black churches, Shiloh Baptist on L Street and Second Baptist in Navy Yard, applied for membership in the association.[64] Both churches had long enjoyed informal relationships with White Baptist churches in the city. When Shiloh Baptist Church was formed in 1863 by twenty-one former slaves who had fled Fredericksburg as refugees with the protection of the Union Army, no Black churches responded to their request for a council to recognize them as a regularly constituted church. The White churches of the city, however, sent delegates, deacons, and pastors to form a committee that celebrated God's deliverance of "these His children, from the fetters of bondage" and heartily approved their recognition as a church.[65]

When the association received the applications of Shiloh Baptist and Second Baptist for membership, their applications were referred to a special committee for consideration.[66] Although this was standard practice for the

---

63 *Minutes of the Second Annual Meeting of the Columbia Association of Baptist Churches, Held in the Meeting House of the Fifth Baptist Church, Washington, D.C., November 18th and 20th, 1879* (Washington, DC: Rufus H. Darby, 1879), 9, District of Columbia Baptist Convention Archives, Washington, DC (hereafter, DCBC Archives).

64 *Minutes of the Third Annual Meeting of the Columbia Association of Baptist Churches, Held in the Meeting House of the Second Baptist Church, Washington, D.C., November 16th and 17th, 1880* (Washington, DC: Rufus H. Darby, 1880), 4, DCBC Archives.

65 John W. Cromwell, "The First Negro Churches in the District of Columbia," *The Journal of Negro History* 7, no. 1 (January 1922): 90n33.

66 *Minutes of the Third Annual Meeting,* 4.

association to examine whether the churches were of like faith and practice, the action gave offense to the pastor of Shiloh Baptist, William J. Walker. For Walker, who had pastored Shiloh for eighteen years and played an active role in establishing other Black churches in the District, the association's action of delaying his church's reception seemed like racial discrimination. As he explained to the delegates of the Columbia Association in a five-minute speech on November 17, 1880, it gave the impression that his church was "under investigation," despite the fact that during the past eighteen years his public character and ministry were well known.[67]

In an attempt to assuage Walker's concerns, the association rushed to adopt a resolution clarifying that the Columbia Association was "formed on the broad basis of 'No distinction on account of color.'" Addressing Walker's frustration head-on, the association acknowledged that an "impression prevails" that the association "is not ready to welcome colored churches (so-called)" into membership in its body. Nevertheless, the association unanimously reiterated its "cordial invitation" to any Baptist church in the district, "assuring them that their application will be welcomed, and no barrier other than those mentioned in article vii of our constitution"—requiring agreement in matters of faith and polity—"will be raised against them."[68] For a White denomination in the nation's capital in 1879, this was quite the statement.

Sadly, Walker was determined to take offense. Referring to the committee's "inquisitorial proceedings," Walker stated that it was "plainly evident" that his church was not wanted in the association on account of its being "colored." Walker requested his application be returned to him and left the church building without another word.[69]

Disappointed, the thoughts of everyone present immediately turned to Madison Gaskins, pastor of Second Baptist, who had likewise applied for

67 "Our Baptist Brethren," *National Republican*, November 18, 1880, 4; "The Columbia Baptist Association," *Evening Star*, November 17, 1880, 4.
68 *Minutes of the Third Annual Meeting*, 18.
69 "Our Baptist Brethren," 4; "The Columbia Baptist Association," 4.

application to the association. Unlike Walker, however, Gaskins stayed. The next year, 1881, the appointed committee returned their unanimous decision to recommend "Second Baptist (colored)" to the association.

As Parker rose to offer "the right hand of fellowship" to Gaskins and the other delegates from Second Baptist, everyone present understood the significance of what was happening. With hands solemnly clasped, Parker and Gaskins were demonstrating the world-defying, gospel-displaying power of Christ to reconcile across ethnic and racial lines. "This was done in a most hearty and impressive manner," a local paper reported, "and some of the delegates were greatly moved."[70]

Figure 2.2. Tombstone of Joseph W. Parker at Angelus Rosedale Cemetery in Los Angeles, California, inscribed with the words of 2 Timothy 1:12: "I know whom I have believed."

70 *The Baptist Beacon,* December 3, 1881, Library of Congress Special Collections.

Between 1878 and 1882, Joseph W. Parker was used by God to bring reconciliation to churches in Washington, DC, and unity to Metropolitan Baptist Church. When Parker was forced to resign on October 15, 1882, due to his failing health, he moved to Los Angeles, California, where he died on November 9, 1887, at age eighty-two. On hearing of his death, churches across the country responded with notes of condolence and tributes to Parker's character. One such church was Berean Baptist Church, an African American congregation in Washington, DC, established with Parker's help in 1877. In their minutes, the members of Berean acknowledged their gratefulness for Parker's ministry. After commending him as "an earnest worker, a faithful Pastor, a man of unblemished reputation and a conscientious Christian Gentleman," their tribute concluded with this description: "a Christian Minister, and a helper of the downtrodden and lowly."[71]

Of the many lessons that can be gleaned from these first years of Metropolitan Baptist Church, two are worth highlighting. First, crucial stability can be provided by a faithful and seasoned pastor. Parker had no reason, humanly speaking, to accept Metropolitan's invitation. There was nothing easy about beginning a new work in his old age. But like Celestia Ferris, Parker was willing to set personal comfort aside and be spent for the sake of the spread of the gospel and the establishment of local churches, in ways that are still being felt today.

Another lesson concerns the importance of church polity. With less than fifty members and little means available to support a pastor, what did the members of Metropolitan Baptist Church give their attention to as a matter of first importance? Their governing documents: the statement of faith, church covenant, and rules of church order and discipline.

71 Minutes of the Berean Baptist Church, January 11, 1888, 36–37.

They did not regard these documents as of nominal importance but spent months deliberating and drafting them so that they could stand the test of time. No one thinks polity matters until something goes wrong. Within only a few years of forming, the church worked through several difficult cases of church discipline. But rather than destroying the church, these difficult cases served to further strengthen their commitment to, in the words of their church covenant, "exercise a Christian care and watchfulness over each other."

With Parker's help, a solid foundation had been laid for Metropolitan to shine as a light on the Hill. As Parker later reflected, "More was accomplished than I anticipated. The labors have been successful, and souls have been comforted and saved."[72] What neither Parker nor the members could have imagined, however, was how quickly after Parker's departure their polity would be tested. Within only a few years the church would find itself divided within and on the brink of destruction.

---

72 Parker Memoirs, 309.

3

"With Conscience Void of Offence toward God and Man"

1882–1884

IN 1884, A SUFFOCATING CONFLICT plagued Metropolitan Baptist Church, leaving its members exhausted and its pastor at his wits' end. The issue began with seemingly trivial matters but quickly escalated into a full-blown crisis. Meetings were fraught with division, investigations into financial impropriety were launched, and the votes were excruciatingly close. By the end of the year, the church was reeling. It had lost its pastor, was in deep debt, and its once-thriving congregation had dwindled to a mere sixty members. After dividing the church over a disputable matter, the church's new pastor, Wilbur M. Ingersoll, insisted that his conscience was "void of offence toward God and toward man."[1] The church claimed the same.[2] How had it come to this?

---

1   "But allow me to say that with a conscience void of offence toward God and toward man, I have served you with some measure of faithfulness for nearly two years." Letter of Resignation of W. M. Ingersoll, October 23, 1884, MS 1093, box 5, folder 5, Capitol Hill Baptist Church Archives, Washington, DC (hereafter, CHBC Archives).
2   "We still live, and have conscience void of offence toward God and toward man." Clerk's Annual Report, January 1, 1885, MS 1582, box 6, folder 5, CHBC Archives.

When Parker resigned as pastor of Metropolitan on October 15, 1882, he expressed two hopes for the church he had pastored for over three years. First, Parker hoped that they would soon be able to build a new chapel to meet the needs of the rapidly growing congregation on Capitol Hill. Second, he expressed his wish that they would call another pastor as soon as possible.[3] The members that he had described in 1878 as "few and poor" and in possession of "a small chapel in an undesirable location" had grown such that the small chapel could no longer accommodate the hundred or more who attended each Sunday.[4] But of even more pressing concern than Sunday services was the Sunday school, which by 1882 included nearly three hundred students. "We had no room for enlargement," Parker wrote in 1881.[5] The only option was to acquire property and erect a larger building.

Building Plans

Before leaving, Parker had gifted the church with an adjacent lot on A Street NE.[6] Having completely paid off the debt on their chapel by the end of 1881, the church was poised to begin construction of a new building on the property donated to them by Parker. There was only one problem. The church could not agree on where to build the new chapel, and the disagreement started with the church's one-armed treasurer, Lester Edwin Forrest Spofford.

<hr/>

3   Metropolitan Baptist Church Minutes, October 31, 1882, MS 1602, p. 68, box 6, folder 7, CHBC Archives.
4   Joseph Whiting Parker Memoirs, 1880, MS 14909, p. 307, Special Collections, University of Virginia Library, Charlottesville.
5   Parker Memoirs, 309.
6   Reports of Board of Trustees, January 1, 1882, MS 654, box 2, folder 2, CHBC Archives. In his memoirs, Parker writes, "Near the close [of my second year] or about the first of 1881, I suggested that we make an effort to pay the old indebtedness and also to pay for the new lot of land which I had purchased for them at $1,000. Some favored, but most hesitated. Finally it was agreed that an attempt to diminish the debt for the new purchase might be attempted, and now all has been pledged to be paid on or before the first of October [1881]." Parker Memoirs, 310.

Spofford and his wife had attended the first prayer meeting at Celestia's home in November 1867. A fiery Yankee, Spofford had enlisted in the Eighth Connecticut at the tender age of eighteen. Like Abraham Ferris, Spofford was no stranger to the horrors of war. In his regiment, 194 men were killed during a charge at the Battle of Antietam. Spofford was fortunate: he only lost his left arm. After convalescing, Spofford could have been honorably discharged, but he was not one to shy away from a fight. The one-armed soldier returned to the fray, rising to the rank of sergeant major, only to suffer an additional injury to his remaining arm at the Battle of Port Waltham Junction in 1864.[7] Later he took a job with the Department of Treasury and built himself a fine home at 508 East Capitol Street NE.[8] Like Celestia and Abraham Ferris, Spofford was a member of E Street Baptist Church and played no small role in the organization of Metropolitan Baptist Church, serving as the church's first treasurer.

Spofford dreamed of erecting a magnificent structure on East Capitol Street, next to his own home. As the church's annual letter explained in 1883, "We desire to have an attractive, convenient and useful Church of the Baptist persuasion on Capitol Hill, located on East Capitol Street."[9] As the main thoroughfare on Capitol Hill, East Capitol Street was an exceedingly superior location to Sixth and A, but it was also more expensive. When Metropolitan's new pastor, Wilbur M. Ingersoll, commenced his labors at Metropolitan on December 3, 1882, Spofford quickly began scheming with the new pastor to buy property on East Capitol Street. But first, they needed the church to grow.

7 Buck Zaidel, "MEN OF CONNECTICUT! TO ARMS!!!," *Military Images* 33, no. 2 (2015): 24–33, https://www.jstor.org/stable/24864378.

8 Tenth Census of the United States, 1880 (NARA microfilm publication T9, 1,454 rolls). Records of the Bureau of the Census, record group 29, National Archives, Washington, DC. United States Department of the Interior, *Official Register of the United States: Containing a List of Officers and Employees in the Civil, Military, and Naval Service* (Washington, DC: US Government Printing Office, 1872), 164.

9 Francis McLean to the Columbia Association of Baptist Churches, November 15, 1883, MS 901, pp. 254–55, box 3, folder 1, CHBC Archives.

Figure 3.1. Lester Edwin Forrest Spofford (1843–1887) lost his left arm at the Battle of Antietam where 194 members of his regiment were killed. He eventually rejoined his unit, serving in the Bermuda Hundred Campaign.

Ingersoll, who was known to the members as the former pastor of Second Baptist Church in Navy Yard, immediately commenced a series of protracted revival meetings the first week of January 1883.[10] In his zeal for protracted meetings, Ingersoll seemed to affirm the dictum of revivalist Jacob Knapp that it was "never so easy to pay off a debt as when it is in the full tide of a religious revival."[11] As long as the church was growing numerically, he believed, members would give everything that was needed to build a new and larger building.

Spofford and Ingersoll wasted little time in bringing their plans to the church. Rather than constructing the new chapel on the adjacent lot

10 Metropolitan Baptist Church Minutes, January 4, 1883, 71.
11 Jacob Knapp, *Autobiography of Elder Jacob Knapp* (New York: Sheldon, 1868), xi.

donated by Parker, they proposed purchasing an expensive plot of land facing East Capitol Street, between Sixth and Seventh streets NE at a cost of $7,400—over four times the church's annual budget. To simply buy the land—before even beginning construction—the cash-starved church would be forced to take out a major loan and surrender the deed of trust on its current property as collateral. The annual interest payments on the loan amounted to nearly $400—a quarter of the church's annual budget. Failing to make loan payments would result in losing its fully paid-off property and chapel. If ever there was an aggressive financial plan, this was it.[12]

To Benjamin F. Bingham, a member of the church's board of trustees, the plan was foolhardy. "It is well known that I was opposed to the purchase of the 'Lots,'" Bingham wrote in October 1883. "I voted against them, both in the Church meeting and Board of Trustees." Like his namesake, Benjamin Franklin, Bingham believed in thrift and thought it imprudent to take on so large a debt. As he explained axiomatically, "A large debt must always be injurious to a Church of small resources."[13]

On April 18, 1883, Spofford brought a motion to take out a loan of $7,400 and buy the new properties. Though a significant financial decision, Spofford stressed the urgency of making the deal, insisting that the motion be voted on the following week. As Bingham later complained, the matter was "hastily brought into the Church and pressed to a vote, not giving sufficient time to carefully consider and weigh the serious questions involved on the proposition."[14] Bingham's concerns notwithstanding, the church voted overwhelmingly in support of Spofford's motion.[15]

Debt and Division

When the debt-saddled church failed to grow numerically the way Ingersoll had hoped, Metropolitan found itself in desperate straits

12 B. F. Bingham to Metropolitan Baptist Church, October 15, 1883, MS 654, box 2, folder 2, CHBC Archives.
13 B. F. Bingham to Metropolitan Baptist Church, October 15, 1883, CHBC Archives.
14 B. F. Bingham to Metropolitan Baptist Church, October 15, 1883, CHBC Archives.
15 Metropolitan Baptist Church Minutes, April 18, 1883, 72.

as the members realized they lacked funds to make the first payment of $2,300. As the first loan payment date of November 8, 1883, approached, bottled-up feelings and antagonisms from the decision earlier that year erupted. Bingham, who had resolved after losing the vote in April to "yield to the majority" and heartily do his part to carry out the will of the church, could remain silent no longer. On October 24, 1883, Bingham made his dissenting view known to the church and warned the members of their precarious financial position.[16] At the last moment, when all hope seemed lost, help arrived in the form of a gift from Joseph Parker, who "remembered us substantially from distant California." A second helper also came along in the form of an anonymous donor from Calvary Baptist Church. Writing a few weeks later on January 1, 1884, church clerk Francis McLean warned the congregation, "I need scarcely remind you that we are in debt. We may thank a kind providence—not ourselves—that we have escaped disaster. We cannot afford again to come so near."[17]

After their close call with bankruptcy, more members seemed willing to take Bingham's view of the church's financial situation. As McLean summed up their predicament in the form of a poem:

> Our logic is interest,
> Our basis is debt,
> We're tied up in two bags,
> To be dumped out yet.[18]

For a growing section of members, the indebtedness felt increasingly like a noose strangling the life out of the church. They had had enough and were ready to rid themselves of the East Capitol Street property and start over again.

16 Metropolitan Baptist Church Minutes, October 24, 1883, 74.
17 Clerk's Annual Report, January 1, 1884, MS 1581b, box 6, folder 5, CHBC Archives.
18 Clerk's Annual Report, January 1, 1884.

On May 16, 1884, a member brought a motion at the church's business meeting to sell the East Capitol Street property and free the church from debt.[19] Spofford opposed this motion, asking for two weeks delay—twice the amount of time given to deliberate taking on the debt—in order to survey the members using printed circulars as to their point of view on the question. When the fateful meeting began on May 30, 1884, the small chapel was packed. Once the circulars were tallied, McLean announced the result: fifty-three supported selling the property on East Capitol Street; fifty-two opposed. Seeing his plan outnumbered, Ingersoll quickly ended the meeting before a final decision could be made about the property.

After a two-month summer vacation, Ingersoll returned to the church in September and asked the church to vote in favor of calling an external council of pastors to help adjudicate the dispute over the church property. To the majority of members, this seemed like an unnecessary tactic of further delay. As they explained, "We claim that the Church is competent to manage its own affairs and settle all differences."[20]

To the shock of the congregation, Ingersoll proceeded to call a church council of ministers against the express will of the congregation. For the members of Metropolitan, this was a bridge too far. Few principles were more zealously guarded and universally agreed on in nineteenth-century Baptist churches than the will of the majority. "The will of majorities," McLean wrote in 1883, "should be respected. When disregarded there's always recoil."[21]

The church's "recoil" took the form of a demand letter with sixty signatures, calling for Ingersoll's immediate resignation as pastor.[22] The letter, dated October 4, 1884, specified Ingersoll's pastoral overreach, domineering leadership, and violation of the church's will as grounds for his resignation. "Why any person should have an ambition to absolutely

19 Metropolitan Baptist Church Minutes, May 16, 1884, 78.

20 Members of Metropolitan Baptist Church to W. M. Ingersoll, October 4, 1884, MS 1096, box 5, folder 5, CHBC Archives.

21 Clerk's Annual Report, January 1, 1883, MS 1581a, box 6, folder 5, CHBC Archives.

22 Members of Metropolitan Baptist Church to W. M. Ingersoll, October 4, 1884, CHBC Archives.

direct the affairs of any church is more than I can fathom," McLean would later write in 1885. "We were like the frogs who clamored for a king and got one." Far from being unruly, McLean insisted, "This church has borne and forborne beyond all reason. Patience and forbearance at last ceased to be cardinal virtues. Simply history repeating itself."[23]

When the church gathered for business on October 23, 1884, Bingham asked Ingersoll to state by what authority he had called a council and proceeded to publish and distribute the recommendations of the council to the church. Ingersoll, however, refused to answer Bingham's questions, leading another member to move that the findings of the church council be deemed inadmissible to the church's proceedings.[24] Still divided, that motion carried only by a vote of 49 to 41.[25] At that same meeting, by a slim majority, the church finally voted to sell the property on East Capitol Street. As soon as the vote passed, showing that Ingersoll's faction had been defeated, Ingersoll stood, handed a hastily scribbled note to the moderator, and left the room, never to return.

McLean opened the note, revealing a succinct letter of resignation. "It is not satisfactory that a statement should be here made of the painful causes precipitating this strife," Ingersoll wrote.

> But allow me to say that with a conscience void of offence toward God and toward man, I have served you with some measure of faithfulness for nearly two years, and borne my share of the sacrifices looking to the largest success of the master's cause. Hoping that you may be best served and the Lord most glorified by my withdrawal from the field, I beg that action may be now taken on this resignation.[26]

Action was indeed taken. By a vote 54 to 43, the divided church accepted Ingersoll's resignation.

23 Clerk's Annual Report, January 1, 1885.
24 Metropolitan Baptist Church Minutes, October 23, 1884, 87.
25 Metropolitan Baptist Church Minutes, October 23, 1884, 87.
26 Wilbur M. Ingersoll to Metropolitan Baptist Church, October 23, 1884, MS 1093, box 5, folder 5, CHBC Archives.

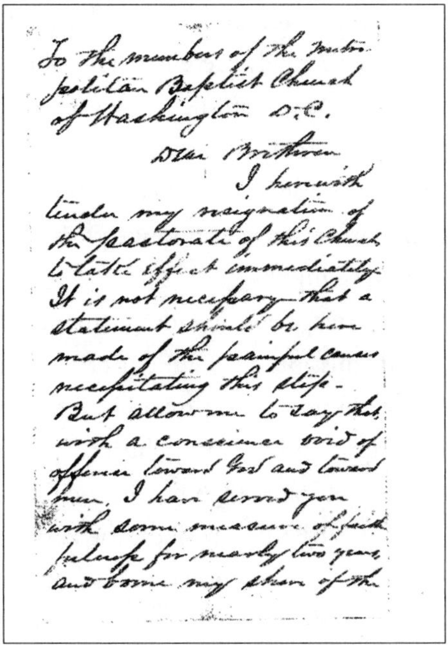

Figure 3.2. Letter of resignation of W. M. Ingersoll, October 23, 1884.

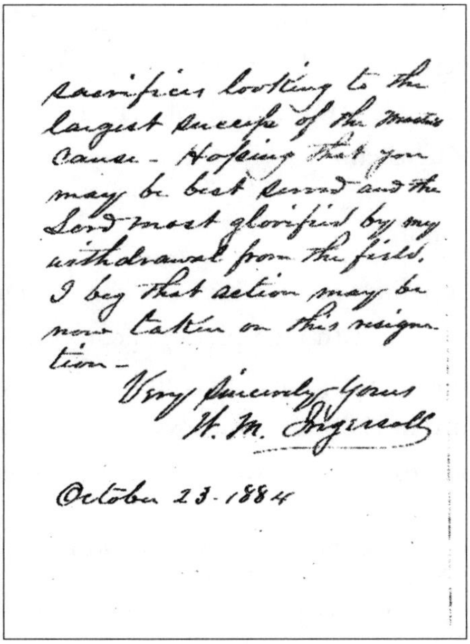

After the church voted to accept Ingersoll's letter of resignation, the dissenting members immediately presented a list of names to the moderator for resignation. If they could not have their way, a large faction was determined to leave. Tempers flared as some in Ingersoll's party cast aspersions on their opponents, predicting the imminent demise of the church.[27] As one former trustee announced, "I am anxious to sever all connection with this church."[28]

All told, thirty-three members, including church treasurer Spofford, requested letters of dismission on the night of Ingersoll's resignation. But to the horror of the remaining members of Metropolitan, they immediately proceeded to form a rival church, just two blocks away, taking East Capitol Street Baptist Church as their name and Ingersoll as their pastor. Meeting at Baum's Hall on the corner of East Capitol and Fourth Street SE, the church soon began advertising its services in local newspapers. The worst of it, however, was that they took most of Metropolitan's Sunday school students with them, organizing a Sunday school just three days later.[29] The members of Metropolitan were incensed. Such actions, they felt, were "contrary to 'Baptist usage,' and good church fellowship" and seemed calculated to "injure the interest of the Met. Bap. Church."[30]

Charity amid Conflict

To say that Metropolitan was in crisis would be a vast understatement. Weakened in number, without a pastor, encumbered with debt, and still without a new building, they were in far worse straits than when Parker had resigned in 1882. Yet somehow, they pulled through without allowing bitterness to cloud their judgment. On December 17, 1884,

27 Benjamin F. Bingham, "Retrospective," *The Metropolitan Baptist*, June 1892, 12, MS 1551, box 6, folder 4, CHBC Archives.
28 A. P. Steward to the Metropolitan Baptist Church, December 16, 1884, MS 654, box 2, folder 2, CHBC Archives.
29 Metropolitan Baptist Church Minutes, November 13, 1884, 91.
30 Metropolitan Baptist Church Minutes, November 13, 1884, 91.

they voted to adopt a resolution, stating that "in the interest of reconciliation, harmony, peace, and Christian spirit," they desired to place
on their records "a declaration of [MBC's] duty toward those who have
severed, and those who are about to sever their connection" with the
church. In this remarkable statement, the hurting members resolved
"that while we may entertain different views, we recognize that we are
in the service of the same Master, and should not entertain other than
a forgiving spirit." Beyond forgiveness, they further resolved "that now
and hereafter it shall be our object to endeavor to cultivate, by kind
word and deed, Christian relations, and we earnestly hope that many
of their number may eventually see fit to return to our membership."[31]
A copy of the resolution was sent to every departing member.

By the fall of 1885, Metropolitan had sold the debt-ridden property
on East Capitol Street and could celebrate "being *once more* free from
Debt."[32] Though there is no record of any reply, the members who
stayed took the additional step of returning any money that had been
contributed to their building project to the members who had left. "If
anybody has formally thanked the church," McLean wrote, "the trustees have not been informed of it." Still, they were unwilling to hold a
grudge. "The matter seems to be closed," McLean wrote, "and we say,
'*requiescat in pace*'"—that is, rest in peace.[33]

A year later, perhaps in response to Metropolitan's gesture, the East
Capitol Street Baptist Church formally invited Metropolitan to send
delegates to meet in council on October 19, 1885, to consider the
"propriety" of recognizing them as a "regular and independent Church
of Christ."[34] The members of Metropolitan voted unanimously to
send delegates and offer their full support and recognition of the new

31 Metropolitan Baptist Church Minutes, December 17, 1884, 93–94.
32 Report of Board of Trustees, December 31, 1886, MS 654, box 2, folder 2, CHBC Archives
    (emphasis in original). For discussion of the sale, see Metropolitan Baptist Church Minutes,
    April 15, 1885, 98.
33 Report of Board of Trustees, December 31, 1887, MS 654, box 2, folder 2, CHBC Archives.
34 Metropolitan Baptist Church Minutes, October 8, 1885, 106.

congregation. When Metropolitan was invited to participate in services in recognition of the new church on October 26, the church adopted a resolution, encouraging "as many of the members attend as practicable."[35] While East Capitol Street Baptist Church was in the process of erecting its own building at the corner of South Carolina Avenue and Ninth Street SE in 1887, Metropolitan offered them the use of their baptistry "whenever they may desire, either in a union service" or as "a special service," adding that "we will esteem it a privilege to prepare the place at any time" for East Capitol Street's use.[36]

GRACE BAPTIST CHURCH.

Figure 3.3. The new building of Grace Baptist Church at South Carolina Avenue and 9th Street SE, built by East Capitol Street Baptist Church in 1891. In the 1980s, the building was sold to a developer who converted it into an apartment building now known as Grace Condominiums.

In a city famous for its acrimony, divisions, and hostility, where did this remarkable display of civility and charity come from? How did two warring factions transform their relationship from one of bitter conflict to amicable cooperation, allowing them to coexist peacefully on Capitol Hill for almost a century? The answer can be traced back to a solemn vow they made to each other on February 27, 1878, which they repeated at every monthly communion service for six years: "We

35 Metropolitan Baptist Church Minutes, October 21, 1885, 107.
36 Metropolitan Baptist Church Minutes, February 5, 1887, 118.

will seek to cultivate and maintain Christian sympathy and courtesy and earnestly endeavor to avoid doing, or giving utterance to anything which may grieve or offend any from the least to the greatest of those for whom Christ died."[37] They understood that, despite their divergent beliefs on certain issues, they were both serving the same Lord who loved and died for them. Their church covenant was the foundation of their enduring reconciliation and serves as a powerful reminder of the transformative power of forgiveness.

Grace Baptist Church, as East Capitol Street Baptist Church became known after completing their building in 1891, experienced growth throughout much of the twentieth century, boasting a membership of over 1,200 in the 1950s. This predominantly White, conservative, middle-class congregation prided itself on its striking architecture, dynamic members, and extensive community outreach. However, like many churches in Washington, DC, Grace struggled to retain its members following the destructive riots of 1968, reportedly losing between forty and fifty members each month. In 1970, Grace sold its beloved building to Faith Baptist Church, a predominantly African American congregation, and relocated to Camp Springs, Maryland. Unfortunately, Faith Baptist, with a membership of just 250, could not afford to maintain the historic building and was forced to sell it to a developer in 1985, who converted it into twenty-four condominiums.[38]

———

"History can only be carefully written in the light of subsequent events," Francis McLean penned in 1885.[39] The story of Ingersoll and the church split of 1884 is a sobering reminder of how sin, pride, and

37 Metropolitan Baptist Church Minutes, March 15, 1878, 18–19.
38 DeNeen L. Brown, "Developer Takes Over Deserted SE Church," *Washington Post*, December 3, 1987, https://www.washingtonpost.com/.
39 Clerk's Annual Report, January 1, 1885.

factionalism can decimate a church community. However, it is also a tale of how God's grace operates in the midst of human imperfection and frailty. It is a story of believers who, although being hurt and wronged, responded with graciousness and forgiveness and joined hands for the sake of the gospel, despite their past differences. The wounds of the past year were still raw, but McLean's words revealed a spirit of compassion and reconciliation: "We wish our erring brethren and sisters well, and manifest that spirit in inviting most of them to return."[40]

McLean's prayers were answered on June 11, 1885, when the members of Metropolitan witnessed a remarkable act of reconciliation. Six months after the group of dissatisfied members had broken away to form East Capitol Street Baptist Church, Carrie E. Trumble, one of their number, stood before the congregation and expressed her heartfelt desire to return to Metropolitan's fold. With tearful embraces and a unanimous vote, sister Trumble was reinstated, welcomed back to her "old church home" with open arms.[41]

As in most conflicts, there were probably many mistakes made on both sides. In some ways, it would have been good for the congregation to agree to the ex parte council called for by Ingersoll, even if they would not have been bound by its decision, humbly accepting outside advice and allowing other pastors to speak into their difficulties. That was one of the weaknesses of not having a plurality of elders. At the same time, Ingersoll clearly overstepped his authority by calling a council apart from the will of the congregation. But in the end, we cannot adjudicate the conflict. We can and should learn lessons from history, but ultimately God is the Lord of history. And it is before his bar of justice that every congregation and pastor will be judged (2 Cor. 1:14). Each one of us—pastor and member—will be judged for whether we, like the members of Metropolitan in 1884, have cultivated and maintained

40 Clerk's Annual Report, January 1, 1885.
41 Metropolitan Baptist Church Minutes, February 2, 1888, 100.

a spirit of sympathy and charity, endeavoring to speak only of what is good and true, even toward those who have hurt us.

Through the most trying of circumstances, Metropolitan Baptist Church found the grace to forgive that can only be found in the gospel of Jesus Christ. The light on the Hill, diminished but not quenched, continued to shine despite the darkness of 1884. In fact, the darkness only made the light shine brighter.

4

"We Do Our Own Thinking in This Church"

1885–1889

IN 1885 METROPOLITAN BAPTIST CHURCH was a shell of its former self. Riven by the bitter schism of the previous year, the church was leaderless, debt-ridden, and still without a new building. At least the members could console themselves that an overcrowded building was no longer a problem. Yet against all odds, the next half decade witnessed a stunning rebirth. By 1890, the church had doubled in size, constructed a grand new edifice, and established itself as one of Capitol Hill's most prosperous and influential religious institutions. How did they do it?

On March 1, 1885, Metropolitan secured the services of William Henry Young, a rising preaching star. Although only thirty-two years old, Young brought a gravitas beyond his years. A formidable figure, his father, Edward Young, was Chief of the US Bureau of Statistics, and Young had initially planned to follow in his father's scientific footsteps before he felt the pull of ministry. With engineering degrees from Yale and Cornell and theological training from Crozer Theological

Seminary, Young brought the youth, energy, and enthusiasm needed by the dwindling church.[1]

William Henry Young

From the outset, Young threw himself into preaching, organizing, and evangelizing. Although he received a meager salary of twenty-five dollars a month, which covered only his Sunday morning services, he insisted on holding two services every Sunday, regardless of pay.[2] With his encouragement, the church printed five hundred cards with its name, service times, Scripture quotations, and instructions on how to join a Baptist church, which they distributed throughout the area.[3] Even though he had only signed on for a six-month interim pastorate, he was determined to help the church in any way he could. Encouraged by the fruit from Young's labors, Metropolitan unanimously called him to serve as pastor on September 5, 1885, installing him on October 8, 1885. The church made a special note to invite Ingersoll and East Capitol Street Baptist Church to the service.[4]

Given that the church had effectively fired its previous pastor, in his letter of acceptance Young was careful to articulate his understanding of the proper relationship of pastor and church. Recognizing his predecessor's heavy-handedness in church finances, Young insisted, first, that his personal views as pastor were not inerrant. He was content to withdraw from any entanglement in church business and finance, citing the example of the apostles when the deacons were first chosen (Acts 6:2–4). He explained that, as an individual, his position among the members was that of a mere brother with no inherent authority.[5]

1 "Science and the Gospel," *National Republican*, October 18, 1886.
2 Metropolitan Baptist Church Minutes, March 6, 1885, MS 1602, p. 97, box 6, folder 7, Capitol Hill Baptist Church Archives, Washington DC (hereafter, CHBC Archives).
3 Metropolitan Baptist Church Minutes, May 29, 1885, 100.
4 Metropolitan Baptist Church Minutes, September 10, 1885, 104.
5 William H. Young to Metropolitan Baptist Church, December 16, 1885, MS 1090, box 5, folder 4, CHBC Archives.

Recognizing the congregation's democratic tendencies, however, Young also emphasized the church's obligation to submit to their pastor in his official capacity. "This gives me an authority, that is unquestioned," he explained, "inasmuch as it is accorded me by your deliberate and untrammeled election." In this official capacity as pastor, Young explained, "directions and decisions are no longer my own but yours, since I represent the church, and not myself." In order to avoid the kind of conflicts that would undermine its cohesion and government, the church needed to support their chosen pastor as the "executive of the whole church." Such authority did not concern "matters of opinion" but only the interpretation and application of Scripture. With these principles in mind, Young trusted that the church would become one living, active, and earnest body of Christians whose chief aim was to honor and obey their Lord and Savior.[6]

Figure 4.1. A photograph of William H. Young (1853–1915) from his 1896 book *How to Preach with Power*.

6 William H. Young to Metropolitan Baptist Church, December 16, 1885.

It did not take long for Young's leadership skills to be tested. Tensions that had lain dormant since the split of 1884 resurfaced at the annual meeting of the Columbia Association of Baptist Churches in 1887. Metropolitan, which had felt betrayed by their Baptist brethren in Washington since 1884, hoped to finally explain their actions and experience some degree of vindication. They hoped to explain to the body, which seemed to have sided with the East Capitol Street Baptist Church, that they had done everything they could for the cause of peace, even returning $638.38 in funds contributed toward its building project to departing members. Nevertheless "vapid talk and misrepresentation" continued to be circulated.[7]

In 1887 Metropolitan resolved to act. They drafted a letter that would set the record straight once and for all. In it, they proclaimed their determination to defend the church's reputation against all challengers. The letter was sent to the Columbia Association to be read at its annual meeting on November 15, 1887.[8]

When the day of the annual meeting came, all was well until the chair turned to read Metropolitan's letter. Some delegates seemed to shift nervously in their seats, anticipating a stir as the meeting chair approached the section of the letter related to the conflict with East Capitol Street Baptist Church. But the stir never came. Or at least not as the members of Metropolitan had expected. Instead of reading the letter in its entirety, the chair deliberately skipped over the section related to the conflict with East Capitol Street. When Young demanded an explanation, he was informed that the executive committee of the Columbia Association had made the decision not to read the entire letter. Infuriated, the delegates of Metropolitan protested vehemently. But their protests fell on deaf ears.[9]

7 Metropolitan Baptist Church to the Columbia Association of Baptist Churches, November 15, 1887, MS 901, box 3, folder 1, CHBC Archives.
8 Metropolitan Baptist Church to the Columbia Association of Baptist Churches, November 15, 1887.
9 "Disagreeing Baptists," *National Republican*, November 16, 1887, 1.

To Metropolitan's members, the insult was the final straw in a long train of abuses and usurpations. The association's apparent "disposition to bulldoze our church" had begun when they failed to come to Metropolitan's defense during Ingersoll's unauthorized 1884 church council.[10] The association's decision to suppress the evidence securing Metropolitan's vindication only confirmed their lack of impartiality. As one sister put it, the association had been using them "as a doormat" for too long.[11] Angered by the slight, Young stood and announced that his delegation would be leaving the meeting.[12]

With a firm resolve to chart their own course, Metropolitan voted the next week to formally withdraw from the Columbia Association.[13] In their annual letter for 1887, the church trustees congratulated the church on "the blessing of being virtually freed from the so-called 'Columbia Association of Baptist Churches.'"[14] The act seemed like the direct fulfilment of Francis McLean's declaration of two years earlier: "We will not be a fifth wheel to somebody's coach," McLean declared. "We do our own thinking in this church and base our actions upon the product of thought."[15] Metropolitan was committed to charting its own course and letting the fruit of their labors be their vindication.

Vindication by Numbers

Freed from the constraining shackles of associational life, the members of Metropolitan were driven by an unyielding determination to succeed. With the taunt that they would inevitably "go under" still ringing in

10 "Cause: MBC vs. Association, 1887, Paper Clippings," MS 901, box 3, folder 1, CHBC Archives.
11 Clerk's Annual Report, December 31, 1887, MS 1585, box 6, folder 5, CHBC Archives.
12 "Disagreeing Baptists," 1.
13 Metropolitan Baptist Church Minutes, December 21, 1887, 129.
14 Reports of Board of Trustees, December 31, 1887, MS 654, box 2, folder 2, CHBC Archives.
15 Clerk's Annual Report, December 31, 1885, MS 1583a, box 6, folder 5, CHBC Archives.

their ears, Metropolitan's members engaged in an ambitious project to grow their church, whatever the cost. If the association and the East Capitol Street Baptist Church had doubts about their survival, Metropolitan would prove them wrong by erecting a new structure that would be "a credit to the Baptist denomination and an ornament to the city."[16]

In a bold attempt to fund their grand vision, the church embarked on an ambitious fundraising campaign, sending letters to "every public man of any note" across the country and printing circulars bearing the signatures of the pastor, treasurer, and clerk.[17] One was even sent to Charles H. Spurgeon in London! When their letter to the "Prince of Preachers" went unanswered, the church treasurer concluded wryly that "Englishmen like to receive presents but not to give any to foreigners."[18]

Metropolitan's financial appeal was compelling, citing the unstable nature of work for the many government workers among their congregation. And with an eye-catching engraving of the proposed building, the circulars left no doubt that this was a project worth investing in. As McLean, wrote in 1886, "We are working partly for those who come after us."[19]

The architectural plan was stunning. With a handsome price tag of $41,000, the ambitious congregation aimed to erect an ornate Gothic structure on Capitol Hill. The design was visionary, allowing the project to be completed in stages. The first stage involved erecting a small, three-hundred-seat chapel for $5,000 and then later adding the impressive spire and main sanctuary once the additional $36,000 could be raised. Construction of the new chapel began in 1887, and by

16 Metropolitan Baptist Church to the Columbia Association of Baptist Churches, November 15, 1886, MS 901, box 3, folder 1, CHBC Archives.
17 "Metropolitan Baptist Church," *Washington Times*, September 9, 1894, 5.
18 "Pickles," *The Metropolitan Baptist*, June 1893, 11, MS 1558, p. 11, box 6, folder 4, CHBC Archives.
19 Clerk's Annual Report, December 31, 1886, MS 1583b, box 6, folder 5, CHBC Archives.

March of the following year, the first part of the building was complete: a chapel that could hold up to three hundred people.[20]

Figure 4.2. Sketch of proposed new church building at corner of 6th and A Streets NE from 1887. The entire structure with the stunning spire was never completed, leaving Metropolitan with only the smaller chapel pictured on the right.

Young was a man on a mission. He wanted to vindicate Metropolitan's reputation by raising the additional $36,000 to complete the new building. But to do so, he resorted to the original revivalistic methods that had contributed to Ingersoll's departure. Like Ingersoll and so many other churches during the late nineteenth century, Young began aggressively holding protracted meetings to grow the church and fund the new building.

20 "The Metropolitan Baptist Church," *Evening Star*, 7 April 7, 1888, 9.

Figure 4.3. The 1876 and 1888 church buildings side by side. The chapel on the right could seat up to three hundred persons. The congregation planned to demolish the first chapel (left) once the additional $36,000 was raised for the new building. These plans never materialized, and the original chapel continued in use as the Sunday school building until both buildings were demolished in 1911.

Protracted meetings had been a regular feature of Metropolitan Baptist Church since 1884. Each year around the New Year, a revivalist would be invited. Nightly prayer meetings would be held with sermons, singing, prayer, and ample opportunities for nonmembers to share their testimonies and be received for baptism the following Sunday. As for other Baptist churches in the nineteenth century, the criteria of church health were primarily quantitative, measured by the number of days a revival lasted and by the number of conversions obtained.[21] Generally speaking, for a revival to be considered a success it had to result in sixteen or more baptisms within a three-month period.[22] With the exception of 1886

---

21 William G. McLoughlin, *Modern Revivalism: Charles Grandison Finney to Billy Graham* (Eugene, OR: Wipf and Stock, 2004), 129.

22 Curtis D. Johnson, "The Protracted Meeting Myth: Awakenings, Revivals, and New York State Baptists, 1789–1850," *Journal of the Early Republic* 34, no. 3 (2014): 355.

when no protracted meetings were held, four such "revivals" occurred between 1884 and 1888 at Metropolitan Baptist Church, adding a total of 117 members by baptism over the course of just five years (see table 4.1).

Table 4.1 Protracted meetings at Metropolitan Baptist Church, 1884–1888 (none held in 1886)

Year	Annual baptisms	Annual baptisms from protracted meetings	Percentage of annual baptisms from protracted meetings
1884	20	20	100
1885	24	17	71
1887	25	24	96
1888	45	45	100

Source: Metropolitan Baptist Church Membership Book, MS 1538, box 6, folder 1, CHBC Archives.

Numerically speaking, Young's efforts at growing the church through revivals were a roaring success. To the delight of its members, and the chagrin of its detractors, Metropolitan's baptismal numbers exceeded every other church in the Columbia Association. Even more staggering, 91 percent of these baptisms occurred in conjunction with protracted meetings, demonstrating the method's success in generating decisions. "No Baptist church in the District compares favorably with ours," McLean wrote smugly in 1887. "Continual increase year after year that convinces people we are fast becoming a power."[23]

Numerical Growth without Lasting Fruit

Under the surface, however, cracks were emerging. As the number of members increased through protracted meetings, from 60 in 1884 to over 200 by 1889, so did the proportion of non-attending and non-giving members. At the end of 1889, 18 percent of the church's 206

23 Clerk's Annual Report, December 31, 1887.

members were known to have neither given nor attended. The following year, this number increased to 21 percent of the church's 208 members.

Although he tried to make light of it in his annual report for 1888, McLean was evidently concerned by the growing trend. "Some birds of flight get registered for safe-keeping, and like Noah's Raven never return," he joked. "Whether in the body, or out of the body, it is hard to keep track. There's a remedy in the magic word 'dropped.'"[24] As table 4.2 indicates, of the 106 members baptized at protracted meetings between 1884 and 1888, an astonishing 44 percent stopped attending and were eventually dropped from membership.

Table 4.2 Measures of effectiveness of protracted meetings at Metropolitan Baptist Church, 1884–1888 (none held in 1886)

Year	Annual baptisms	Annual baptisms from protracted meetings	Percentage of baptisms from protracted meetings	Average membership duration of revival converts (in years)	Percentage of revival converts dropped from membership
1884	20	20	100	4.82	30
1885	24	17	71	6.86	53
1887	25	24	96	6.81	42
1888	45	45	100	5.55	51

Source: Metropolitan Baptist Church Membership Book, MS 1538, box 6, folder 1, CHBC Archives.

Despite the efforts of the pastors and deacons, nonattendance and non-giving continued to be a problem. A resolution was passed in 1888 warning that non-attending and non-contributing members would be subject to disciplinary actions.[25] Still the problem persisted. When Young issued an ultimatum to the church in June of 1888 stating that

24 Clerk's Annual Report, December 31, 1888, MS 1586, box 6, folder 5, CHBC Archives.
25 Metropolitan Baptist Church Minutes, October 7, 1888, 137.

if they could not increase his income by the following fall, he would have to go elsewhere, the church reluctantly responded that increasing his salary was an impossibility.[26] Although Young later claimed in 1890 that his resignation had nothing to do with salary, there is little doubt that he was deeply disappointed in the fruits of his labors. The church had grown numerically—it even had a bigger building. But where were the members who had recently been baptized? Were they growing spiritually? Why were they not gathering? To what extent did the church's reliance on revivalistic techniques contribute to a cheapening of church membership and a weakening of the church's culture of discipling? Those were the questions that plagued Young for years, long after he had left Metropolitan Baptist Church.

Years later, Young reflected on his experience pastoring Metropolitan and the mixed results of his evangelistic methods by calling for patience over spontaneity and inward fruit over external responses. "Impatience" in evangelism, Young wrote, "leads to a change of methods and remedies without reason, and very commonly urges the sinner to profess conversion and 'join church,' before he is even convicted of sin—because 'additions' are regarded more important than regeneration."[27] Such methods, Young warned, lead to a church filled with "more fishes than sheep. They are tame, graceful, beautiful but they are nothing but fish! No 'conversion,' not a change of nature but merely a change of habit."[28]

———

From a purely materialistic standpoint, Metropolitan appeared on the path to success. Despite the split of 1884 and the conflict with the Columbia Association in 1887, the church had bounced back with a new building and a growing membership. But serious questions

26 Metropolitan Baptist Church Minutes, July 18, 1888, 134.
27 William Henry Young, *Tactology: The Science of Personal Work* (Athens, GA: How, 1905), 65.
28 Young, *Tactology*, 139.

remained regarding the church's future. Had the church saved itself from debt and disgrace by sacrificing its integrity and purity?

One implication of the supernatural nature of Christian ministry is that there is no shortcut to success. A church can attract a crowd. A church can even baptize them, erect a building, and fill it. But if the people are not converted, the work will have been built on sinking sand, destined to be washed away with the rain because it is not built on the rock (see Matt. 7:24–27). Rushing the work of the Holy Spirit, even when the goal is to secure a good end such as increasing giving, constructing a building, or reaching the community, will have a tendency to undermine the nature of the church and its mission. Alternatively, when you build a church that is truly composed of believers, those good fruits that you desire will come with time as a natural result of the Spirit's work through changed lives. There is no shortcut in the process—just the ordinary means of grace.

Metropolitan had survived its darkest moment yet. It had emerged from a church split with a resolve to vindicate its rightness by adopting an aggressive growth plan to vindicate worldly ambitions. But the church had changed in the process. Could they recover the spiritual zeal of their founding? Or would they succumb to the all-too-common maladies of nominalism and spiritual apathy that plagued so many churches in the District?

The answer to these pressing questions lay, at least in part, in the arrival of a decorated Civil War general in Washington, DC, in 1890, whose final pastoral stint before his death would leave an indelible mark on the nation's capital. His influence would be crucial in helping Metropolitan rekindle the spiritual zeal of its founding and chart a course toward its future as a light on the Hill.

5

"We Have a Leader of National Reputation"

1890–1895

PETER H. YOUNG lay battered and bloodied when a neighbor found him on the desolate streets of Third and A Street NE in the early hours of June 22, 1892. A dim streetlight cast an eerie glow on the scene, illuminating a pick handle covered in blood and hair, discarded beside a barely breathing body. Carried to his brother-in-law's home at 302 East Capitol Street, Young died shortly after, victim to a senseless crime.

Forty-eight-year-old Young had served in the Union Army during the Civil War, leaving him permanently scarred and paralyzed in his left arm. Though his eyesight was poor, Young operated a small grocery store at Fourth and D Streets SE, a few blocks from where he was viciously attacked. Months earlier, he had been robbed of $200, but instead of seeking justice, he showed mercy to his assailants, declining to prosecute them. Little did he know that this act of kindness would be repaid with a brutal and fatal beating.

On the night of June 22, Young's assailants reappeared at his store. One purchased a cent's worth of cigarettes before following Young as he made his way home. Unaware that he was being followed, Young crossed Pennsylvania Avenue SE and reached Third Street, where his assailants approached him under a nearby streetlamp. Asked by one of the attackers for a light for his cigarette, Young paused to pull a pack of matches from his pocket. Struck without warning, Young fell to the ground in a pool of his own blood. The assailants snatched his satchel and fled into the darkness. But they were not alone. A young girl witnessed the crime from inside her home, providing a crucial eyewitness account that would aid the police investigation.[1]

The murder of Peter Young shocked the Capitol Hill community. It also shocked the members of Metropolitan Baptist Church, of which Peter Young was a member. Since joining by baptism on April 29, 1888, during one of William H. Young's revival services, Peter H. Young had been a faithful and consistent church member.[2] "He never lost an opportunity of saying a word for the Master," James O'Connor eulogized in *The Metropolitan Baptist*, "and he was often heard speaking to a customer about his soul's welfare."[3] As a symbol of his sacrificial nature, Young's final act was to offer assistance to his assailant.

For those living on Capitol Hill, Young's murder represented the social decay and moral regress enveloping the urban centers of the nation. As America shifted from a nation dominated by small towns to one shaped by cities, urbanization wrested social control from small, tight-knit communities, creating a vacuum of moral authority. Laissez-faire market policies struggled to rein in economic empires that exploited immigrants and African Americans, leaving them to dwell in overcrowded alleys and tenement houses. Daily papers shocked audiences with stories of murders, divorce, and decadence, contributing to

1   The story of Young's murder has been reconstructed from "A Pick Handle the Weapon," *Evening Star*, July 23, 1892, 6; "The Capitol Hill Murder," *Evening Star*, July 25, 1892, 7.
2   Metropolitan Baptist Church Minutes, April 26, 1888, MS 1602, p. 132, box 6, folder 7, Capitol Hill Baptist Church Archives, Washington DC (hereafter, CHBC Archives).
3   "Peter H. Young," *The Metropolitan Baptist*, August 1892, MS 1552, p. 22, box 6, folder 4, CHBC Archives.

an overall sense of gloom. As one member of Metropolitan lamented in 1892, "The opening of our present century in this country was an age animated by great statesmen with pure and lofty sentiments, but the close of it seems to be animated by a desire for money and power more than for the public welfare."[4]

But as a growing evangelical congregation in the emerging Capitol Hill neighborhood of the nation's capital, Metropolitan Baptist Church was determined to do its part to push back the darkness of the decadent age. They started by calling Green Clay Smith as their pastor.

Figure 5.1.   General Green Clay Smith (1826–1895) in 1862 shortly after his election to Congress.

4   Fannie Bingham, "Stray Thoughts," *The Metropolitan Baptist*, March 1892, 50, Kiplinger Research Library, Washington, DC. For instance, George Marsden writes of the final decades of the nineteenth century, "America was changing rapidly from a culture dominated by small towns and the countryside to one shaped by cities and suburbs. Waves of 'uprooted immigrants,' together with rapid industrialization, created virtually insurmountable urban problems." George M. Marsden, *Fundamentalism and American Culture: The Shaping of Twentieth Century Evangelicalism, 1870–1925* (New York: Oxford University Press, 1980), 21.

Green Clay Smith

When Gen. Green Clay Smith arrived in Washington on September 14, 1890, to preach at Metropolitan in view of a call, the city was abuzz with excitement. The *Washington Post* ran an extensive article the next day titled "From Politics to Preaching," providing a lengthy biography of the renowned lawyer turned soldier turned politician turned preacher.[5] When the esteemed general graciously accepted the church's call a few weeks later, church clerk Francis McLean could hardly contain his enthusiasm, "Ring the bells! Ring the change!" he wrote excitedly. "We have a leader of national reputation."[6] After a quarter of a century away from the capital, General Smith had returned to Washington.

Born in 1826, Smith was a member of the famous Clay family of Kentucky. A nephew to Cassius M. Clay, Smith married Lena Duke, the niece of Supreme Court Chief Justice John Marshall. Before he answered the call to the pastorate, Smith's illustrious career included serving as a second lieutenant during the Mexican-American War, a Union brigadier general during the Civil War, a two-term congressman from Kentucky, and the first territorial governor of Montana.

What Smith was most famous for—at least during his day—was reputedly coming one vote short of becoming president of the United States. The story, frequently recounted, was that as a delegate to the Republican National Convention in Baltimore in 1864, Smith was one of two nominees put forward to run on the same ticket as Abraham Lincoln as vice president. The other nominee was Andrew Johnson of Tennessee. But when the votes were tallied, the result was a tie, leading the chairman, who was obligated to break the tie, to vote in favor of Andrew Johnson.[7] Although Smith later denied and downplayed the

---

5   "From Politics to Preaching," *Washington Post*, September 15, 1890, 1.
6   Clerk's Annual Report, December 31, 1890, MS 1587, box 6, folder 5, CHBC Archives.
7   *Contributions to the Historical Society of Montana*, vol. 7 (Helena, MT: Historical and Miscellaneous Library of Montana, 1910), 217–18, https://archive.org/details/contributionstohvol7hist1910rich /page/216/mode/2up.

story, the legend continued to live for decades, even during Smith's pastorate in Washington, DC, leaving him to be remembered as the man who almost became president.[8]

To the shock of Smith's family, at the end of his term as territorial governor of Montana, he abruptly announced in 1869 that he intended to enter the ministry. Despite protests that such work was beneath him, Smith was ordained as a preacher at the old Viney Fork country church in Madison County, Kentucky.[9] From that day until his death, as one friend remarked, where he had often before been heard as a "lawyer, politician and warrior," he was now "heard as a preacher of the gospel."[10]

Over the next two decades, Smith held numerous pastorates and traveled extensively as an evangelist and church planter. He was respected throughout Kentucky, being chosen for nine consecutive years (1879–1887) as moderator of the Kentucky Baptist General Association. As a preacher, his gifts were remembered as being "much above the average,"[11] a fact unsurprising given his reputation as an orator in Congress.[12] As an accomplished raconteur, like his friend Lincoln, Smith had been awarded a gold-headed cane by his colleagues

8   The apocryphal nature of this story is best demonstrated by an examination of the minutes of the Republican National Convention for 1864, which show that although Green Clay Smith was present as a delegate for Kentucky, he was never nominated for vice president. In fact, the narrow vote was between Johnson and Hannibal Hamlin—with Smith being one of the first to change his vote from Hamlin to Johnson after the men were locked in a tie vote. *Presidential Election, 1864: Proceedings of the National Union Convention Held in Baltimore, Md., June 7th and 8th, 1864* (New York: Baker and Godwin, 1864), 68–76. Furthermore, a newspaper account from 1895 acknowledged the widespread rumor that Smith had nearly won the nomination for vice president but asserted that Green Clay Smith had personally denied the story: "There was a severe contest between him and Andrew Johnson, and Smith was defeated for the nomination. . . . A story has been going the rounds that he came within one-half a vote of securing the place on the ticket with Abraham Lincoln, but Gen. Smith himself denied this story." *Courier-Journal*, June 30, 1895.

9   *Contributions to the Historical Society of Montana*, vol. 5 (Helena: Independent, 1904), 182, https://archive.org/details/contributionstohvol5hist1904rich/page/182/mode/2up. This volume contains six essays on Green Clay Smith (see 5:108–86).

10 *Contributions to the Historical Society of Montana*, 5:180.

11 *Contributions to the Historical Society of Montana*, 5:183–84.

12 "Metropolitan Baptist Church: A Wide-Awake and Pushing Organization on Capitol Hill," *Washington Times*, September 9, 1894, MS 1323, box 5, folder 22, CHBC Archives.

in Congress as "ablest speaker of that body."[13] As one contemporary put it, he belonged to "the old school of preachers who made the doctrines of the Bible the themes of their discourses and illustrated them with their own experiences."[14] Wherever he went, whether as pastor of the prestigious First Baptist Church of Frankfort where Kentucky Governor Preston H. Leslie was a member, or smaller, lesser known congregations such as the Baptist Church at Williamsburg in Whitley County, with only seven charter members,[15] Smith preached the undiluted gospel of Jesus Christ—with a healthy dose of temperance mixed in.

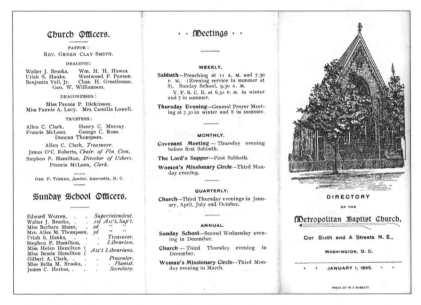

Figure 5.2. A church directory from 1895 indicates the regular schedule of the church and features a drawing of the newly constructed chapel.

Temperance Man and Baptist Reformer

Smith was not just a preacher and a church organizer but also a prominent figure in the temperance movement, both locally in Kentucky

13   "Bravely Faced Death," *Washington Post*, June 30, 1895, 3.
14   *Contributions to the Historical Society of Montana*, 5:184.
15   *Courier-Journal*, June 30, 1895.

and on a national level. As a young man, he had been involved in the liquor business and had opposed the expansion of taxes on liquor as a congressman. In fact, in 1864 he wrote to President Lincoln, pleading with him not to approve a proposed liquor bill but to instead let Congress more carefully consider the question of taxing liquor.[16]

Everything changed after the Civil War. Legend has it that Smith spent a week at a Washington hotel and was charged an exorbitant rate of $1,200 by a greedy proprietor. To recoup the cost, he presented the hotel owner with a bottle of Kentucky whiskey, which the owner declared was the best whiskey he had ever tasted. The owner agreed to purchase five barrels at a rate of ten dollars per gallon, unaware that Smith could buy the whiskey wholesale for only three dollars per gallon. Smith returned to Kentucky, shipped off the liquor and returned to Washington to collect the bill. But on entering the hotel saloon, Smith found several large posters hanging over the counter advertising "General Green Clay Smith's Old Crow Kentucky Bourbon Whisky! Guaranteed to be twenty-five years old! Only 50 cents a drink!" Furious, and embarrassed, Smith demanded that the posters be taken down and vowed never to buy, sell, or drink a drop of liquor again.[17]

True to his word, after becoming a minister, Smith emerged as a leading figure in the temperance movement in America. In 1874, he coedited the temperance journal *The True Reformer* with Elder B. B. Taylor.[18] Two years later, he was unanimously nominated at the Prohibition Convention in Cleveland to run as a presidential candidate for the Prohibition Party.[19] In fact, when the Southern Baptist Convention took the dramatic step of passing a resolution condemning the liquor trade and calling for temperance legislation, who else could

16 Green Clay Smith to Abraham Lincoln (telegram concerning tax on liquor), December 27, 1864, Abraham Lincoln Papers, Series 1, General Correspondence, 1833 to 1916, Library of Congress, https://www.loc.gov/item/mal3958800/.
17 "General Green Clay Smith," *Indiana State Sentinel,* June 29, 1887, 5.
18 *Owensboro Monitor,* April 15, 1874, 2.
19 *Courier-Journal,* June 30, 1895.

have presented the resolution to the convention floor but Green Clay Smith?[20] Although his attempts to disrupt the two-party system never resulted in major campaign victories (of the 8 million popular votes cast, Smith received only 9,737 as the Prohibition Reform Party candidate in 1876), he did bring attention to the social and moral consequences of alcohol consumption, driving both parties to acknowledge the need for temperance legislation in America.[21]

As a Baptist and a preacher, Smith never conceived of anything akin to a separation of religion and politics. "The Word of God," he declared in his inaugural sermon as pastor of Metropolitan, "is the foundation of all that is good in human laws." "We put a penalty on our statute books for murder," he explained, "but it was God who said: 'thou shalt not commit murder.'" So it was with all other earthly laws.[22]

Smith was keenly aware of the social and intellectual forces seeking to sever Christianity's influence on government, law, and culture. He saw how materialism and naturalism were creeping into American intellectual circles, and he derided "liberalism" as "the most illiberal position to assume." Although God had entrusted to America the gift of liberty, that freedom was not a license to do as one pleased but the Spirit-wrought moral obligation to submit to God's law. Individual liberty, Smith taught, entitled everyone to a degree of respect to their own opinions but did not entitle them to "break up churches, override the Sabbath, and destroy the religion of Christ."[23]

---

20 *Proceedings (Thirty-First Session—Forty-First Year) of the Southern Baptist Convention* (Atlanta: Jas. P. Harrison, 1886), 19, http://media2.sbhla.org.s3.amazonaws.com/annuals/SBC_Annual_1886.pdf.

21 For a study of the limited success of the Prohibition Party and Green Clay Smith's role in it, see Lisa M. F. Andersen, *The Politics of Prohibition: American Governance and the Prohibition Party, 1869–1933* (Cambridge University Press, 2013). Another historian makes the case that, far from being an abject failure, "the prohibition experiment worked surprisingly well, reducing both individual consumption and the social and health problems associated with alcohol abuse." Gaines M. Foster, *Moral Reconstruction: Christian Lobbyists and the Federal Legislation of Morality, 1865–1920* (Chapel Hill, NC: University of North Carolina Press, 2002), 224.

22 "Soldier and Preacher," *Washington Post*, January 5, 1891, 2.

23 Green Clay Smith, "Liberalism," *The Metropolitan Baptist*, February 1893, 45, Kiplinger Research Library.

As Smith traced God's sovereign hand in history, he could not help but conclude that America had a special, God-given mission to the world. From the Mayflower to the Civil War, Smith proclaimed that "it was God fighting for liberty . . . for the independence of nations." What was America's mission in the world? Smith stated the matter unmistakably: "to plant the gospel in all the dark spots of the earth, to be the great chandelier hung out between heaven and earth to give light unto the nations of the world and make them Republican and Christian and free."[24]

The freedom toward which history was tending, in Smith's view, would only be realized as the nation embraced Christianity as the foundation of its laws and the means of making its citizens righteous. Echoing the language of George Washington's Farewell Address, Smith argued that only a godly and moral populace could faithfully steward the responsibilities of republican citizenship, and only Christianity could produce such righteousness. This simple syllogism yielded only one conclusion. The fate of the world rested with America. And America's future lay in the hands of the church. If the church was tasked with making America a light to the nations, then Smith was determined to make Metropolitan Baptist Church a light to America.

The Nursery of the Church

Smith had returned to Washington, in part, because of his fondness for politics. But it was not fundamentally a political mission that brought him back to the nation's capital.[25] True, Metropolitan occasionally endorsed legislation and even petitioned Congress directly in favor of temperance legislation. But for Smith and members of Metropolitan, reform and renewal did not start with the legislation being debated by Congress down the street but with the children in their neighborhood. One could almost say that for members of Metropolitan in the nineteenth century, changing the world started with changing diapers in the nursery.

24 Green Clay Smith, "Memorial Sermon," *The Metropolitan Baptist*, June 1891, 11. Kiplinger Research Library.
25 "Bravely Faced Death," *Washington Post*, June 30, 1895, 3.

To careful observers, America's youth were facing a crisis. Never before had vice, impurity, and obscenity been so accessible to American children. Because of cheap books and dirty magazines, Christians feared that the soft soil of the rising generation's consciences would be too hardened to receive the sacred seed of the gospel message. As Metropolitan's Sunday school superintendent Benjamin F. Bingham explained, "Without these lessons implanted in the hearts and minds of the young by faithful teachers, at home as well as in the school-room, whereby they are led into right ways of living and doing, what would become of thousands?" Bingham knew the answer to his question. "They would add numbers to our almshouses, penitentiaries, prisons, and reform schools, already too crowded with idlers and wrongdoers, thus adding misery to themselves and being a burden to the community."[26]

Figure 5.3. A Sunday school class, photographed in the 1920s, standing in front of Metropolitan's new building, completed in 1912.

26 Benjamin F. Bingham, "Between Ourselves," *The Metropolitan Baptist*, March 1892, 48.

To offset the harmful effects of public immorality, the members of Metropolitan gave themselves tirelessly to the work of teaching the gospel to neighborhood children through the church's Sunday school ministry. Members fully expected that seeds sown in childhood would result in fervent and faithful church membership.[27] To use a favorite metaphor of the day, the Sabbath school was the "Nursery of the Church."[28] The imagery of gardening made this a favorite metaphor of Sunday school workers: gospel seeds were to be sown in the good soil of young and tender hearts, nurtured with the love and affection of teachers, in the hope of bearing lasting fruit of true conversion in time. Thus, the Sunday school was a key part of Metropolitan's hope for America's future. "We owe it to the cause for which we labor," Bingham wrote in 1891, "and we owe it to all we hope for America's stability in the future, to do something—the very best something possible, and that right speedily."[29] The moral and civilizational consequences of failing were too catastrophic to contemplate. Sadly, Metropolitan did not need to look far for an example of the consequences of immorality.

In 1892, a salacious disciplinary case enveloped the church and scandalized the city. It started with a twenty-seven-year-old man named Warren C. Brundage. Brundage was well known to the church. His mother Alice P. Brundage had been a member since 1880, and Brundage had joined Metropolitan by baptism during the protracted meetings of 1885. Shortly after his wedding night, however, Brundage began staying out until 2:00 or 3:00 a.m. Before long, rumors started circulating that Brundage was frequenting a "house of ill fame," where he was reputed to be infatuated with a "woman of the town." The woman, who went by the name "Pauline Gerard," was really named Annie Pullman. And though rumors circulated freely, the church had

---

27 As Boylan writes, by 1880, the American Sunday school had become "the primary recruiting ground for church members." Anne M. Boylan, *Sunday School: The Formation of an American Institution, 1790–1880* (New Haven, CT: Yale University Press, 1988), 166.

28 Clerk's Annual Report, December 31, 1879, MS 1575, box 6, folder 5, CHBC Archives.

29 "Between Ourselves," *The Metropolitan Baptist*, December 1891, 36, Kiplinger Research Library.

no evidence to act on.[30] That is, until Brundage attempted to take out a life insurance policy.

One day, the deacons of Metropolitan Baptist Church were approached by a life insurance agent and his medical examiner who produced evidence of Brundage's guilt. Brundage had applied for a life insurance policy, naming his liaison, Annie Pullman, as the beneficiary in the event of his death. More shockingly, the address listed on his application was the very house of ill fame Brundage had been suspected of frequenting. Though not members of Metropolitan themselves, the insurance agent and medical examiner were aware of Brundage's church membership and held the church in such high regard that they informed Metropolitan's deacons of Brundage's scandalous actions, producing copies of his insurance policy application as incontrovertible evidence of his marital infidelity.[31] On February 11, 1892, on motion of the deacons, Brundage was excluded from membership as an act of discipline.[32]

For the parents and Sunday school workers of Metropolitan Baptist Church, the unfortunate case of Warren Brundage was a cautionary tale they hoped their children and students would avoid. They understood that the little boys and girls who occupied the seats of the Baptist chapel on Sixth and A Streets NE were the mothers, fathers, workers, and leaders of the future. They knew the importance of good role models for children from broken homes. And they knew what was likely to happen to those who failed to learn lessons of thrift, delayed gratification, and honesty in childhood. The jails, saloons, and houses of ill fame were living proof.

As the "nursery of the church," the Sunday school played a critical role in Metropolitan's growth during the nineteenth century. In 1892 the Sunday school outnumbered the church members, 269 to 228. By 1896 this had increased to 314 to 276. Although most students did not

30 "For the Benefit of Another Woman," *Baltimore Sun*, July 26, 1892, 6.
31 "The Brundage Case" 1892, June 10, 1891–April 16, 1892, MS 8, box 1, folder 1,CHBC Archives. Cf. "Mrs. Brundage's Plea for A Divorce," *Evening Star*, July 26, 1892, 8; "Two Divorces Granted," *Washington Times*, April 9, 1895, 6.
32 Metropolitan Baptist Church Minutes, February 11, 1892, 171.

Figure 5.4. Warren C. Brundage's life insurance policy application naming his "friend" Annie Pullman, as the beneficiary.

join the church by baptism until adulthood, some became members as young as nine years old. Thus, Sunday school students constituted a growing proportion of Metropolitan's membership. In 1881, 17 of Metropolitan's 82 members (21 percent) were Sunday school scholars. By 1900, this ratio had grown to 145 of 353 (41 percent).

One Sunday in September 1891, during a service in which Smith invited new members to come forward to be given "the right hand of fellowship," two came forward: a white-haired follower of Christ for over fifty years, and a thirteen-year-old girl who attended Sunday school. The sight of these two vastly different individuals overwhelmed the pastor, causing his voice to falter and tears to stream down his face as he welcomed them both into the church's fellowship and its mission in the Master's vineyard.[33] For Metropolitan Baptist Church, each Sunday school student baptized into membership represented a beacon of hope, indicating that all was not lost and that the forces of light were still prevailing over the forces of darkness. America was not yet without hope.

33 "Current Events," *The Metropolitan Baptist*, September 1891, 25, Kiplinger Research Library.

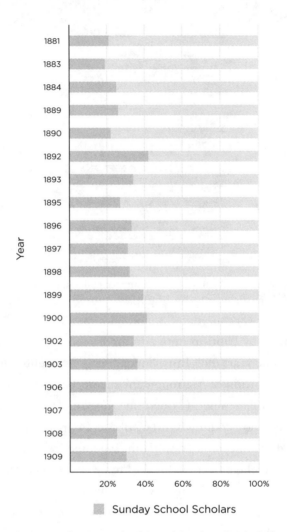

Figure 5.5. Metropolitan's membership and Sunday school scholars (data is missing for the omitted years).

Social Reform Efforts

As pastor, Green Clay Smith led the church in engaging politically in the pressing moral reform causes of the day, including prohibition, Sabbath keeping, and immigration. By the nineteenth century, liquor consumption reached epidemic levels in America. Particularly in urban areas, the devastating effects of liquor traffic were everywhere to be seen in broken families and starving children. Poverty, violence, adultery, divorce, gambling, and Sabbath breaking all shared the common denominator of alcohol.[34] As George Marsden explains, "Prohibition was widely considered the most effective way of attacking urban problems at their root."[35] Even by modern standards, nineteenth-century drinking habits were extreme. In 1830, the average American adult drank anywhere from 4 to 7 gallons of pure alcohol per year, compared to the modern average of 2.8 gallons.[36] While temperance advocates recognized that they may not be able to eradicate alcohol entirely, they could limit its expansion by stigmatizing, restricting, and limiting its sale and consumption. All this lay at the heart of evangelical efforts to the moral, spiritual, and material elevation of the urban poor.

In 1893, the churches of Washington, DC—White and Black—came together to form the Anti-Saloon League of the District of Columbia.[37] Over the next few decades, they worked tirelessly to pass laws through Congress restricting the sale of liquor in the District. Metropolitan Baptist Church was active in temperance work through its preaching and teaching and even through direct political advocacy. For instance, on July 29, 1894, Metropolitan authorized its pastor and deacons on behalf of the church "to sign petitions to both houses of Congress, that manufacture and sale of alcoholic beverages within the District of Columbia, be prohibited."[38]

---

34 According to Carol Crawford Holcomb, "Ultimately, [Baptists] became convinced that alcohol constituted a social problem because it was responsible for family violence, poverty, racial conflict, and a host of other evils." Carol Crawford Holcomb, *Home Without Walls: Southern Baptist Women and Social Reform in the Progressive Era* (Tuscaloosa, AL: University of Alabama Press, 2020), 5.

35 Marsden, *Fundamentalism and American Culture*, 83.

36 Thomas Pegram, *Battling Demon Rum: The Struggle for a Dry America, 1800–1933* (Chicago: Ivan R. Dee, 1998), 7, 31.

37 For instance, Walter H. Brooks, pastor for sixty-eight years of Nineteenth Street Baptist Church in Washington, DC, and one of the most prominent Black preachers of his day, served on the Anti-Saloon League's executive committee from its inception in 1893. Ernest Hurst Cherrington, *History of the Anti-Saloon League* (Westerville, OH: American Issue Publishing Company, 1913), 26.

38 Minutes of the Metropolitan Baptist Church, July 29, 1894, 188.

While their ultimate goal was prohibition, the Anti-Saloon League worked to gradually restrict the sale of liquor by regulating it to death. They petitioned authorities to enforce a clause in the liquor law of the District of Columbia, stating that "licenses shall not be granted to any person to conduct such business within 400 feet of a public or private school *or place of religious worship*."[39] It worked. In time, through persistent lobbying, even prominent Washington hotels—Chamberlin's, Wormley's, Welcker's, the Normandie, the Shoreham, and the Oxford—were barred from serving alcohol as a result of their proximity to churches.[40]

Another pressing area of moral and social reform was Sabbath laws. Questions over the delivery of mail and the legitimacy of printing newspapers on Sunday reached fever pitch in the early 1890s.[41] Recall that in 1861 following the firing on Fort Sumter, no newspapers were printed in Washington on Sunday. Most evangelicals stood decidedly against mail delivery on Sunday, being convinced that the fourth commandment was perpetually binding.[42] "When Christ rose from the grave on the morning of the first day of the week that occasion was called by the apostles and recognized by Christ as the Lord's day," Smith preached. Thus, he explained, "The Sabbath or Lord's Day . . . should be so observed . . . as perpetually binding upon mankind in all ages."[43] On April 17, 1892, Metropolitan's members agreed to stand in solidarity with "the Icemen of the city" and to "unite with them in the effort to observe the Sabbath" by agreeing to "arrange to take ice on Saturday so as to relieve them on the Sabbath day."[44] This was not a case where

---

39 "The Anti-Saloon League is Pursuing an Aggressive Policy," *Washington Post*, July 27, 1893, 3 (emphasis added).

40 "Licenses are Denied," *Washington Post*, May 2, 1894, 8.

41 Wayne Edison Fuller, *Morality and the Mail in Nineteenth-Century America* (Urbana, IL: University of Illinois Press, 2003).

42 Kyle G. Volk, *Moral Minorities and the Making of American Democracy* (New York: Oxford University Press, 2014), 42.

43 "Which is the Lord's Day?" *Washington Post*, June 29 1891, 7.

44 Minutes of the Metropolitan Baptist Church, April 17, 1892, 172. Cf. Stephen T. Hamilton, "Current Events," *The Metropolitan Baptist*, May 1892, MS 1550, p. 5, box 6, folder 4, CHBC Archives.

the church as an institution was out of step with Sabbath observance. There were no ice deliveries to Metropolitan on Sundays. Rather, it was a decision of church members to act in concert in their individual lives as a corporate expression of their conviction on a moral issue.

Another area of moral concern was immigration. However, rather than taking a restrictive stance toward immigration, as might be expected of a church concerned with the toxic spread of "rum, Romanism, and rebellion,"[45] Metropolitan was outspoken in condemning the Chinese Exclusion Act. This law, passed by Congress and signed by President Chester A. Arthur in 1882, excluded skilled and unskilled laborers from China from entering the country. It was the first federal law in American history designed to prevent all members of a specific nation from emigrating to the United States and was closely tied to rising anti-Chinese sentiments. The law was set to last for only ten years, but in 1892 Congress voted to renew the act along with several other dehumanizing requirements for ethnically Chinese-background Americans legally residing in the United States. In May 1893, the Supreme Court voted to uphold the discriminatory law.[46]

In response to the Supreme Court's decision, Metropolitan published an article in the church's newspaper in June 1893 entitled "Our Chinese Brethren," in which the church treasurer, Allen C. Clark, represented the church in condemning the act as contrary to the United States Constitution and Christian morality:

> The primal truth enunciated in the Declaration of Independence is, "that all men are created equal; that they are endowed by their Creator with certain unalienable rights; that among these are life, liberty, and the pursuit of happiness." The word of God declares: "He hath made of one blood all nations of men for to dwell on the face of the earth."

45 Mark Wahlgren Summers, *Rum, Romanism, and Rebellion* (Chapel Hill, NC: University of North Carolina Press, 2000), 282.

46 Andrew Gyory, *Closing the Gate: Race, Politics, and the Chinese Exclusion Act* (Chapel Hill, NC: University of North Carolina Press, 2000), 1, 253, 315–316.

Our highest department of the judiciary in upholding the constitutionality of the Chinese Exclusion Act have construed our Declaration of Rights into a mere platitudinous glitter and defied the instincts of humanity and laws of God. Some solace it is that the most gifted minds of the Supreme Bench scored the drastic measure.

The enforcement of the Act to eject and exclude the Chinese would be the most infamous act in our history. The atrocity of slavery would not equal it. That institution was fostered several centuries; property in human servitude was transmitted from sire to son; it had its palliating circumstances; its abolition by practical and peaceable measures was nigh impossible. The Act in question involves cold-blooded, premeditated perpetration of barbarity.[47]

Supporting the civil rights of ethnic minorities, restricting the traffic of harmful substances, and calling for more restrictive Sabbath laws may seem like mutually exclusive political positions today. But the members of Metropolitan Baptist Church saw no inconsistency—simply a desire to protect the dignity of those made in God's image and see the nation's laws conform to the law of God.

Women's Work at Metropolitan

As the majority of Metropolitan's members were women (on average 65 percent of the membership between 1891 and 1896), much of the temperance, educational, and evangelistic work of the church was driven by women. Metropolitan's women were active in the Women's Missionary Union and the Women's Christian Temperance Union.[48] Moreover, the minutes of the Women's Missionary Union show how

47 Allen C. Clark, "Our Chinese Brethren," *The Metropolitan Baptist*, June 1893, MS 1558, p. 10, box 6, folder 4, CHBC Archives.

48 For more on this women's work in nineteenth- and twentieth-century Baptist churches, see Holcomb, *Home Without Walls*. For a study of the role of women in Black Baptist churches, see Evelyn Brooks Higginbotham, *Righteous Discontent: The Women's Movement in the Black Baptist Church, 1880–1920* (Cambridge, MA: Harvard University Press, 1994).

educated these late-nineteenth-century American women were on global issues.[49] They shared stories from Japan, Mexico, Burma, and the Belgian Congo. They read papers that they had personally composed on the latest trends in missions and the leading figures in various countries. Moreover, they were educated in missionary history, familiar with figures like William Carey, Adoniram Judson, and Henry Martyn. Beyond church history, they were steeped in the Scriptures. They led Bible readings, discussions, and lessons related to missions, the Christian life, and the role of women in God's plan of redemption.

Figure 5.6. A women's Sunday school class, taught by Annie Hanie, pictured in 1945.

At one meeting of the Women's Missionary Union, Celestia A. Ferris led a discussion of Baptist work among African Americans in the District of Columbia. As the minutes report, "The program of the evening

49 Minutes of Women's Baptist Missionary Society (1899–1910), MS 662, box 2, folder 5, CHBC Archives; Secretary's Book of the Women's Missionary Circle of the Metropolitan Baptist Church (June 7, 1878–June 13, 1889), MS 664, box 2, folder 6, CHBC Archives; Women's Missionary Society Record of Contributions (October 16, 1892–April 17, 1899), MS 666, box 2, folder 7, CHBC Archives.

was in charge of Mrs. Ferris who gave an interesting talk on the early Mission work of the Baptists among the colored people of the District of Columbia, and read extracts from the 'Tidings' on Miss [Joanna P.] Moore's work among the colored people of the South." Her talk demonstrated a fervent interest in the spiritual needs of former slaves, and Ferris commended the pioneering missionary work of Joanna P. Moore, who spent her life organizing Sunday schools among former slaves across the Southern states. As the members of Metropolitan Baptist Church met each week to pray and labor together, they were fueled by a shared vision for the betterment of society and the spread of the gospel, both in their city and throughout the world.[50]

What most surprised other churches about the role of women at Metropolitan was the decision to adopt female deaconesses. Under the heading "Some Innovations," an 1894 article in the *Washington Times* described Metropolitan's appointment "some years ago" as "an experiment" that far exceeded "the expectations of the church officials."[51] What was this novel innovation? On June 4, 1891, the church recognized, for the first time, women as deaconesses to oversee the church's benevolent ministries and assist women in preparing for baptism.[52]

As the newspaper noted,

Metropolitan has managed to make itself known over the United States not only among Baptists, but among public men of all. . . . It has taken the lead in woman's work and has two deaconesses, and two of the assistant superintendents of the Sunday-school and . . .

50 Women's Missionary Society Minutes, June 20, 1898, MS 666, p. 37, box 2, folder 7, CHBC Archives. For an account of Moore's evangelistic work among former slaves, see Joanna P. Moore, *"In Christ's Stead": Autobiographical Sketches* (Chicago: Women's Baptist Home Mission Society, 1902).

51 "Metropolitan Baptist Church," *Washington Times*, September 9, 1894, 5.

52 Minutes of the Metropolitan Baptist Church, June 12, 1891, 164–165: "Resolved, That the Board of Deacons shall consist of seven members, instead of five as now constituted. Resolved, That three Sisters of this church be elected, to be known and recognized as a Board of Deaconesses."

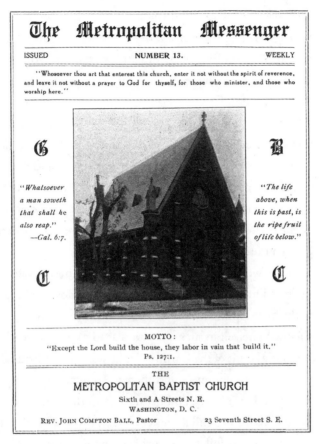

Figure 5.7. The front cover of the *Metropolitan Messenger* in 1910, a weekly newsletter published by the church.

the assistant librarians are ladies. If any of the ladies will take charge of any branch of the work the male members of the congregation are willing to turn it over to them.[53]

When a visiting pastor asked about deaconesses, stating incredulously, "Women at work? How do they do?" "Elegantly," was the enthusiastic response. "It's the best change we have made for years."[54]

53 "Metropolitan Baptist Church," 5.
54 "Metropolitan Baptist Church," 5.

One such woman, who loved the church and embodied the same sacrificial love that had characterized Peter H. Young, was Hattie M. Vail. As wife to Deacon Benjamin Vail and mother of two young boys, Hattie Vail, according to her eulogy in the *Metropolitan Baptist*, "gave her life to save her child":

> One more of our members gone. . . . This time a tender, gentle loving wife and mother has been taken from a happy home, and the vacant chair and tender prattle of baby for mama makes the grief more keen and the burden almost too heavy. And yet there is consolation, for we have the divine invitation, "Come all ye that are heavy laden and I will give you rest."
>
> Sister Vail gave her life to save her child. A few months ago while carrying little Dudley, aged two years, she started downstairs, and in making the first step she stumbled. Seeing that she would fall on her baby, she threw herself in such a position as to protect her child and took the whole brunt of the fearful fall. She was terribly bruised, but baby was safe and unharmed, and she was content. She never fully recovered from her injuries, and her death was the result.
>
> O, what love for her child! She showed in this act her true character, in that she was following Christ, even willing to give her life for her loved one. "Greater love than this hath no man, that he lay down his life for his friends."
>
> Her last moments were spent in talking of her Saviour, and requesting that her two little children should be taught the word of God, that they might meet her again. The day after her death her oldest child, George, aged five years, was heard telling his little brother that mama was with Jesus, and that they must go and see her.
>
> Yes, dear children, mama is with Jesus, and God grant that you, papa and all may meet her up there.[55]

---

55 James O'Connor Roberts, "Hattie M. Vail," *The Metropolitan Baptist* 2, no. 7 (October 1892), MS 1553, p. 29, box 6, folder 4, CHBC Archives.

Twelve years later, Hattie Vail's prayers were answered when her sons, George and Dudley, were both baptized into membership on the same day.

——

Hattie Vail died the way she had lived: laying down her life for others. Peter Young, likewise, after serving his country in war, laid down his life performing an act of kindness to the very ones who took his life. In doing so, Vail and Young exemplified their Savior, who "came not to be served but to serve, and to give his life as a ransom for many" (Mark 10:45).

After a career in politics, Green Clay Smith finished his race like Hattie Vail and Peter Young, by laying down his life for others and for the spread of the gospel. Smith died on June 29, 1895, at sixty-eight years of age, forty-three years to the day after the death of his famous great uncle, Henry Clay.[56] His five years as pastor left Metropolitan in a stronger position than when he had found it. With 276 committed members, a thriving Sunday school, and a growing civic and religious presence on Capitol Hill, the members of Metropolitan were ready to recommence their dream of erecting a truly "metropolitan" building on Capitol Hill. No longer a doubtful experiment, Metropolitan Baptist Church was ready to assume its place as a leading church in the nation's capital.

56 "General Smith Dead," *Evening Star*, June 29, 1895, 1.

6

"The Future Is Bright with Promise"

1896–1912

THE WEIGHT AND TERROR of the Titanic disaster descended slowly on Washington. Initially, optimistic statements by the press allayed public fears, indicating that it was "probable that all of the passengers of the Titanic are safe." But their hopes were soon shattered by the tragic reality. Despite the insistence of Philip Franklin, the chief officer and vice president of the British shipping line White Star, that the Titanic was "absolutely unsinkable," the final death toll exceeded 1,500 people.[1]

When Metropolitan's pastor John Compton Ball addressed the assembled congregation on the Sunday following the disaster, every seat was occupied. For Ball, the tragedy was a microcosm of the world's plight as outlined in Scripture. As Ball explained, all of mankind was on a voyage—the voyage of life. Like the Titanic's passengers, many were unprepared for God's sudden and decisive judgment. Christ, he proclaimed, was mankind's only hope, and we must sound forth a spiritual SOS to seek his salvation.[2]

1   "Passengers of Titanic in Crash with Iceberg Safe on Other Vessels," *Evening Star*, April, 15, 1912, 1–2.
2   "Memorial Rites in All Churches Here for Wreck Victims," *Washington Times*, April 20, 1912.

The service drew thousands of Washingtonians to the church to grieve
and pay their respects. As the *Washington Times* reported, "Never in the
history of Washington has such a tribute been paid."[3] Eyewitnesses recalled
that the Titanic's string ensemble played the hymn "Nearer My God to
Thee" as women and children boarded the life rafts of the sinking ship. No
eye was dry as Ball selected that very hymn to conclude the service, and
a thousand voices reverberated across the walls, singing, "So by my woes
to be nearer, my God, to thee; nearer, my God, to thee, nearer to thee!"[4]

A Growing, Southern Congregation

Between 1896 and 1912, Metropolitan Baptist Church accomplished
several significant milestones that transformed its trajectory. The church
not only paid off its debt and constructed its present building but also
welcomed as its new pastor John Compton Ball, who led the church
for nearly half a century from 1903 to 1944. However, this period
was also marked by a profound transition as the church shifted in a
distinctly Southern direction. Despite its Northern roots, the number
of members joining from the South between 1896 and 1912 exceeded
Northerners more than twofold. For instance, in 1896, twenty-six new
members joined from Southern Baptist churches in comparison to one
who joined from the North. Socially, politically, and temperamentally,
by 1912 Metropolitan was unmistakably a Southern church.

One of the church's most notable acknowledgments of its growing
Southern constituency was the selection of Granville S. Williams as
Green Clay Smith's successor in 1896.[5] A proud Southerner, Williams
was born in Decatur, Tennessee, on September 30, 1847, and possessed
an exceptional education and nearly thirty years of ministry experience.
Thus, his appointment as pastor was a conscious effort by the church

3   "Church Records Broken at Service for Titanic's Dead," *Washington Times*, April 22, 1912, 4.
4   "Church Records Broken at Service for Titanic's Dead," 4.
5   Biographical features summarized based on the entry in William Cathcart, *The Baptist Encyclo-paedia* (Philadelphia: L. H. Everts, 1883), 1247; "Site on Capitol Hill," *Washington Post*, June 29, 1901, 11.

to acknowledge and embrace its new Southern identity. As the Boston-based Baptist newspaper *The Watchman* wrote glowingly in 1901, "The future of this growing church is bright with promise."[6]

An early sign of its growing Southern leanings took place in 1888 when Metropolitan admitted its first known Confederate veteran—the venerable William Carey Maupin.[7] Remarkably, the Union general, Green Clay Smith, baptized Maupin's son John, providing a striking picture of the reconciling power of the gospel, as a former Union general stood in the baptistry with the son of a Confederate soldier—welcoming him into membership in Christ's body.

One of the hundreds of Southerners who joined Metropolitan under Granville Williams was Liston D. Bass, who by all accounts seemed to have it all. Bass boasted an impressive academic background that included the Southern Baptist Theological Seminary in Louisville, Kentucky, and the University of Chicago and possessed a knack for captivating audiences with his public lectures. But Bass had a dark secret that he was running from and a current swindling scheme that would land him in jail within just a few years.

Bass created a phony institution called the Bureau of Civil Service Instruction and preyed on individuals by promising jobs in the civil service in exchange for a modest fee. Bass convinced desperate job seekers to send money in exchange for a course of instruction in his "bureau." However, it was all a sham, and none of the individuals received any instruction or appointment, leading his victims to file a complaint with the United States Civil Service Commission in 1900. It was not the first time that Bass had gotten himself in trouble. Eight years earlier, while head of a female college in Alabama, Bass had been dismissed after entering a student's quarters at night for "improper purposes."[8]

6   *The Watchman*, March 14, 1901, 26, Library of Congress.
7   Kevin Fair, "Metropolitan Baptist Church and United States Military Service 1846–1947" (Unpublished essay, n.d.), 9–10.
8   *Eufaula Daily Times*, November 27, 1892, 1.

Since Bass had used the mail to lure his victims, the Civil Service Commission forwarded the matter to the Post Office Department, citing statutes prohibiting the use of the mail for fraudulent schemes. The postmaster general conducted a hearing and issued an order banning Bass from using the mail to circulate literature about his phony institution.

But the drama didn't end there. The authorities presented the matter to the grand jury of the District of Columbia, leading to Bass's indictment, trial, and conviction. He was sentenced to three years in prison and a $1,000 fine, the maximum penalty allowed by law.[9] All this occurred while Bass was a member of Metropolitan Baptist Church. Undeniably, the tragic story of Liston Bass illustrates that theological education is no guarantee of godliness.

THE REV. LISTON D. BASS IN TWO CHARACTERISTIC POSES.

Figure 6.1. Liston D. Bass (1854–1930), the swindler, pictured in a newspaper article from 1908.

9 "Got Three Years: Dr. Liston D. Bass in Trouble," *Birmingham News*, June 1, 1901, 15.

Not all of the lives of Metropolitan's Southern members ended as shamefully. Socrates and John Maupin were sons of the aforementioned Confederate veteran William Carey Maupin. As brothers and recent high school graduates, both responded to the call to fight for their country during the Spanish-American War in 1898. In Havana, tragedy struck when nineteen-year-old Socrates fell ill with typhoid fever. Despite the best efforts of his brother and the army medics, Socrates could not be saved. He died not a victim of a bullet or sword but of typhoid. In Cuba, he had been serving alongside his older brother John, who was with him at his death and accompanied his body to Washington.[10]

"Sorrowful Home-Coming" read the title of the story in the *Evening Star*: "Two Soldier Boys Back from Cuba, One Dead, the Other Ill." "Soc," as he was known to his friends, had been a star in his own right, a talented athlete, and a leader among his peers. He had captained the Eastern High School's football team to victory, leading his teammates in the championship of 1897. Loved and respected by all who knew him, he had also been a devoted church member and youth leader in the Young People's Society of Christian Endeavor. He was just nineteen years old at the time of his death.

As during the pastorate of Green Clay Smith, Metropolitan remained active in the social causes of the day. On January 14, 1897, the church voted to endorse a bill in the House and Senate that raised the age of consent from sixteen to eighteen. Passing so-called age-of-consent laws was part of a larger effort by evangelicals in the late nineteenth century to combat human trafficking and prostitution that targeted underage girls.[11] A month later, the church once again made its voice heard by voting to petition the US Senate and House of Representatives for a bill that would ban the sale of alcoholic liquors in government buildings in the District of Columbia.[12]

10 "Sorrowful Home-Coming," *Evening Star*, September 9, 1898, 11
11 Minutes of the Metropolitan Baptist Church, January 14, 1897, MS 1602, p. 212, box 6, folder 7, Capitol Hill Baptist Church Archives, Washington, DC (hereafter, CHBC Archives). Cf. Age of Protection for Girls in the District of Columbia, S. 1500, 54th Cong., 2nd Ses. (1897).
12 Minutes of the Metropolitan Baptist Church, February 10, 1898, 222.

While their new building, completed in 1888, was sufficient for the present needs of the congregation, the church had not forgotten their original dream of erecting a structure that would be "a credit to the Baptist denomination and an ornament to the city." From 1896 to 1900, the congregation tirelessly fundraised and hosted various entertainments with the aim of eradicating the debt and commencing work on a larger, more commodious church building. Finally, on February 20, 1901, just a week before its twenty-third anniversary, the church finished paying off the remainder of the debt.[13] Granville S. Williams, who had led the congregation into the twentieth century, resigned in August 1902 due to ill health. With the debt fully paid off and the church's foundation solidified, Metropolitan was no longer a fledgling congregation but was poised to assume its place as a leading church in the nation's capital. Williams could resign in good conscience, knowing that he had helped steer the congregation toward a brighter and more promising future under its next pastor, John Compton Ball.

John Compton Ball

John Compton Ball was born on January 23, 1863, in Mears Ashby, Northamptonshire, England. His parents, though Baptists, had him christened at eight months old so that he could attend public school. Apparently, he had yelled throughout the christening, leading his parents to remark that, "because he was a Baptist, he knew better."[14] His father, a tailor and shopkeeper, moved the family to Philadelphia, Pennsylvania, when John was seven, and he attended public schools while working as a clerk at Wanamaker's Department Store and studying at Temple University. At seventeen, Ball was converted through the ministry of James Good, pastor of the Heidelberg Reformed Church in

13 "85 Years on Capitol Hill," *Metropolitan Messenger*, February 20, 1963, MS 1751, box 8a, folder 14, CHBC Archives.
14 John Compton Ball, "God's Five Writings" (sermon, Metropolitan Baptist Church, Washington, DC, April 26, 1936), 11–13, Kelley family private collection, Waterford, Virginia.

Philadelphia. He married Jenetta A. Loder on December 27, 1887, and was baptized into membership of First Baptist Church, Lambertville, New Jersey, at age twenty-four.[15]

While working at Wanamaker's, Ball began to sense a call to ministry. John Wanamaker, a businessman, Presbyterian elder, and philanthropist, was thrilled at Ball's decision to pursue full-time ministry and supported his decision to attend seminary. As Wanamaker later wrote to Ball, "I am glad to know that the time spent in business education in the store has become valuable to you in your ministry, which is a better work than storekeeping."[16]

Figure 6.2. John Compton Ball (1863–1950), Metropolitan's seventh pastor.

15 William Powell Hill, "John Compton Ball," *The Temple Review*, February 20, 1903, Kelley family private collection. The Heidelberg Reformed Church grew under Good's ministry from sixty members in 1877 to over seven hundred in 1890. Cf. Carl H. Gramm, *The Life and Labors of the Reverend Prof. James I. Good* (Webster Groves, MO : Old Orchard, 1944), 42.

16 John Wanamaker to John Compton Ball, December 5, 1905, Kelley family private collection.

Another lasting influence on Ball's life was his friendship with the famous Philadelphia pastor Russell Conwell. Ball received a scholarship from Conwell to begin full-time studies at Crozer Theological Seminary. Conwell's sermon *Acres of Diamonds*[17] was preached over six thousand times, the proceeds of which went toward seminary scholarships for promising young men and later funded Gordon-Conwell Theological Seminary outside of Boston.[18] Conwell licensed John Compton Ball for gospel ministry on December 2, 1898.[19] He also helped Ball secure his first pastorate and, in 1903, recommended Ball to Metropolitan.[20]

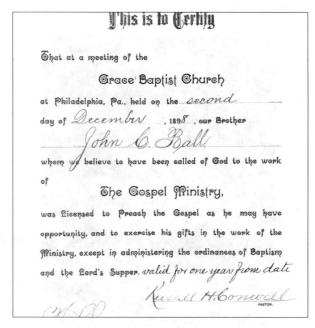

Figure 6.3. John Compton Ball's preaching license, dated December 2, 1898, was signed by Russell H. Conwell, pastor of the Baptist Temple in Philadelphia.

---

17 Russell H. Conwell, *Acres of Diamonds* (Philadelphia: John D. Morris, 1901).

18 "Dr. Conwell's lecture income has always been a means of supporting hundreds of students in college and seminary, year by year; many of these becoming preachers of the Gospel." *The Watchman-Examiner*, February 13, 1913, 20. Cf. Gary Scott Smith, *The Search for Social Salvation: Social Christianity and America, 1880–1925* (Lanham, MD: Lexington, 2000), 107.

19 Preaching license, John Compton Ball, December 2, 1898, Kelley family private collection.

20 H. B. Mahan to John Compton Ball, March 19, 1903, Kelley family private collection.

Wanamaker and Conwell embodied the evangelical ethos that would characterize Ball's ministry at Metropolitan. Both, though active in social Christian causes, were avowed theological conservatives.[21] Both were devout supporters of the projects of urban renewal, evangelism, and revival. For instance, Wanamaker brought D. L. Moody and Ira Sankey to Philadelphia in 1876 and Billy Sunday in 1915 by personally financing both campaigns. Undoubtedly, something of Wanamaker's knack for promotional stunts and showmanship and Russell Conwell's flair for topical evangelistic preaching would influence Ball's later ministry.[22]

While a student at Crozer, Ball would have imbibed conservative denominational and theological views under the leadership of President Henry Griggs Weston.[23] As a student, Ball "engaged assiduously in gospel work," including preaching, evangelism, and Sunday school work. In a newspaper article describing how he had filled the pulpit of an ill pastor, Ball was described as "a rising young man" who "created a very favorable impression."[24] Another article from Ball's seminary days poked fun at his name: "One of the rising young theologians in this country is named Ball. He knows how to put the sermon over the plate before the people make a home run."[25]

Ball graduated from Crozer on June 7, 1899, as part of a class of thirty students.[26] Upon graduation, he began a four-year ministry at New Bethlehem Baptist Church, a rural congregation in the extremely

21 Smith, *The Search for Social Salvation*, 9.

22 Smith, *The Search for Social Salvation*, 246–47.

23 Jeffrey Paul Straub, *The Making of a Battle Royal: The Rise of Liberalism in Northern Baptist Life, 1870–1920*, Monographs in Baptist History (Eugene, OR: Pickwick, 2018), 241. It was not until Weston's retirement in 1909 that Crozer took a sharp turn toward the liberal tradition. William H. Brackney, *Congregation and Campus: Baptists in Higher Education* (Macon, GA: Mercer University Press, 2008), 278–79.

24 "The Upland Baptists," Kelley family private collection.

25 T. M. Eastwood, "Commencement at Crozer," *The Baptist Commonwealth*, June 15, 1899, Kelley family private collection.

26 Eastwood, "Commencement at Crozer," Kelley family private collection.

poor region of New Bethlehem, Pennsylvania, on October 19, 1899. In the small town of just over one thousand residents, Ball was "popular from the first."[27] "Besides being very popular with his people," the *New Bethlehem Vindicator* reported, "his ministry has been blessed with success to the extent of a very considerable accession to the church."[28] Less than four years into his pastorate, however, on March 19, 1903, Henry B. Mahan, a deacon at Metropolitan, wrote to Ball, inviting him to preach at the Washington church at the recommendation of Conwell:

Washington, DC,
March 19, 1903

Rev. John C. Ball,
Dear Brother:
   The Metropolitan Baptist Church of this City, of which I am a member, is without a Pastor. I have been instructed by the Board of Deacons to invite you to preach for us some Sunday at as early a date as will suit you. Please let me know if you can come and on what date. We have a membership of about 350—a good field for work. . . . You were recommended to me by Rev. Drs. Conwell and Pelt of the Temple Church, Phila.
   I would be pleased to entertain you at my home during your stay in Washington.
   Very truly yours,
   H. B. Mahan
   1007 East Capitol Street[29]

Accepting Mahan's invitation, Ball preached two sermons at Metropolitan on May 17, 1903. In the morning, he chose Romans 8:28

27 "Pennsylvania," *Commonwealth*, April 2, 1903, Kelley family private collection.
28 *New Bethlehem Vindicator*, June 21, 1901, 7.
29 H. B. Mahan to John Compton Ball, March 19, 1903, Kelley family private collection.

for his text, highlighting the apostle Paul's sufferings as a model for Christians.[30]

When Metropolitan gathered to vote on its next pastor on June 4, the support was so overwhelmingly in favor of Ball that no runoff vote was needed.[31] Ball wrote to the church on June 20 to accept their invitation and proposed to commence his ministry at Metropolitan on September 1.[32]

When John Compton Ball, his wife Jeanette, and daughter Ruth carted their belongings to the New Bethlehem Station on Monday, August 31, 1903, they found dozens of their congregants waiting.[33] They had gathered to say a last farewell. As the train pulled away from the station, and the tearful faces disappeared in the distance, Ball knew that a new chapter of his life was about to begin.

Figure 6.4. The newly constructed Metropolitan Baptist Church in 1912.

30 "Strength in Paul's Words," *Washington Post*, May 18, 1903, 12, quotes Ball's sermon: "Paul was an able scholar, a prominent man in the politics and the religion of the times. He was persecuted, imprisoned, scourged. His life was the reverse of an easy or pleasant one. . . . It is easy for us in our smooth lives when suffering and tribulation do not press us down, to quote this text from Paul. It is not until we have suffered that it can really mean anything to us. That we can know its truth in any other than an intellectual way: that we can know it with our hearts."

31 Minutes of the Metropolitan Baptist Church, June 4, 1903, 258–59.

32 Minutes of the Metropolitan Baptist Church, July 2, 1903, 263.

33 *New Bethlehem Vindicator*, September 4, 1903, 7.

Ball's most significant legacy as pastor of Metropolitan was to guide the church's next building project. In 1909, Metropolitan appealed to the Columbia Baptist Association for assistance in constructing a new building, which they could not afford to construct alone. Francis McLean stated the request bluntly, "We now plead for definite action."[34] After years of labor, they received the good news on February 24, 1910, that the association would contribute $10,000 to their cause, with $6,500 coming from Calvary and Fifth Baptist alone.[35] The long-awaited building project could finally begin.

Figure 6.5. With the women in white dresses and the men in suits, the members of Metropolitan gathered for the cornerstone-laying ceremony of their new building on June 28, 1911.

Metropolitan broke ground on April 17, 1911. While they constructed the new building on the corner of Sixth and A Street NE,

34 Francis McLean to the Columbia Association of Baptist Churches, November 1, 1909, MS 901, box 3, folder 1 CHBC Archives.
35 Minutes of the Metropolitan Baptist Church, June 29, 1910, MS 1604, pp. 36–38, box 6, folder 8, CHBC Archives.

the site of the original chapel, Metropolitan held Sunday worship in a massive tent erected across the street. Designed by Appleton P. Clark, brother of church treasurer Allen C. Clark, the new building would feature a two-story, square Gothic tower and a striking stone coping surrounding the structure. Anticipating the congregation's growth, the wall separating the main sanctuary from the Sunday School auditorium could easily be removed, expanding the capacity of the main auditorium to accommodate 1,300 attendees. Including furnishings, the entire project cost $50,000.[36]

The cornerstone-laying ceremony on June 28, 1911, was attended by hundreds of supporters who shared in the excitement of this monumental occasion. Finally, on December 24 Metropolitan celebrated its first Sunday service in the new church as five new members were baptized. They dedicated the structure on January 14, 1912—just weeks before the Titanic disaster.

———

A church is so much more than a building. But since the earliest decades of Christianity, Christians have found buildings immensely helpful as spaces to gather for public worship and prayer. Imagine the cost of purchasing land and constructing a comparable building a half mile from the US Capitol today. It would be cost prohibitive even to a church of a thousand members. One architect estimated that such a project, if attempted today, would cost between $40 and $90 million dollars.

It is remarkable that the members of Metropolitan Baptist Church had the foresight to construct a building that could accommodate over a thousand. They had no wealthy benefactor like Amos Kendall who personally financed Calvary Baptist Church's building. Instead, they

36 "New Church Opened," *Washington Post*, December 25, 1911, 10; Minutes of the Metropolitan Baptist Church, June 29, 1910, 36.

made mighty personal sacrifices to construct a building that has served generations. When one considers all of the sermons preached, converts baptized, services held, couples married, and conferences hosted since 1912, is there any doubt that their sacrifices were worth it? Is there any question that in heaven they are grateful for every dollar given to support the work of erecting a church building on Capitol Hill?

Today the original stained-glass windows honor the members who sacrificed to begin, sustain, and grow the church: Celestia Ferris, Francis McLean, Green Clay Smith, and others. They had a sense that Washington, DC, was growing and that God might bless the church in such a way that every seat was needed. They were right. With a young and gifted pastor, a new building, and room to grow, Metropolitan was ready to be a light on the Hill.[37]

---

37 Minutes of the Metropolitan Baptist Church, January 14, 1912, 57–60.

7

"War, Fuel Famine, and Influenza Epidemics"

1913–1918

STEPHEN TYREE EARLY (1889–1951) is remembered as one of the most influential men of mid-twentieth-century America. As press secretary for three terms of Franklin Delano Roosevelt's presidency, Early revolutionized the way US presidents relate to the press, introducing daily press conferences and even allowing reporters direct access to the president. Early's key role in shaping Roosevelt's public image during some of the most tumultuous times in American history included proposing the famous fireside chats and guiding FDR's response to the Pearl Harbor attack. To historians, Early is remembered as America's first modern press secretary.[1] To members of Metropolitan, he was just another Sunday school student who grew up in the church.

Known as Steve to his friends and church family, Early was born on August 27, 1889, in the Shenandoah Mountains outside of Charlottesville, Virginia, where his parents were members of the Mountain

---

1   Linda Lotridge Levin, *The Making of FDR: The Story of Stephen T. Early, America's First Modern Press Secretary* (Buffalo, NY: Prometheus, 2010).

Plain Baptist Church of Albemarle County. When he was ten, his family moved to Washington, DC, where they settled in the working-class neighborhood of Capitol Hill. Early's parents, Thomas and Ida, joined Metropolitan Baptist Church on September 21, 1899, and less than a year later, on April 1, 1900, ten-year-old Stephen Tyree Early followed their example and joined Metropolitan by baptism.[2]

As a young adult, Early worked his way up in the news industry while remaining an active member of Metropolitan Baptist Church. He even taught Sunday school for the Baptist Young People's Union on occasion.[3] Early remained a member through World War I, the Great Depression, New Deal era, and World War II. Regardless of his accomplishments, Early never forgot the church that had shaped him, remaining a member until his death in 1951.[4]

World War I

When the US could no longer avoid the war that had been raging in Europe for almost three years, Early was ready. In May of 1917, Early quit his job with the Washington bureau of the Associated Press to enlist for military service. His early enlistment enabled him to join the army as an officer—a crucial step for his future career. As a second lieutenant, he was assigned to the 317th Infantry of the 80th Division. After only a few weeks of machine gun training, Early and his division set sail for France in late May of 1917.[5]

Early faced his first combat experience just two months later in the region of Picardy, France, during which he displayed exceptional bravery

2 Membership Cards for Mrs. Ida V. Early and Thomas J. Early, Metropolitan Baptist Church, Capitol Hill Baptist Church Archives, Washington, DC (hereafter, CHBC Archives). For Stephen T. Early's membership information, see Deacons Meeting Minutes, March 22, 1900, MS 16, p. 25, box 1, folder 2, CHBC Archives. Three of Stephen's siblings, Elisha Eugene Early, Felix E. Early, and Thomas Joseph Early Jr., joined the church as well.

3 "Order of Services," *Metropolitan Messenger*, November 10, 1910, MS 1738, box 8a, folder 1, CHBC Archives.

4 Membership Card for Stephen T. Early, CHBC Archives.

5 Levin, *The Making of FDR*, 31.

and leadership and was quickly promoted to first lieutenant. Later, at
the brutal Battle of the Argonne, a fellow soldier was wounded in a blast
and unable to fall back with the troops to the rear. Early, fighting only
a few feet away, rushed to his aid, picked him up, and carried him to a
nearby shell hole. Early's bravery and selflessness were just a few of the
qualities that would mark him as a public servant in the years to come.[6]

Figure 7.1. Stephen T. Early (1889–1951) in his White House office in 1939.

In 1918, Early was just one of the eighty-nine blue stars on the service
flag that adorned the pulpit of Metropolitan Baptist Church. Each star
signified a church member in military service—over ten percent of the
church's membership. By the time the guns of war sounded their final
salvo in 1918, two of the stars had turned gold, honoring the men who
had paid the ultimate sacrifice.[7]

As pastor, John Compton Ball knew the devastating effects of war
firsthand. He had been in England on June 28, 1914, when Archduke
Franz Ferdinand of Austria was assassinated, triggering the war. He

6   Levin, *The Making of FDR*, 34–36.
7   "Church Service Flag Lowered," *Washington Herald*, September 22, 1919.

had witnessed the "appalling condition" of Europe with his own eyes. Everywhere, signs reading "Men Wanted" bore witness to the unspeakable loss of human life that war always brought in its train.[8]

Returning to Washington with his wife Jeanette in September, Ball made it his mission to advocate for peace and restraint.[9] "War was not the answer," Ball explained to his congregation in a sermon entitled "The Secret of Permanent Peace." Increased armies did not guarantee a nation's safety. Instead, Ball decried the foolishness of armament, arguing that a "continual contest in armament" was "conducive to conflict." "We may talk about civilization, write books on culture, and boast of morality," Ball thundered, "but until we, as individuals and as a nation, practice Christ's teachings, there can be no abiding peace."[10]

Ball's warnings about war and his skepticism of achieving permanent peace through arms set him squarely in opposition to the overwhelming flood of theological liberalism during his day. For those optimistic liberals, the Great War was widely viewed as the war to end all wars and to usher in a postmillennial vision of peace and progress, built on the foundations of ecumenical cooperation and the abandonment of denominational dogmatism.[11] But for the more conservative evangelicals, the still fresh

8   Minutes of the Metropolitan Baptist Church, MS 1604, p. 85, box 6, folder 8, CHBC Archives; "Call to the Colors Is Sounded by Pastor," *Washington Herald*, April 16, 1917, 3; "Pastor and People," *Evening Star*, September 19, 1914, 13.

9   "Plan Reception to Returning Pastor," *Washington Times*, September 19, 1914, 5.

10 "God, Not Arms, Insures Peace," *Washington Herald*, September 28, 1914, 2. In his calls for peace, Ball resembled other peace-loving conservative evangelicals leading up to the war, epitomized by the anti-war posture of Secretary of State William Jennings Bryan. Lawrence W. Levine, *Defender of the Faith: William Jennings Bryan: The Last Decade, 1915–1925* (Cambridge, MA: Harvard University Press, 1987), 1-4. William G. McCloughlin writes that even Billy Sunday, so famous for his bloodthirsty support of America's victory during World War I, "from 1914 until the very month of America's entry in April, 1917, rarely mentioned the war, and, when he did, it was to express the opinion held by the great mass of Americans that Europe should be left to stew in its own juice." William Gerald McLoughlin, *Billy Sunday Was His Real Name* (Chicago: University of Chicago Press, 1955), 255.

11 For the origins of the clash between fundamentalists and modernists, see George M. Marsden, *Fundamentalism and American Culture: The Shaping of Twentieth-Century Evangelicalism, 1870–1925* (New York: Oxford University Press, 1980); Matthew Avery Sutton, *American Apocalypse: A History of Modern Evangelicalism* (Cambridge, MA: Belknap Press of Harvard University Press, 2014).

wounds of the Civil War had permanently shaken their faith in human progress. "Believe me when I say," Ball told his congregation on April 1, 1917, "that while the most powerful nations may win the war, it will not be a real, permanent or abiding peace."[12] For Ball, as for other evangelicals, the world would be redeemed only by Christ's bodily return not through the material, scientific, or economic progress of America or any nation.

For theological liberals, Ball's pessimistic outlook threatened to undermine the war effort. In fact, some—like Shailer Matthews, dean of the University of Chicago's School of Divinity—even accused conservatives of receiving funding from Germany. But conservatives had a rejoinder of their own. For them, the social and moral decay of Germany was evidence of the devastating consequences of adopting the same higher-critical methods in interpreting Scripture that were being taught by liberal seminaries like the University of Chicago.[13]

Until April 1917, Ball refused to back down from his calls for peace and an end to aggression. But when the United States entered the war on April 6, 1917, Ball flipped his script. The man who had vehemently opposed war during peace assumed the responsibility of advocating for victory through war. He called for military service, urging men to join the cause as a matter of Christian duty. In sermons, he valorized military service, likening it to Christian martyrdom and casting it as a righteous cause. To Ball, military service for a just cause was unambiguously Christian service, an act of upholding the principles of a Christian nation. "Victory for a soldier of Christ," he proclaimed, "meant eternal happiness," and "the bugler of Christ never blew a retreat." Ball saw the call to the colors as a serious one—one that demanded the church's attention and support. His message was clear: preserving a Christian nation was undoubtedly a just cause, and military service was an act of service to God and country.[14]

12 "Peace Will Not Last When It Comes—Ball," *Washington Herald*, April 2, 1917, 4.
13 Marsden, *Fundamentalism and American Culture*, 92–99.
14 "Call to the Colors Is Sounded by Pastor," *Washington Herald*, April 16, 1917, 3.

Figure 7.2. The interior of Metropolitan's sanctuary decorated for Palm Sunday, pictured sometime before 1919 when an organ was installed.

Figure 7.3. Folding chairs are visible in the Sunday school auditorium (west hall) for overflow seating, as the sanctuary was expected to be crowded for Palm Sunday.

From April 6 onward, Ball's sermons marched in lockstep with the American war effort. Ball bordered on conflating democracy and Christianity when he argued that America had a responsibility to take up arms to defend "the liberty of all nations all the time."[15] While the church was decorated with twenty large flags draped throughout the sanctuary, Ball's message "How to Keep the Flag Waving" recounted the history of the American flag, proclaiming it had never trailed in defeat nor unfurled in an unrighteous cause.[16]

As the war wore on, Ball's preaching grew more aggressive. He began referring to the Germans as "Huns," and argued that the magnitude of their brutality made the Roman emperor Nero look like a mere beginner.[17] In a service culminating in the singing of "God Bless and Guard Our Men," Ball urged his congregation to pray for victory in the war, Christianizing America's participation in the conflict by likening the Central Powers to Nero, the great persecutor of Christians.[18] He hoped that his endeavors to support the war effort would be rewarded and appreciated. But to the dismay of Ball and other pastors in the District, when a coal shortage hit the country in January of 1918, the churches of Washington were treated as nonessential and dispensable.

Billy Sunday and the Fuel Crisis

In the winter of 1918, fiery evangelist Billy Sunday arrived in Washington, DC, bringing with him his world-famous pulpit antics, shocking rhetoric, and common-man slang. His eight-week evangelistic campaign was aimed at promoting the war effort, saving souls, and strengthening the churches. But he had not expected to find Washington in the midst of a fuel crisis.[19]

15 "Scripture Shows Reason for America's Joining the War, Asserts Rev. John Compton Ball," *Washington Herald*, May 7, 1917, 12.
16 "Flag Never Trailed in Dust of Defeat," *Washington Herald*, June 11, 1917, 2.
17 "Make Nero 'A Beginner,'" *Washington Post*, October 29, 1917, 12.
18 "Prayers by Washington Pastors, in Response to President's Call, for Victory for American Arms," *Washington Post*, October 29, 1917, 2.
19 "Billy Sunday As People Have Seen Him During His Campaign," *Washington Times*, March 3, 1918, 2.

As the Billy Sunday Tabernacle was being constructed to seat over ten thousand people, a growing coal shortage, combined with subzero temperatures, was creating a national disaster and a political quagmire. The military needed coal for the ongoing war in Europe. But so did Americans at home. In response, on January 24, 1918, John L. Weaver, the fuel administrator for the District of Columbia, made the controversial decision to shut down two-thirds of the city's churches for a three-week period.

Weaver's plan called for denominations to hold joint services in convenient locations throughout the city, allowing churches only enough coal to keep their pipes from bursting. However, the plan left it up to each denomination to decide which churches would remain open for Sunday services. Billy Sunday's campaign was exempted from the order. Churches were certainly willing to do their part in the war effort as they had been doing from the beginning. But church leaders were shocked at Weaver's unfair targeting of churches while leaving theaters, moving picture shows, and dance halls open.[20]

Before long, the DC government had a full-blown mutiny on its hands. Catholics led the way, refusing to stop holding mass, as congregants gathered in freezing temperatures inside their unheated buildings.[21] The Protestants followed suit, filing formal protests with the District's government. As a joint resolution of the Baptist churches explained, "For patriotic reasons we obey the order, but at the same time we most emphatically protest against it as unfair, unnecessary and an unwarranted abridgement of religious liberty."[22] But it was Walter H.

20 "Two-Thirds of D.C. Churches Closed for 3-Week Period," *Evening Star*, January 24, 1918, 1.
21 "Protest Fuel Order," *Washington Post*, January 28, 1918, 1.
22 As Monsignor Thomas S. Lee of what is today the Cathedral of St. Matthew the Apostle explained, "To stop our people from hearing mass, a purely spiritual matter, is a thing which Mr. Weaver has no right to do. Cardinal Gibbons is the only one in this jurisdiction who can issue a general dispensation relieving our churches from holding mass, and such dispensation was not issued. . . . Mr. Weaver has made a great mistake. It amounts to persecution." Or as one Presbyterian Church protested, "We, members of the Church of the Covenant and its congregation, residents of the District of Columbia, do respectfully and heartily protest against the unjust, incongruous and mysterious discrimination

Brooks, the esteemed African American pastor of Nineteenth Street Baptist Church, who raised the constitutional question of the city's action. "I concede to the government the right to withhold light and fuel," Brooks acknowledged. "Let the fuel administration regulate the church's fuel. But say nothing as to the matter of public worship, a matter which pertains to God and not to the will of human governments."[23] For Brooks, as for other churches in the city, the unequal and unfair treatment of churches in comparison with less essential activities marked a dangerous precedent. Holding public services was part of their spiritual duty and a distinctive contribution to the war effort. The churches were willing to do their part but not at the cost of their religious liberty.

Figure 7.4. In February 1918, snow covered Billy Sunday's outdoor tabernacle between Union Station and the Capitol building. The Library of Congress's Thomas Jefferson Building is visible in the background.

---

of the District fuel administrator in closing two-thirds of the churches of the District for a period of three weeks seven days in the week, while theaters, moving picture houses and all other places of amusement are to remain open six days in seven. . . . Such an order, issued without explanation, seemingly appraising the church as of less service to the city than playhouses, will conserve some fuel, but at the high cost of weakened confidence of the public in all persons responsible for an attempt to obtain an end so desirable by a means so illogical." "Protest Fuel Order," 8.

23 "Churches Comply With Fuel Order," *Evening Star*, January 26, 1918, 8.

Only one man defied expectations as a supporter of the fuel administrator's orders. Among a crowd of eager listeners at his tabernacle on Sunday, January 24, 1918, Billy Sunday stated his controversial opinion. "I wish they would shut up all the churches," Sunday proclaimed amid laughter and raucous applause from the crowds. "If you haven't got fuel in your church, come down here!"[24] In fact, even before the fuel shortage, Metropolitan, like many other churches, had been cancelling Sunday morning services in order to allow their members to attend the Billy Sunday rallies.[25] But just a week later, on February 3, 1918, perhaps in protest to Weaver's order, both morning and evening Sunday services were held in the Sunday School auditorium at Metropolitan. Even though Weaver's order was not set to expire until February 11, Metropolitan, like most churches in the District, decided to hold services anyway. "All usual services resumed," read the notices of most church advertisements in daily papers, a not-so-subtle statement of defiance against what they perceived as government overreach.[26] Heat or no heat, coal or no coal, the churches of Washington were determined to have their own way. Although they did not know it yet, the question of emergency powers and shutting down churches would explode again later that year when the Spanish flu struck DC.

The Spanish Flu

Like other churches in the District, Metropolitan made great sacrifices for the war effort. They also received a bounty in return. From 1917 to 1919, Metropolitan's congregation swelled to 837 as thousands moved to Washington for work and quickly found their way to Sunday school classes and services.[27] The Columbia Association of Baptist Churches

---

24 "Will Preach For All," *Washington Post*, January 25, 1918, 4.

25 "Church Announcements," *Evening Star*, January 5, 1918, 8.

26 "Church Announcements," *Evening Star*, February 2, 1918, 10.

27 *Minutes of the Thirty-Ninth Annual Meeting of the Columbia Association of Baptist Churches Washington, D.C. November 20, 21, 22, 23, 1916* (Washington, DC: Judd & Detweiler, 1916), MS 921, p. 68, box 3, folder 4, CHBC Archives.

lauded the efforts of its churches in their support of the government in "peace and war."[28] But as World War I was coming to a close, still another enemy was making its way toward the nation's capital: the Spanish flu.

Between October 1918 and February 1919, an estimated fifty thousand cases of influenza were reported in the District of Columbia, and some three thousand residents lost their lives.[29] At the peak of the pandemic, the District government banned all public gatherings, including churches, for three weeks. Metropolitan, like the other churches of Washington, DC, begrudgingly complied.

When the first active cases in the District were reported in September 1918, only six people had died because of the flu. On September 26, the city's health officer, W. C. Fowler, warned the public to be cautious about influenza but said he did not yet expect a full-on pandemic.[30] He was wrong. The next day saw three more deaths and forty-two new cases.[31] From that point on, cases multiplied exponentially, with death rates soaring thereafter. As children proved most susceptible to the virus, the morgues of Washington began filling with infants and children.

When 162 new cases were reported on October 1, city officials took action. Public schools were ordered to close indefinitely, and operating hours for stores were limited to 10:00 a.m. to 6:00 p.m.[32] More closings followed in the next few days. On October 3, private schools and beaches were ordered to be closed. On October 4, the number of cases spiked as 618 new cases were reported. As a result, Fowler called for additional bans on public gatherings, including church services,

28 Minutes of the Forty-First Annual Meeting of the Columbia Association of Baptist Churches Washington, D.C. November 18, 19, 20, 21, 1918 (Washington, DC: Judd & Detweiler, Inc. 1918), MS 922, p. 40, box 3, folder 4, CHBC Archives.
29 Elliot Williams, "The Forgotten Epidemic: A Century Ago, DC Lost Nearly 3,000 Residents to Influenza," Washingtonian, October 31, 2018, https://www.washingtonian.com/.
30 "Washington, DC," The American Influenza Epidemic of 1918–1919, Influenza Encyclopedia, University of Michigan Center for the History of Medicine, https://www.influenzaarchive.org/.
31 "Influenza Brings Death to Three More," Evening Star, September 27, 1918, 1.
32 "DC Schools End Sessions in Fight Against Epidemic," Evening Star, October 2, 1918, 1.

playgrounds, theaters, dance halls, and other places of amusement. According to official orders, commissioners of the District of Columbia "requested" clergy to "omit all church services until further action by the Commissioners."[33] Apparently, the city government had learned from past mistakes that requests would be more readily received by churches than orders.

At a gathering of the Pastors Federation of Washington the next day, the Protestant churches of the city agreed to comply with the safety measures called for by the city, recognizing that a unified response was necessary to combat this deadly disease. Gathering at the New York Avenue Presbyterian Church, the pastors released a public statement, acknowledging that "the prevailing condition of our city" led them to place themselves on record as "cheerfully complying" with the commissioners' "request" to close all churches in the city for the safety of all. They urged their congregants to conduct their own forms of religious worship at home for the next three weeks, offering up prayers for the sick and the allied nations at war.[34]

Some churches got creative in the face of the recommendation against indoor gatherings, choosing to gather outdoors instead. Across the city, churches obtained permits to gather in public parks or simply met in front of their own buildings. As the *Washington Times* reported, "Numerous permits have been obtained to hold services in various Government parks in the city. These open air services will continue each Sunday until such time as the District Commissioners decide the influenza epidemic is sufficiently abated to warrant resumption of meetings in church buildings."[35] Unfortunately, the churches' creativity was not well received by the District health commissioner, who issued a further order on October 9, 1918, to ban outdoor gatherings. "This order includes all indoor and outdoor services in churches,"

33 "Churches Closed While Influenza Threatens DC," *Evening Star*, October 4, 1918, 1.
34 "Influenza Spread Not Checked Yet," *Evening Star*, October 6, 1918, 7.
35 "Church Services in Open Planned," *Washington Times*, October 5, 1918, 2.

Commissioner Brownlow explained. "No outdoor gatherings will be allowed."[36] In a remarkable display of patience, the churches complied with these additional restrictions, waiting and praying for the virus to subside.

The number of new cases and fatalities rose steadily until reaching its peak on October 18 when 91 deaths and 934 new cases were reported.[37] Then, slowly, the virus began to decline. As the curve began to flatten, churches began to agitate for a lifting of the ban on gatherings. They argued that intelligent regulation and strict adherence to guidelines could prevent any further spread of the virus. Moreover, they contended that the very nature of religious gatherings made them uniquely entitled to be treated as regulated, rather than prohibited, assemblies. Theodore Noyes, the influential editor of the *Evening Star*, spoke for many Washingtonians when he argued that church gatherings should only be prohibited when absolutely necessary, because banning church gatherings constituted a direct assault on the free exercise of religious liberty. "The authorities know that through national and civil loyalty their prohibitive order will be obeyed," Noyes explained. For that very reason, "they should be reluctant to prevent men and women from doing that which their consciences and, in the belief of some of them, God's command impel them to do."[38]

By October 26, the Pastors Federation of Washington had changed their tack and were now squarely opposed to any continued adherence to the health commissioner's orders. Meeting with Health Commissioner Fowler, who was recovering from the flu, and the surgeon general, the Federation demanded that churches open the following day. To their great disappointment, the commissioner remained resolute in his continued opposition to public gatherings. Though he explained that he had no desire to "interfere any longer than necessary" until the

36 "Forty Deaths in Day from 'Flu,'" *Washington Times*, October 9, 1918, 3.
37 "Epidemic Decline Seen by Officials," *Evening Star*, October 28, 1918, 2.
38 Theodore W. Noyes, "Open Churches for Public Worship," *Evening Star*, October 25, 1918, 6.

danger of the spread of infection through large public gatherings had abated, the ban on gatherings would not be lifted.[39]

The pastors of the city were livid. They had met with the city commissioners, hoping to reason with them but found that their arguments fell on deaf ears. The commissioners, they felt, were motivated purely by "materialistic grounds" and had no regard for the power of prayer or the comfort that religious gatherings could provide. In an opinion piece the following day, Pastor Randolph H. McKim of the Church of the Epiphany lamented the "state of panic" that had seized the city and attributed it to the "disorganization" of normal religious life.[40]

But the pastors did not give up. They wrote letters, made appeals, and fought tooth and nail to have the ban lifted. They knew that their congregations needed them now more than ever and that the spiritual strength of the community was essential to weathering the storm of the influenza pandemic. Pastor J. Milton Waldron of the Shiloh Baptist Church, a prominent African American congregation, spoke for many when he decried the city officials' "interference with the freedom of religious worship." He argued that the church was not a luxury but a necessity to the life and perpetuity of the nation and that the authorities were woefully lacking in reverence to God and the church's mission.[41] Despite the ongoing appeals, it would be several more days before the ban was lifted, and the city's churches could once again open their doors to their congregations.

Finally, on October 29, the commissioners released an order to lift the ban. Health Commissioner Fowler requested that his order of October 4, 1918, "requesting the clergy of Washington to omit all church services until further action by the Commissioners, be terminated."[42] Theaters, schools, and other public gatherings would be reopened the

---

39 "Influenza Keeps Ban on Gatherings," *Evening Star*, October 26, 1918, 1.
40 Randolph H. McKim, "Closing of the Churches," *Evening Star*, October 26, 1918, 7.
41 J. Milton Waldron, "Prohibition of Public Worship," *Evening Star*, October 29, 1918, 24.
42 "Movies, Schools and Churches Are to Be Reopened," *Evening Star*, October 29, 1918, 1.

following week. The churches had been the last public gatherings to close and the first to reopen.

Advertisements flooded the papers, announcing the resumption of services, and people joyfully flocked back to their beloved houses of worship. On that first Sunday back at Metropolitan on November 2, 1918—their first public gathering in four weeks—John Compton Ball preached a scarcely veiled sermon entitled "The Value of the Church."[43] Despite the hardships they had endured, the churches of Washington remained steadfast in their faith, and as the city slowly began to recover, they emerged stronger than ever.

Figure 7.5. John Compton Ball greeting Steven T. Early's wheel-chair-bound brother, Thomas Joseph Early Jr., also a member of the church, in 1944.

The toll of the epidemic had been severe, with many churches reporting multiple deaths among their congregations. Fifth Baptist Church reported twenty-six deaths. Second Baptist Church lost several members, including two sisters who died three days apart. Temple Baptist Church lost fifteen members, including Pastor J. J. Muir's firstborn son, Edward. And when Stephen T. Early returned to Washington after the war, he found his family grieving the loss of his sister-in-law, Ethelyn Callaway Early, wife to his brother Felix Early and beloved member of Metropolitan Baptist Church. She had succumbed to the Spanish flu.[44] She was twenty-five years old, and they had been married only sixteen months.

There is no question that Metropolitan was devastated by the pandemic of 1918. The loss of life and disruption of church services, combined with the lingering effects of war, took an incredible toll on the church. Nevertheless, they had a resolute confidence in God's sovereignty and continued goodness.

———

As Capitol Hill Baptist Church faced significant hardship on an individual and corporate level during the COVID-19 pandemic of 2020, the church's elders and members were encouraged by the knowledge that they were not the first to encounter such challenges. One hundred years earlier, the church had grappled with how to respond to government regulations related to a virus far more lethal than COVID-19, and the church had emerged stronger. God sustained Capitol Hill Baptist during that difficult season in 2020 partly through the knowledge that he had previously sustained the church during an even more difficult season in 1918.

No generation can perfectly predict what trials will come. Future generations may face far worse challenges than COVID-19 or the Spanish flu. But all believers can take comfort in the fact that the way

44 "Organist of Metropolitan Baptist Church Influenza Victim," *Washington Post*, January 13, 1919, 10.

they trust the Lord with the trials he sends may be part of the way he sustains future believers. The consolation the Lord gives his saints in any trial is the knowledge that trials are not given to hoard but to steward; patient endurance in suffering is often how the Lord brings comfort to others (2 Cor. 1:3–7).

Looking back on 1918, Ball called it a year of "war, fuel famine, and influenza epidemics."[45] Certainly the church had struggled, wept, and rejoiced. But as troops began to return home and families were reunited, glimmers of hope shone through the darkness. Ball was convinced, and the church with him, that Metropolitan's best days were still ahead of them.

45 *Minutes of the Forty-First Annual Meeting of the Columbia Association of Baptist Churches Washington, D.C.*, 68.

8

"No Modernism Will Be Tolerated at All in This Church"

1919–1943

THE STAGE WAS SET. The audience was ready. Crowds filled the auditorium of Calvary Baptist Church in New York City on Sunday morning, February 20, 1921, to hear the sensation of the West Coast preach.[1] After a period of singing, Calvary's pastor, John Roach Straton, strode on stage to introduce his special guest. The consummate entertainer and fundamentalist firebrand, Straton knew he had discovered an irresistible evangelistic tool in the young preacher from the West Coast. Though many had come to mock and scoff, by the time the sermon began, everyone was spellbound. "In the world of religion," the preacher explained, "there isn't any 'No Man's Land.' You are either a Christian or a disbeliever. What are you?"[2] With short, punchy sentences, interspersed with slang and illustrations from everyday life, the nineteen-year-old female preacher captivated the audience. The effect was electric. Hundreds made professions

1 "Church Advertisements," *New-York Tribune*, February 19, 1921, 15
2 "Woman Preacher in Pulpit," *Brooklyn Daily Eagle*, February 1921, 23.

of faith as the campaign continued throughout New York City and down the East Coast. Amy Lee Stockton had stepped into her own as a female preacher and was ready to take her place in the fundamentalist movement. But was fundamentalism ready for Amy Lee Stockton?

During the Roaring Twenties and Depressing Thirties, Amy Lee Stockton was a household name among conservative Christians in America. She preached on behalf of and alongside nearly all of the leading fundamentalists of her day, including Oliver Willis Van Osdel at Wealthy Street Baptist Church in Grand Rapids, Michigan, and Henry H. Savage of First Baptist Pontiac, Michigan.[3] In fact, when the famous Temple Baptist Church of Detroit, Michigan—of which J. Frank Norris would become pastor in 1934—found itself in need of pulpit supply in 1931, they called for none other than Amy Lee Stockton.[4]

Figure 8.1. Amy Lee Stockton (1892–1988) in a 1920 New York newspaper, describing her as "the first regularly ordained co-pastor of her sex in New York" and as the "assistant of Dr. John Roach Straton."

3   Kevin Bauder and Robert Delnay, *One in Hope and Doctrine: Origins of Baptist Fundamentalism, 1870–1950* (Schaumburg: IL: Regular Baptist Books, 2014), 201.
4   "Woman Fills Pulpit Here," *Detroit Free Press*, August 1, 1931, 12.

Far from a progressive or liberal, Stockton held to conservative theological views on the authority of Scripture as she had been taught by
John Marvin Dean at the Northern Baptist Theological Seminary in
Chicago.[5] Dean, who founded the school in 1913 as a counterweight to
the liberal University of Chicago, recruited Stockton as one of his first
students and helped jumpstart her preaching career as she accompanied
him on evangelistic tours throughout the United States. Dean would go
on to start Western Seminary in Portland, Oregon, and briefly pastor
Portland's Hinson Memorial Baptist Church, but he never withdrew
his endorsement of Stockton's preaching ministry.

Stockton first spoke at Metropolitan Baptist Church when Dean
brought her with him on the evangelistic tour through Washington, DC,
in 1919.[6] It would not be the last time. Between 1930 and 1942, Stockton visited Metropolitan over a dozen times, nearly always preaching on
Sunday morning. In fact, when John Compton Ball took an extended
vacation for six weeks in June and July of 1930, the congregation voted
overwhelmingly that Stockton return to fill the pulpit in Ball's absence.[7]

The Battle for Baptist Fundamentals

For twenty-first-century evangelicals, a woman preaching from the
pulpit might be taken as an undisputable sign of theological liberalism.
Surprisingly, however, this was not the case among many nominally
conservative churches in the early twentieth century. Like Amy Lee
Stockton, Metropolitan held to conservative theological views on Scripture and doctrine. In fact, when a Louisiana congressman named Asa
Leonard Allen wrote to his home church of his impressions of attending
Metropolitan Baptist Church in 1937, he offered this encomium: "No
modernism will be tolerated at all in this church." As Allen would go

5 Bauder and Delnay, *One in Hope and Doctrine*, 74.
6 "Church Announcements," *Evening Star*, October 18, 1919, 24.
7 Deacons Meeting Minutes, March 6, 1930, MS 26, pp. 56–57, box 1, folder 7, Capitol Hill Baptist
   Church Archives, Washington, DC (hereafter, CHBC Archives); "Woman to Hold Meetings,"
   Evening Star, July 26, 1930, 8–9.

on to describe, the church thoroughly examined anyone who would be teaching the Bible at the church. "No person will be permitted to teach in the Sunday school," Allen explained, "until he or she has been pronounced absolutely orthodox in every way."[8] Hosting a female preacher was not a sign of liberalism because the issue had not yet emerged as a line of demarcation between liberals and conservatives.

As a church, Metropolitan was fixedly aligned with the denominational conservatives. When conservatives launched a shot across liberalism's bow in 1919 with a petition calling for a conference on "Baptist Fundamentals" as part of a pre-convention gathering of Northern Baptists in 1920, Metropolitan's pastor, John Compton Ball, was one of the signatories.[9] The initial Baptist Fundamentals meeting in 1920 led to the formation of the Baptist Bible Union of North America, which aimed to check the spread of liberalism within Baptist denominations in America and Canada. In 1926, the fourth annual meeting of this organization was held at Metropolitan Baptist Church.

By 1926, Baptists in partnership with the Northern Baptist Convention were deadlocked in mortal combat over the question of believer's baptism and its relationship to church membership. On the far left of the spectrum was Harry Emerson Fosdick, the famous preacher and avowed liberal, who had recently been called to pastor the prestigious Park Avenue Baptist Church in New York, home to the Rockefellers. Among other liberal positions, Fosdick was famous for his advocacy of open membership—that is, not requiring believer's baptism as a prerequisite for church membership and the Lord's Supper. At the previous year's convention in Seattle in 1925, conservatives had raised this point with the enrollment committee, arguing that Park Avenue should be disfellowshipped and barred from the conven-

8   "Washington Religious Activities Impress Congressman Allen," *Baptist Message*, March 25, 1937. For more on Asa Leonard Allen's relationship to Metropolitan, see K. Owen White, interview by A. Ronald Tonks, January 17, 1974, and February 1, 1976, Oral History Program, Historical Commission, Southern Baptist Convention, 74, https://sbhla.org/wp-content/uploads/oh-white.pdf.

9   American Baptist Convention, *Baptist Fundamentals: Being Addresses Delivered at the Pre-Convention Conference at Buffalo, June 21 and 22, 1920* (Philadelphia: Judson, 1920).

tion, since they were effectively no longer a Baptist church. However, in an unnerving act of equivocation, the chair ruled that the convention did not possess any definition of what a Baptist church was and, therefore, no grounds for excluding the Park Avenue delegates. The conservatives were livid. The following year, they were determined to come ready to fight.[10]

On the conservative extreme of the denominational spectrum was the usual cast of the Baptist Bible Union, which had gathered at Metropolitan Baptist Church the week before the annual meeting of the Northern Baptist Convention to strategize how to challenge the previous year's decision. Present were the "big three" of fundamentalism: the gun-slinging J. Frank Norris of Fort Worth, Texas; the fiery W. B. Riley of Minneapolis, Minnesota; and the world-famous president of the Baptist Bible Union, T. T. Shields of Toronto, Canada.[11] Each delivered messages at Metropolitan Baptist Church on Sunday, May 23, 1926, castigating Harry Emerson Fosdick as "one of the outstanding enemies of the Christian faith."[12]

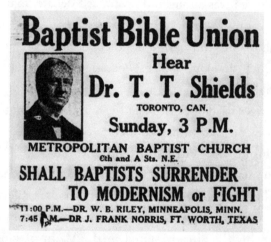

Figure 8.2. Metropolitan's advertisement in the *Evening Star* indicating that fundamentalism's three greatest preachers—T. T. Shields, W. B. Riley, and J. Frank Norris—would be occupying the pulpit on Sunday, May 23, 1926.

10 "Upheavel in Baptist Church Is Looked For," *Washington Post*, May 23, 1926, M1.
11 "Baptist Bible Union Meets Here Today," *Washington Post*, May 19, 1926, 10.
12 "Baptists to Open Modernist Fight," *Evening Star*, May 24, 1926, 1.

The conservatives gathered at Metropolitan Baptist Church during the lead-up to the 1926 Northern Baptist Convention. All agreed that the issue of open membership was a fundamental matter of the Christian faith and a hill to die on. If the convention voted to allow churches that practiced open membership to remain in, the conservatives all agreed that they would leave the denomination. As the *Washington Post* reported, "The fight looms over this issue."[13]

When the Northern Baptist Convention opened on Tuesday, May 25, over three thousand delegates from Baptist churches filled the Washington auditorium. At the appointed time, on Wednesday, May 26, W. B. Riley, pastor of First Baptist Church of Minneapolis, brought Baptist Bible Union's motion to require that "the Northern Baptist Convention recognize its constituency as consisting solely of those Baptist churches in which the immersion of believers is recognized and practiced as a pre-requisite to membership."[14]

What followed was a long and protracted debate, marked by jeers and cheers. As the *Watchman-Examiner* later recounted, "Never before in the annals of the Convention has there been debate quite like this one."[15] "Frequent and loud applause" occasionally interrupted a general "tense feeling."[16]

Conservatives tried to clarify that the question was not about what authority the convention had to dictate the faith and practice of a local church but whether the convention could define its terms for cooperation in any other way than the Bible commanded. "Though we have fellowship with our pedobaptist friends," Riley explained, "we do not express [this] in our approval of any form of baptism other than which is already stated in the Word of God." Earl V. Pierce of Minnesota argued similarly that "the great fundamental

13 "Upheavel in Baptist Church Is Looked For," M1.
14 *Watchman-Examiner*, June 3, 1926, 684.
15 *Watchman-Examiner*, June 3, 1926, 683.
16 *Watchman-Examiner*, June 3, 1926, 683–84.

of a Baptist church is not freedom but obedience. Our freedom is to believe as God pleases, and that alone." John Roach Straton of New York summed up the crux of the matter: "Shall we stand for the original commission of Christ and obey his, 'Whatsoever I have commanded you?' "[17]

To the dismay of the conservatives, however, when the debate ended and the time to vote finally came, Riley's motion lost by a vote of 2,020 to 1,084.[18] For conservatives, this marked the beginning of the end.[19] This decisive meeting in Washington, DC, proved a watershed for the Northern Baptist Convention. After failing to get their resolutions passed in Washington, many conservatives began to organize independent structures or leave the Northern Baptist Convention altogether.[20]

Arguably the single most significant factor that contributed to the theological decline of the Northern Baptist Convention in the twentieth century was its rejection of confessionalism. Whether voting on adopting the New Hampshire Confession of Faith or defining its position on baptism, the Northern Convention consistently chose inclusivism over conviction and ambiguity over exclusivity. In contrast, in 1925, the Southern Baptist Convention adopted the Baptist Faith and Message—a revised version of the New Hampshire Confession of Faith—as a confessional basis of cooperation.[21] Adopting the Baptist Faith and Message (which has been revised and expanded over the years) was not an act of division but a means of ensuring unity. As the chairman of

17 *Watchman-Examiner*, June 3, 1926, 684.
18 *Watchman-Examiner*, June 3, 1926, 684.
19 As William Vance Trollinger Jr. writes in his biography of W. B. Riley, "This crushing defeat . . . closed the [Baptist Bible Union] campaign." William Vance Trollinger Jr., *God's Empire: William Bell Riley and Midwestern Fundamentalism* (Madison, WI: University of Wisconsin Press, 1990), 59.
20 J. Michael Utzinger, *Yet Saints Their Watch Are Keeping: Fundamentalists, Modernists, and the Development of Evangelical Ecclesiology, 1887–1937* (Macon, GA: Mercer University Press, 2006), 201–10.
21 *Annual of the Southern Baptist Convention 1925* (Nashville: Marshall & Bruce, 1925), 71, http://media2.sbhla.org.s3.amazonaws.com/annuals/SBC_Annual_1925.pdf.

the committee explained, adopting a statement of faith would "clarify the atmosphere and remove the causes of misunderstanding, friction, and apprehension."[22]

The Northern Baptist Convention never adopted any such statement of faith. In fact, every time conservatives attempted to get the convention to adopt a statement of faith, it was shot down. Arguably, a significant reason that the Southern Baptist Convention has remained theologically orthodox is that it defined a statement of faith that would serve as a test of orthodoxy.

Like other Baptist churches in the District of Columbia, Metropolitan continued to partner with both denominations, notwithstanding their misgivings about the Northern Convention. As John Compton Ball explained to the church in 1929, "We have no governing body that rules over us. . . . Every Baptist church is independent." Nevertheless, "a mutual tie binds Baptist congregations in helpful fellowship and a unity of purpose in our work for the Lord Jesus." As a church, Metropolitan gave contributions to the District of Columbia Association of Baptist Churches (DCBC), which were then divided evenly between Northern and Southern Conventions. As a result, Ball explained, "We should have delegates from this church to BOTH conventions."[23] For Ball, as for several others, there remained hope of reforming the Northern Convention.

Not all of Metropolitan's members were comfortable with this dual affiliation. In 1942 and 1943, several members sought, albeit unsuccessfully, to sever Metropolitan's financial ties with the Northern Baptist Convention.[24] It was not until 1947, however, under K. Owen White, that Metropolitan formally cut ties with

22 *Annual of the Southern Baptist Convention 1925*, 71.
23 John Compton Ball, "Pastor's Page," Metropolitan Baptist Church Bulletin, May 5, 1929, MS 1790, box 9a, folder 4, CHBC Archives (emphasis in orginal).
24 Metropolitan Baptist Church Minutes, December 17, 1942, MS 1608, p. 110, box 6, folder 9, CHBC Archives; Deacons Meeting Minutes, April 6, 1943, MS 32, p. 16, box 1, folder 10, CHBC Archives.

the Northern Baptists. They did this by designating their giving to the DCBC, which was affiliated with both Northern and Southern Baptist Conventions, so that none of their contributions went to the Northern Baptist Convention. As White explained in June 1947, "We do not approve the policies or program of the Federal Council of the Churches of Christ in America; we are definitely opposed to any move toward organic church union."[25] From 1947 on, Metropolitan Baptist Church would be identified only with the Southern Baptist Convention.

By that time, however, the disposition of conservative churches toward female preachers had shifted markedly. As members of the Baptist Bible Union turned from fighting the shared opponent of modernism in 1926 and instead sought to work together to form alternative denominational structures, female preachers like Amy Lee Stockton quickly became a lightning rod issue. Most Southern Baptists opposed female preachers as a matter of principle. As the Nashville-based *Baptist and Reflector* wrote in 1922, any celebration of Stockton's success in leading converts to Christ needed to be weighed against "Paul's statement: 'Let your women keep silent in the churches.' "[26] On the other hand, leading fundamentalists in the north like Oliver Van Osdel in Michigan and John Roach Straton in New York were firmly in favor of female preachers.[27] The matter was bound to come to a head.

25 K. Owen White, "Pastor's Paragraphs," Metropolitan Baptist Church Bulletin, June 1, 1947, MS 1805, box 9a, folder 11, CHBC Archives.
26 Fleetwood Ball, "Among the Brethren," *Baptist and Reflector*, April 20, 1922, 15.
27 Bauder and Delnay write that Oliver Van Osdel's mind was changed by reading George F. Wilkin, *The Prophesying of Women* (Chicago: Fleming H. Revell, 1895), such that he was opening his pulpit to Amy Lee Stockton by 1928. Bauder and Delnay, *One in Hope and Doctrine*, 200–201. Lee Canipe argues that Straton's mind changed after hearing the thirteen-year-old Uldine Utley in Florida in February 1926. The fact that he had Amy Lee Stockton preaching for him in 1920 and 1921 indicates an earlier change of heart than has been previously recognized. Lee Canipe "The Unlikely Argument of a Baptist Fundamentalist: John Roach Straton's Defense of Women in the Pulpit," *Baptist History and Heritage* 40, no. 2 (March 22, 2005): 64–77. Cf. Thomas A.

At the next year's annual session of the Baptist Bible Union, hosted at Straton's own Calvary Baptist Church in New York City in March 1927, the question of female preachers was front and center. When a female member of the audience asked J. W. Gillon of Kentucky "whether a woman should be permitted to speak in a Baptist church," Gillon responded snidely that he could not answer the woman's question since she was in violation of the scriptural injunction of 1 Corinthians 14:34 "that women should keep silent in the churches." Leaping to his feet, Straton took issue with Gillon's treatment of the woman and his interpretation of Scripture. "We haven't yet opened our eyes to the writings of the New Testament in regard to women preaching," Straton insisted. "In this respect we are still stone blind."[28] The tense interaction highlighted a growing rift between northern and southern evangelicals. Within a few years, the Baptist Bible Union would disintegrate over, among other reasons, disagreement on this very question.

Despite denominational tensions, the relationship between Metropolitan and Amy Lee Stockton deepened over the years. In 1940 Ball described Stockton as a "radiant soul winning evangelist" who "need[s] no introduction or recommendation to the people of Washington."[29] In 1942, Ball would refer to her as "our miss Stockton."[30] When Stockton was awarded an honorary doctorate in 1950, members of Metropolitan sent congratulatory messages.[31] "Metropolitan means so much to us," Stockton later wrote to the church in 1978. "Your letter thronged my mind and heart with

Robinson and Lanette R. Ruff, *Out of the Mouths of Babes: Girl Evangelists in the Flapper Era* (New York: Oxford University Press, 2011).

28 "Woman's Right to Preach Is Argued," *Arizona Daily Star*, March 11, 1927, 1.

29 "The Stockton-Gould Meetings," Metropolitan Baptist Church Bulletin, February 11, 1940, MS 1792, box 9, folder 6, CHBC Archives.

30 John Compton Ball, "Letter from Pastor," Metropolitan Baptist Church Bulletin, October 11, 1942, MS 1792, box 9, folder 6, CHBC Archives.

31 "Honor to Miss Stockton," Metropolitan Baptist Church Bulletin, May 28, 1950, MS 1793, box 9a, folder 7, CHBC Archives.

countless tender, unsurpassed memories . . . [of] the crusades and revel in the priceless friendships that were formed in our fellowship in service."[32]

How do we make sense of this? When Ball's successor, K. Owen White, arrived in 1944 to take over, he was shocked by some of Metropolitan's practices. The church was Bible loving but disorganized. It was run based on Ball's idiosyncratic personality rather than a coherent biblical principle. What shocked White most was that three adult Sunday school classes for men were taught by women—the same women who had been teaching the men when they were children. For White, this seemed to indicate theological immaturity, where men never learned to feed themselves or others.[33]

A Gospel-Preaching Church

Metropolitan continued to hold to traditional Baptist practices of baptism and membership. The church had grown from 363 members in 1903 to 1,585 in 1930. In Ball's twenty-seven years as a pastor, he had seen over 2,200 new members join the church.[34] Standard practice in those days was still for those wishing to join the church to meet with the pastor and deacons for a membership interview on Thursday evenings at 7:00 p.m. As one entry in the deacons' minutes reads, "Kenneth Dean Webster appeared before the pastor and deacons, and, on his profession of faith, was recommended to the church as a candidate for baptism."[35] Throughout the 1930s, the church would "receive new members" and celebrate the Lord's Supper during the morning service followed by the ordinance of baptism at the evening service.[36]

32 Amy Lee Stockton and Rita Gould to Metropolitan Baptist Church, February 21, 1978, MS 1432, box 5, folder 31, CHBC Archives.

33 White, interview, 68.

34 "Rev. John C. Ball Returns to Pulpit," *Washington Post*, October 25, 1930, 4.

35 Deacons' Meeting Minutes, May 6, 1915, MS 20, p. 26, box 1, folder 4, CHBC Archives.

36 "Baptist Church Plans to Hold Special Meeting," *Washington Post*, January 5, 1935, 10.

Figure 8.3. John Compton Ball, pastor for forty-one years at Metropolitan Baptist Church, standing in the pulpit next to the Christian flag under an illuminated cross.

In his preaching, moreover, Ball continued to proclaim the true gospel without shying away from controversial topics. For instance, on January 13, 1935, Ball preached on the subject, "Will Everybody Be Saved?" His answer was unmistakable: "The man who denies the existence of God, will not be saved." Even the man who acknowledges "a first cause of creative force that might be called God" but who "goes on in his wicked way refusing to acknowledge any claim of God on his life will not be saved." In fact, Ball warned his hearers that "the man reared in a Christian home, an attendant of the services of the church, giving of his time and money to the cause of Christ, but for social and business advantages only, living a self-willed and sinful life in secret, will not be saved."[37]

Figure 8.4. Ball in the pulpit on Easter Sunday 1940. The stars on the service flag above the organ represent members serving during World War II.

Alongside clear teaching on God's judgment of sin, Ball also extolled the cross and the necessity of faith in Christ's atonement. On April 5, 1936, he defended the doctrine of substitutionary atonement. "You sung rightly in that hymn," he told the gathered church. " 'There is a fountain filled with blood.' That is being left out of a great many hymn books nowadays, but it never will be left out of the hymn book that I will have used in this church as long as I live."[38] As one pastor testified concerning Ball's ministry in 1936, "In the presence of all the pretentious systems, plausible philosophies and humanitarian schemes

37 "Unrepentant Doomed, Rev. J. C. Ball Declares," *Washington Post*, January 14, 1935, 6.
38 John Compton Ball, "The Glory of the Cross" (sermon, Metropolitan Baptist Church, Washington, DC, April 5, 1936), 10, Kelley family private collection.

that are being pushed to the front today in efforts to better life, he has stood, trumpeting forth his firm conviction that Christ is the wisdom of God and the power of God unto salvation."[39]

Figure 8.5. On February 27, 1943, on the sixty-fifth anniversary of the church's founding, Metropolitan symbolically burned its mortgage, having paid off the debt on its present building. Pictured (left to right) are William Eckhart, chairman of the board of trustees; John M. Ballbach, assistant pastor; and John Compton Ball, Metropolitan's pastor.

One final aspect of Metropolitan's ministry during the 1920s and 1930s concerns the question of the church's race relations. Few mentions of racial issues occur during Ball's forty-one-year pastorate at Metropolitan, which is itself a statement, considering some of Washington's darkest years of racial segregation and discrimination occurred during that time period. Despite the church's cultural context, John Compton Ball enjoyed a strong personal relationship with Walter H. Brooks, the

39 Perry L. Mitchell to Metropolitan Baptist Church, December 28, 1936, Kelley family private collection.

longtime pastor of Nineteenth Street Baptist Church, the leading—and oldest—African American church in the city. Brooks (mentioned in the previous chapter for his criticism of the government during the 1918 Spanish flu) was the longest-serving pastor of any Washington church, ministering at Nineteenth Street Baptist for sixty-three years. On the occasion of Ball's retirement after forty-one years as pastor of Metropolitan, he made sure that his friend Brooks was present and seated in the place of honor next to him—a staggering statement in 1944 at a time when Washington was profoundly segregated.

Figure 8.6. At the service commemorating John Compton Ball's retirement on September 15, 1944, Walter H. Brooks, the ninety-three-year-old pastor of Nineteenth Street Baptist Church, can be seen seated next to Ball on the front row. Brooks died the following year. Left to right: Walter Brooks, John Compton Ball, Oscar Blackwelder, John E. Briggs, and Edwin H. Pruden (DC Baptist Convention president).

In a photobook in the church archives, the caption of the photo of Brooks and Ball reads, "Dr. Ball tells his flock there is no color line drawn in preaching the Gospel of Jesus Christ."[40] To the extent Ball

40 "Dr. Ball Greets Dr. Walter Brooks," photo 128, box C, folder 2, CHBC Archives.

preached that the gospel of Jesus Christ contains no color line—and to the extent that he modeled it with his life—he was swimming upstream from his predominantly Southern cultural context and following the clear teaching of Scripture.

Figure 8.7. In a remarkable display of interracial cooperation, Walter H. Brooks greets John Compton Ball on stage at Ball's retirement celebration.

Although Metropolitan faithfully preached the gospel of Jesus Christ during the entirety of Ball's long pastorate, the church's future was far from certain. As a Southern church in a Southern city, pastored by a Northerner, in partnership with both Northern and Southern Baptist Conventions, Metropolitan was a church of contradictions. In this respect, Metropolitan provides a glimpse into some of the paradoxes of early- to mid-twentieth-century fundamentalism. On the one hand, conservatives like Ball were committed to resisting theological modernism and defending the inspiration of Scripture. On the other hand, a commitment to the authority of Scripture did not settle every theological question or resolve the precise bounds of cooperation, whether within or between churches.

———

During the 1920s and 1930s, the dividing lines between egalitarians and complementarians (as the groups would come to be known much later) over the question of female preachers had yet to be drawn. This is often how theological development occurs. When a new practice emerges—in this case, women preachers—there is often a period of debate and exploration as pastors and churches ask whether the new practice contradicts the Bible, not just their longstanding traditions.

The question that naturally emerges, however, is this: How do we determine whether a particular issue is worth dividing over? Why would baptism be worth dividing over in the 1920s but not female preachers, while a century later many would consider female preachers, not baptism, worth dividing over? One question to answer is this: Will this doctrine or practice have a tendency to undermine the gospel in the long run?

The question is not whether someone can believe in open membership or female preachers and still be a Christian. Or even whether a church that practices open membership or has female elders can be a true church. The question is this: Will these beliefs and practices have a corrosive effect on the church's ability to protect the gospel?

This question cuts both ways. Some beliefs that constituted long-term gospel threats in the past may no longer serve as an ever-present danger to the church. Premillennial eschatology, for example, helped shore up early twentieth-century churches against the denial of the visible, bodily return of Jesus Christ. But a biblically faithful articulation of amillennialism, for instance, might just as suitably clarify a church's position on Christ's second coming. In the 1920s and 1930s, however, it was not yet clear to the members of Metropolitan Baptist Church what down-the-road impact the hermeneutic undergirding support for women preachers would have on the church.

Contradictions may be inevitable in every person and every church— but they make for generational instability. John Compton Ball could maintain the apparent inconsistencies of conservative views on Scripture and support for female preachers through the sheer force of his personality. But the next pastor would likely have to choose one or the other. As Ball's years came to a close and Metropolitan emerged from World War II, who could take the helm of the church after a forty-one-year pastorate, and what direction would he take it?

9

"Holding Forth the Word of Life"

1944–1955

BY THE TIME BILLY GRAHAM took the stage, every seat in the National Guard armory had been taken. Following a brief introduction by J. Walter Carpenter, pastor of Metropolitan Baptist Church and general chairman of the Greater Washington Evangelistic Crusade, Graham strode on stage, jaw clenched and eyes glaring, ready to bring a message from God to the nation's capital.

"I am here to tell you what the Bible has to say," he announced to an estimated crowd of twelve thousand—nearly twice what the fire code had permitted until a Congressional vote expanded its capacity specifically for the occasion. "The Bible says we're all sinners," he told his transfixed audience from in front of a blue banner with the words of John 14:6 written in two-foot capital letters: "I AM THE WAY, THE TRUTH AND THE LIFE."

Striding back and forth across the wide platform, Bible in hand, punctuating the air with his characteristic sharp gestures, Graham preached for an hour, couching his call for repentance in the language of national crisis. "We've been trying to change the world without changing the man. But you can't do it. You've got to change the man first. Many agree that they are sinners," he pressed, "but stop short of the cross. You have to come to Christ," he urged. "Confess that you are a sinner and ask him to cleanse you of sin." He finished with a rallying cry for revival. "I believe that there are millions of Americans praying that Washington can lead the way in a revival," he announced with Bible held aloft, "Let's do it!"[1] Billy Graham had come to Washington, ready to turn the nation to Christ. The nation was ready for him.

Figure 9.1. Billy Graham (1918–2018) preaches to thousands from the east steps of the US Capitol building on February 3, 1952.

1   "200 Ministers Praise Billy Graham's Drive After First Revival," *Evening Star*, January 14, 1952, 6.

Figure 9.2. Metropolitan's choir director speaks with a member of the church in military uniform during World War II.

Between 1944 and 1961, evangelicals would engage in dizzying efforts to establish a presence in the nation's capital. From Billy Graham's Washington crusade of 1952 to the establishment of *Christianity Today* in 1956, evangelicals understood America to be at a critical moment and were determined to not be caught on the sidelines. At the center of these efforts stood Metropolitan Baptist Church.

If World War II had taught evangelicals anything, it was that the fate of the world depended on America and that the fate of America depended on the church. Everywhere they looked, America was in crisis. "America is rapidly becoming more and more pagan," Metropolitan's pastor, K. Owen White, wrote in February 1948. "Only a mighty, soul-stirring revival of New Testament Christianity can help us now!"[2] If the fate of the world hung in the balance, and America held the keys, no city

2 K. Owen White, "Pastor's Paragraphs," Metropolitan Baptist Church Bulletin, February 8, 1948, MS 1792, box 9, folder 6, Capitol Hill Baptist Church Archives, Washington, DC (hereafter, CHBC Archives).

had more potential to shape the history of the world than Washington, DC. The question was, would America assume the mantle of moral and spiritual leadership and be a beacon of peace to the world or continue in spiritual indifference and idolatry?

With the help of Carl F. H. Henry and under the leadership of K. Owen White and J. Walter Carpenter, Metropolitan Baptist Church established its place after the war as one of the most influential churches in the capital and leading evangelical churches in America. In what can only be termed a revival, between 1944 and 1955, the church added thousands of members, saw hundreds sent into the ministry, and became the local hub of Billy Graham's evangelistic crusades in the capital. None of it, however, would have been possible apart from the efforts of Agnes Shankle.

Figure 9.3. Agnes Shankle, long-time Sunday school teacher at Metropolitan Baptist Church, posing with several of the students in her Ask-Seek-Knock Sunday school class. The Greek letters Alpha Sigma Kappa signify the class name. Each star on the class banner represented a student serving in World War II.

Agnes Shankle and K. Owen White

If America was facing an existential crisis in 1944 coming out of the war, so was Metropolitan Baptist Church. After a pastorate of forty-one years, John Compton Ball was finally ready to retire, and Metropolitan was finally looking for a new pastor. "I have heard that your long and faithful tenure as pastor of Metropolitan Baptist Church is drawing to a close," wrote President Franklin D. Roosevelt from the White House:

> I cannot restrain the impulse to join the members of the congregation and other friends in a hearty, "well done, good and faithful servant." I trust all your days may be radiant with the memories of your 41 years spent in our Capital City Community as preacher of the word of God and a leader in all good works.[3]

Due to the stability of Ball's ministry, Metropolitan didn't need to hire a new pastor during the early decades of the twentieth century when the fundamentalist-modernist controversy was roaring. But now the time had come. The nominee of the pulpit committee, hand selected by Ball and unanimously agreed upon by the board of deacons, was Ralph Walker of Portland, Oregon.[4] However, during the congregational meeting preceding his call, Agnes Shankle, a longtime Sunday school teacher, stood up and questioned the soundness of Walker's teaching. She noted that there were "considerable rumors that he was compromising in his dealing with controversial questions between Fundamentalists and Modernists." Other members soon spoke up with similar concerns. The pulpit committee attempted to withdraw its motion and requested three more months to seek suitable candidates, but this was rejected by the congregation. Instead, the name K. Owen White, a recent graduate of the Southern Baptist Theological Seminary and a well-known

3   Press Release, John Compton Ball's Retirement, 1945, MS 1108, box 5, folder 8, CHBC Archives.
4   Deacons' Meeting Minutes, May 28, 1944, MS 32, p. 76, box 1, folder 10, CHBC Archives. Cf. Albert W. Wardin Jr., *Baptists in Oregon* (Portland, OR: Judson Baptist College, 1969), 459.

conservative, was offered from the floor, and after the pulpit committee withdrew their nomination of Walker, White was unanimously called to be the next pastor of Metropolitan Baptist Church.[5]

Figure 9.4. K. Owen White and John Compton Ball shake hands on stage as a portrait of Ball is unveiled on April 22, 1945.

In the history of this church on Capitol Hill, the vote to call K. Owen White may have been its most decisive moment, and it all started with Agnes Shankle. Later in his tenure at the church, White would complain of the church's disorganization and express incredulity over the fact that the church had "three elderly women teaching men's classes." Did he ever learn that one of those women was Agnes Shankle, who spoke up when others were silent, securing his election and possibly saving the church?[6]

5 Metropolitan Baptist Church Minutes, June 14, 1944, MS 1608, pp. 143–44, box 6, folder 9, CHBC Archives.

6 K. Owen White, interview by A. Ronald Tonks, January 17, 1974 and February 1, 1976, Oral History Program, Historical Commission, Southern Baptist Convention, 70, https://sbhla.org /wp-content/uploads/oh-white.pdf.

Though he would later acquire national fame for questioning then Senator John F. Kennedy at a gathering of the Houston Ministerial Association in September 1960 and later serve as president of the Southern Baptist Convention in 1963–64, Kenneth Owen White arrived at Metropolitan on September 17, 1944, as a relatively inexperienced pastor ready to get to work. What he found horrified him. The membership rolls were a mess. The church boasted nearly three thousand members, but White suspected that probably no more than five hundred showed up on Sundays.[7] When he tested his theory by placing attendance cards in the pews unannounced one Sunday in January 1948, he found that only 763 members had been present at the service.[8] "Because of the long pastorate of Dr. Ball," he later explained, "there were second and third generation people there who were tied to the church out of loyalty to him" simply because "it had become traditional to be a member of Metropolitan even though they had moved."[9]

What made things even worse was that Ball refused to cede pastoral leadership to White. Ball remained on the church staff as pastor emeritus, kept 75 percent of his salary, attended deacons meetings, and insisted that White recognize him publicly during services. He asked to retain the middle seat on the stage during services where the pastor typically sat, explaining that "people say unless I'm seated on the platform, it just doesn't seem like Metropolitan." During one of his first pastoral addresses to the church on a Wednesday night, White presented a half-dozen priorities for the church, after which Ball requested to address the church. He came to the front and said, "Well, you have heard our pastor's suggestions. He is a young man, and unknown to most of you. You will not feel free to go to him with your most personal problems, but I want you to remember that

7   K. Owen White, "Pastor's Paragraphs," Metropolitan Baptist Church Bulletin, February 4, 1945, MS 1803, box 9a, folder 9, CHBC Archives.
8   K. Owen White, "Pastor's Paragraphs," Metropolitan Baptist Church Bulletin, January 11, 1948, MS 1806, box 9a, folder 12, CHBC Archives.
9   White, interview, 68.

I am still living right across the street. You can always come to me."[10]
If ever there were a case study in how *not* to handle pastoral succes-
sion, this was it.

White tried to be patient. He emphasized continuity with Ball's
ministry, even choosing 1 Corinthians 2:2 for his inaugural sermon on
September 17, 1944—the same text that Ball had preached forty-one
years earlier in his first sermon as pastor.[11] He sought to always speak
well of the former pastor, declaring early on,

> Metropolitan Baptist Church has always stood by the plain, simple
> message of the Gospel. No schemes, or stunts, or sensational meth-
> ods have characterized its work. Under the leadership of Dr. J. C.
> Ball for 41 years it built upon the one foundation—"Jesus Christ
> and Him crucified." It will continue to do so. Your present Pastor
> has earnestly sought to preach the Word and God has been blessing
> His Word.[12]

Still, Ball refused to let White lead. "[It was] probably the most difficult
experience I have ever had," White recounted in an interview in 1974.
"Mrs. White said my hair turned gray within the first six months. . . .
I have to say, in all frankness, that he didn't make any great effort to
make it easy for the new pastor."[13]

Finally, White had had enough. He confronted the deacons about
the problem at a private meeting. Commendably, all of the deacons
except one took White's side, agreed to speak with Ball, and gave White
the space he needed to lead the church.[14]

---

10 White, interview, 71.
11 A Reception of Welcome for K. Owen White, October 24, 1944, MS 1527, box 5, folder 33,
    CHBC Archives.
12 K. Owen White, "Pastor's Paragraphs," *Metropolitan Baptist Church Bulletin*, September 16,
    1945, MS 1792, box 9a, folder 6, CHBC Archives.
13 White, interview, 68.
14 White, interview, 71–72.

Figure 9.5. K. Owen White places his hand on John Compton Ball's shoulder as White gives a speech, with Agnes Shankle sitting in the background.

One significant difference between Ball's ministry and White's ministry was White's commitment to expositional preaching. Sermons at Metropolitan had always been topical, focusing on a single verse during the Sunday morning service and a single verse during the evening service. White, however, was determined to serially exposit the Scriptures.[15] He chose Nehemiah for his first sermon series to begin on October 1, 1944. He printed the sermon texts and titles in the church bulletin and encouraged the congregation, "Take your Bible and read each week the chapter we are to deal with the following Sunday." White

15 White later recalled, "In Washington I really began more seriously than ever before preaching through books of the Bible." White, interview, 83.

was convinced that the message of Nehemiah was especially suited for their present situation. As he explained, "It is the earnest hope of your pastor that all our work shall be based upon the Word of God. We are to 'preach the Word,' 'teach the Word,' 'honor the Word,' and follow where it leads."[16]

Starting on May 6, 1945, White preached expositionally through the Gospel of John in a twenty-two-part series entitled "That Ye Might Believe." The instructions in the bulletin stated, "Read the appropriate chapter each week."[17] White's preaching was not the feel-good sentimentalism of Ball's latter years. For instance, on Thanksgiving Sunday in 1947, his morning sermon was on "The Judgment of God."[18] He preached forcefully and scripturally because he believed that only God's word could meet man's deepest needs. As he explained in 1947,

> There can never be any substitute for Gospel preaching! Pageantry, dramatics, audio-visual aids, esthetic appeals, personal counseling— all these and many other things may have their place, but they cannot take the place of the plain, positive preaching of the Gospel by one whose heart is afire and whose lips are empowered by the Spirit of God.[19]

As White's preaching ministry grew, Metropolitan began to broadcast their evening services each Sunday over the local radio station, WWDC.[20]

---

16 K. Owen White, "Pastor's Page," Metropolitan Baptist Church Bulletin, October 1, 1944, MS 1792, box 9a, folder 8, CHBC Archives.

17 "That Ye Might Believe," Metropolitan Baptist Church Bulletin, May 6, 1945, MS 1803, box 9a, folder 9, CHBC Archives.

18 "Order of Worship," Metropolitan Baptist Church Bulletin, November 23, 1947, MS 1805, box 9a, folder 11, CHBC Archives.

19 K. Owen White, "The Heavenly Vision," *The King's Business* 38, no. 8 (August 1947): 9, https://digitalcommons.biola.edu/kings-business-all/441/.

20 K. Owen White, "Pastor's Paragraphs," Metropolitan Baptist Church Bulletin, April 27, 1947, MS 1805, box 9a, folder 11, CHBC Archives.

Figure 9.6. Metropolitan's choir, pictured here in 1953, recorded several LPs and traveled far and wide to perform at churches and conferences. The map of the globe behind the choir reminded the church of its responsibility to evangelize the world.

Following preaching, the most important step White took in reforming the church was revising the membership process. Under Ball, candidates for baptism appeared before the pastor and deacons before being recommended to the church.[21] White, however, took the additional step of creating a new members class. The class's four lessons covered "sin, salvation, and security," "the ordinances," "our denomination," and "our church."[22]

---

21 Deacons' Meeting Minutes, May 6, 1915, MS 20, p. 26, box 1, folder 4, CHBC Archives. This practice continued at least until 1937, when Congressman Asa Leonard Allen wrote, "No person is received in the church by experience as we do [in Louisiana]. Everyone desiring to join the church by experience indicates it in open church and is thereafter examined in detail by the pastor and board of deacons so that it may be ascertained for a certainty that he or she fully understands what the step means. After examination, and if the applicant is found to be satisfactory, at another service the person again comes down and joins and then the pastor gives to each person a fine New Testament and gives the party a short lecture." "Washington Religious Activities Impress Congressman Allen," *Baptist Message*, March 25, 1937.

22 C. Michael Warr, Syllabus for the New Members Class, n.d., p. 17, box 15, folder 7, CHBC Archives.

Starting on January 6, 1946, anyone who desired to join the church was required to attend the class on four consecutive Sunday evenings before the evening service.[23] As White wrote in the introduction to the class handbook, "We have long felt that the members of our churches ought to have a better understanding of some of the most vital facts concerning their relationship to their Lord and to their church."[24] Only after completing the class could prospective members meet with White and the deacons on a Wednesday evening to apply for membership.[25]

After clarifying the process of joining the church, White began the laborious process of cleaning up its membership rolls. This had been a long source of concern for White, who had no patience for a church that boasted a membership of three thousand, the majority of whom rarely attended. "We claim a membership of 2,950 or more," he lamented on February 4, 1945, but "probably not much more than 500 MEMBERS attend the average worship service."[26] "The strength of a church is not measured by the number of names on the roll," he preached on January 11, 1948, "but by the actual participation of its members in the work."[27] On February 15, he complained that "nearly a third of the average congregation is composed of visitors. Where are the members?"[28] "We have a fine congregation here this morning," he said on April 4, looking over the sea of faces packed into the auditorium of Metropolitan. "But it does not represent one-third of our own membership. Where are our

23 K. Owen White, "Pastor's Paragraphs," Metropolitan Baptist Church Bulletin, December 30, 1945, MS 1803, box 9a, folder 9, CHBC Archives.
24 Syllabus for the New Members Class.
25 "Church Notes," Metropolitan Baptist Church Bulletin, October 1, 1944, MS 1802, box 9a, folder 8, CHBC Archives.
26 K. Owen White, "Pastor's Paragraphs," Metropolitan Baptist Church Bulletin, February 4, 1945, MS 1803, box 9a, folder 9, CHBC Archives (emphasis in original).
27 K. Owen White, "Pastor's Paragraphs," Metropolitan Baptist Church Bulletin, January 11, 1948, MS 1806, box 9a, folder 12, CHBC Archives.
28 K. Owen White, "Pastor's Paragraphs," Metropolitan Baptist Church Bulletin, February 15, 1948, MS 1806, box 9a, folder 12, CHBC Archives.

members, where are all those Christian people today, the members of our church and others?"[29]

On August 18, 1946, Metropolitan printed the names of over five hundred members whose addresses were unknown. "There is inserted in today's bulletin a list of members for whom we do not have addresses. If you know the addresses for any of these members, please turn them in at the office."[30] After giving the church time to respond, on October 23, White led Metropolitan to drop 480 names from its membership.[31]

As Metropolitan grew in health and in membership, White preached unabashedly about the church's mission in America and about America's mission in the world. As the closest Baptist church to the US Capitol building and the Supreme Court, Metropolitan Baptist Church was especially positioned to prepare America for national revival. "Metropolitan has been placed here to fulfill a sacred mission," White wrote in 1949. "We must not fail."[32] After all, "No group of Baptists anywhere in the world are situated just as we are. We are in the political nerve center of the world. We are in the capital site of a great democratic nation. We are at the crossroads!"[33] The special mission that God had entrusted to White as pastor of Metropolitan was to preach the word and to prepare the way. "I feel that in a special way He has laid His hand upon Metropolitan to bear witness to the truth in Washington," he wrote in 1947. "If we fail we shall be

---

29 A Series of Messages on the Home and the Church by K. O. White, April 4, 1948, 4, MS 1132, box 5, folder 9, CHBC Archives.

30 K. Owen White, "Pastor's Paragraphs," Metropolitan Baptist Church Bulletin, August 18, 1946, MS 1804, box 9a, folder 10, CHBC Archives.

31 "Motion carried that 480 names of members on printed list who could not be found be dropped from the Church membership rolls and such names to be kept on file for future reference." Minutes of the Metropolitan Baptist Church, October 23, 1946, MS 1610, pp. 18–19, box 6, folder 10, CHBC Archives.

32 K. Owen White, "Pastor's Paragraphs," Metropolitan Baptist Church Bulletin, October 9, 1949, MS 1807, box 9a, folder 13, CHBC Archives.

33 K. Owen White, "Pastor's Paragraphs," Metropolitan Baptist Church Bulletin, November 19, 1944, MS 1802, box 9a, folder 8, CHBC Archives.

as guilty as Peter who denied, or as Judas who betrayed the Lord of Glory."[34] White was determined that he would not fail.

Figure 9.7. K. Owen White officiates a baptismal celebration at Metropolitan Baptist Church—one of 848 baptisms during his five years as pastor.

For White and his fellow members at Metropolitan, America was in crisis. "The Devil is having a field day," he lamented in January 1948. "Sin is on the rampage. The spiritual tides are at an appallingly low level. Morals have gone into a 'tailspin.'"[35] White's declensionist outlook was entirely consistent with the eschatology he frequently preached from the pulpit.[36] The world was awash in wickedness, and believers were to expect Christ's return at any moment. "We do not

34 K. Owen White, "Pastor's Paragraphs," Metropolitan Baptist Church Bulletin, Church Bulletin, July 27, 1947, MS 1805, box 9a, folder 11, CHBC Archives.

35 K. Owen White, "Pastor's Paragraphs," Metropolitan Baptist Church Bulletin, Church Bulletin, January 3, 1948, MS 1806, box 9a, folder 12, CHBC Archives.

36 Note the titles of the following sermons from summer 1945 by White: "What About Premillennialism?" (June 24, 1945), "What About the 'Times of the Gentiles'?" (July 1, 1945), "Where Is the Promise of His Coming" (July 15, 1945), Metropolitan Baptist Church Bulletins, MS 1803, box 9a, folder 9, CHBC Archives.

know how many of us shall live to see the end of 1945," he warned in his last sermon for 1944. "[W]e only know that for each of us some day will be the last day. Let's live as though each day were the last we should ever have to serve God."[37]

For White, a national revival represented America's only hope. "Only a mighty, redemptive Gospel with power to regenerate and renew can cope with a world situation like that," he wrote in 1947.[38] America's problems were many and severe, but hope was not yet lost. "The answer to our problems—national, denominational, domestic and personal is still 2 Chron. 7:14. . . . Repentance, confession of sin, full surrender to the Lordship of Christ will even yet bring glorious revival to our hearts and to our church."[39] Such was the mission of White, Metropolitan, and American evangelicalism in the wake of World War II.

Figure 9.8. A highlight of K. Owen White's ministry in Washington was leading a delegation of thirty-five Baptist missionaries to meet with President Harry S. Truman at the White House. White and Truman are in the front row, third and fourth from the right respectively.

37 K. Owen White, "Pastor's Paragraphs," Metropolitan Baptist Church Bulletin, Church Bulletin, December 31, 1944, MS 1802, box 9a, folder 8, CHBC Archives.
38 White, "The Heavenly Vision," 11.
39 K. Owen White, "Pastor's Paragraphs," Metropolitan Baptist Church Bulletin, Church Bulletin, June 26, 1949, MS 1807, box 9a, folder 13, CHBC Archive.

White's efforts were not without fruit. Even with the church's stricter membership practices, Metropolitan added 309 members during the first year of White's pastorate; 124 joined by baptism.[40] At the start of his third year as pastor of Metropolitan, he could proudly note that among the thirty-five churches partnering with the District of Columbia Baptist Association, Metropolitan ranked first in baptisms, first in total additions, first in Training Union enrollment and average attendance.[41] In just three years, Metropolitan added 1,155 new members; 476 of these by baptism.[42] "As far as we can discover from the records available this is the first time that any Baptist Church in D.C. has reported over 100 baptisms for three successive years." However, this provided no grounds for boasting, "since we should have done far more."[43]

By 1948, well over a thousand packed into the building every Sunday where there was standing room only at services. So beginning at Easter 1948, White led Metropolitan to adopt a two-service model for its Sunday morning services. He wrote to the congregation in April 1948, asking for advice on this question of multiple services: "[A] number of our members have spoken of the possibility of having two identical services every Sunday. . . . What is your reaction to such a plan? Let us know. Many other churches are now doing this with considerable success and satisfaction."[44]

After packed Easter services two years in a row, Metropolitan felt ready to proceed with a permanent two-service model not just on Easter but every Sunday.[45] As White explained, over eight hundred

40 K. Owen White, "Pastor's Paragraphs," Metropolitan Baptist Church Bulletin, September 16, 1945, MS 1803, box 9a, folder 9, CHBC Archives.
41 K. Owen White, "Pastor's Paragraphs," Metropolitan Baptist Church Bulletin, December 1, 1946, MS 1804, box 9a, folder 10, CHBC Archives.
42 K. Owen White, "Pastor's Paragraphs," Metropolitan Baptist Church Bulletin, November 2, 1947, MS 1805, box 9a, folder 11, CHBC Archives.
43 White, "Pastor's Paragraphs," November 2, 1947, CHBC Archives.
44 K. Owen White, "Pastor's Paragraphs," Metropolitan Baptist Church Bulletin, April 18, 1948, MS 1806, box 9a, folder 12, CHBC Archives.
45 "Today we are initiating two morning services and we shall continue on this schedule at least until the middle of July. We believe that there are many who would prefer to attend an early service; that there are some who cannot come at 11:00 who could be present at 8:15; that some of our

attended the 8:15 am Easter service, and at 11:00 a.m. "every inch of space was occupied."

> Our congregations have been increasing and have taxed the capacity of our buildings. We have been told that some do not come because they cannot find a comfortable seat where they can both see and hear. We are sure that many more would attend if they could be satisfactorily seated.[46]

Thus, beginning in 1949, Metropolitan would hold its first service every Sunday at 8:15 a.m., Sunday school at 9:30 a.m., and a second service at 11:00 a.m. This would give attendees the opportunity to attend joint Sunday school classes between the two services.

When White announced his resignation at the end of 1949, he had seen nearly two thousand new members join—nearly half by baptism.[47] Without any despondency or discouragement in his work ("the years we spent in Washington were the high point in all our ministry"[48]), White departed in obedience to the call of God because he understood his mission in the capital complete.[49] As a forerunner, he had done his part in preparing the way. The rest of the mission would be left to a lanky North Carolina boy sixteen years his junior named Billy Graham.

J. Walter Carpenter and the Billy Graham Crusade of 1952

Since his rise to fame during the Los Angeles Crusade of 1949, Billy Graham had his eyes set on the grand prize: an extended campaign in the national capital. For over a year, Graham made frequent stops in

---

own members who have been deprived of hearing the morning message because of their duties here will be glad to come." K. Owen White, "Pastor's Paragraphs," Metropolitan Baptist Church Bulletin, May 8, 1949, MS 1807, box 9a, folder 13, CHBC Archive.

46 K. Owen White, "Pastor's Paragraphs," Metropolitan Baptist Church Bulletin, May 1, 1949, MS 1807, box 9a, folder 13, CHBC Archive.

47 "Appreciation For Our Pastor," Metropolitan Baptist Church Bulletin, September 4, 1949, MS 1807, box 9a, folder 13, CHBC Archive.

48 K. Owen White to Charles Trainum, February 2, 1978, MS 1439, box 5, folder 31, CHBC Archives.

49 White, interview, 81–82.

Washington, DC, finding Metropolitan Baptist Church and its new pastor, J. Walter Carpenter, an eager partner for his crusade. Carpenter, who came to Metropolitan after teaching New Testament at Columbia Bible College in South Carolina, readily opened his church to Billy Graham after assuming the pastorate on June 1, 1950.[50]

On a visit in January 1951, Graham preached at an evening evangelistic rally that filled Metropolitan to more than double its seating capacity of 1,300.[51] Graham named Carpenter chairman of the Greater Washington Crusade of 1952 and wrote to him in March 1951 that the crusade was set to commence on January 13, 1952. "Let us begin now," Carpenter urged his congregation, "to pray for revival in Metropolitan and greater Washington. Pray for Revival."[52]

The crusade, however, was not without its obstacles, and Graham was not without detractors. More than one reporter warned that Graham was preparing for a "Waterloo in Washington," a reference to Napoleon's famous defeat in 1815. Skepticism only increased after Graham made the surprising announcement that the crusade would be desegregated. "This meeting," Carpenter wrote approvingly, "will not be conducted on a segregated basis. People will attend the meeting not as colored and white, but only as saved or lost."[53] As Graham explained to a group of pastors gathered at the Mayflower Hotel, "In Christianity there is no color line nor national or international barriers."[54]

Graham's campaign made this decision to operate on a nonsegregated basis while debate over segregation was at a fever pitch in the nation's capital. Arguments over the constitutionality of segregated

50 "New Baptist Pastor to Be Welcomed," *Washington Post*, June 3, 1950, 10.
51 "Evangelist to Address Clerics and Laymen," *Evening Star*, January 3, 1951, 20; "Billy Graham's Meeting Site Shifted," *Washington Post*, January 3, 1951, 10; "Billy Graham Opens Year with Two Week January Tour," *The Northwestern Pilot: The Bible Study Magazine*, February 1951, 17.
52 "Billy Graham Accepts Washington Dates for Revival Meetings," *Metropolitan Messenger*, March 4, 1951, MS 1739, p. 4, box 8a, folder 2, CHBC Archives.
53 "Billy Graham in Washington May 1," *Metropolitan Messenger*, April 29, 1951, MS 1739, p. 1, box 8a, folder 2, CHBC Archives.
54 "Billy Graham's Revival Starts Sunday," *Evening Star*, January 11, 1952, 19.

public schools were being debated in the Supreme Court in *Briggs v. Elliott*, the first of five cases that would be decided by *Brown v. Board of Education* in 1954. Moreover, the District of Columbia was still a deeply segregated city. Just about the only thing African Americans could do in the capital that they could not do in Birmingham or Atlanta was ride in the front of the capital transit buses—that is, until they crossed the river into Virginia, at which point they were relegated to the back of the bus.[55] Despite these obstacles, Carpenter remained optimistic, telling the *Washington Post*, "If anybody has met his Waterloo here it was the devil. God's testimony, work and word are stronger in Washington now than ever before."[56]

Figure 9.9. Newspaper clipping from the *Evening Star* pictures Billy Graham (center) speaking with J. Walter Carpenter (left), pastor of Metropolitan Baptist Church, alongside Graham's music director, Cliff Barrows (right), after breakfast at the Mayflower Hotel on January 11, 1952.

As Washington churches prepared for the crusade, Metropolitan became the base of operations. Members of Metropolitan offered their homes to host "Cottage Prayer Meetings" and were trained to serve as

55 David Brinkley, *Washington Goes to War* (New York: Alfred A. Knopf, 1988), 18.
56 Kenneth Dole, "14,000 Hear Billy Graham's Closing Sermon of Revival," *Washington Post*, February 18, 1952, B1.

personal workers during the crusade.[57] "Pray," Carpenter entreated his congregation, "that this crusade will be the greatest spiritual awakening America has ever known."[58] Graham shared Carpenter's optimism, writing to Metropolitan's pastor on the eve of the crusade and thanking him for his efforts. "I sincerely believe that God is going to do things of which we never dreamed," Graham wrote. "Never have I had such faith and conviction for any campaign that we have ever conducted."[59]

The crusade in Washington far exceeded expectations. Between January 13 and February 2, nightly meetings were held at the National Guard armory, where Graham and his supporters succeeded in lobbying the District's government to expand the occupancy from 5,310 to 8,000 to make room for the crowds. When more than 8,000 began to arrive nightly, Graham decided that in spite of the gloomy February weather, it was time to take the meetings outside. The crusade would continue at the very foot of the US Capitol building.

On Sunday, February 3, 1952, at the invitation of House Speaker Sam Rayburn, Billy Graham commenced a series of historic open-air services from the US Capitol steps.[60] Between thirty thousand and forty thousand gathered in the rain to hear Graham's Sunday address, broadcast over the ABC network to the nation.[61] With one-third of the members of the US Senate and one-fourth of the members of the House of Representatives present, it was an evangelical State of the Union of sorts.

Taking "America's path to world peace" as his theme, Graham spoke with presidential poise. He called for maintaining strong military power

---

57   "Homes Needed," *Metropolitan Messenger*, November 11, 1951, MS 1739, p. 3, box 8a, folder 2, CHBC Archives.

58   "Billy Graham News," *Metropolitan Messenger*, December 30, 1951, MS 1739, p. 4, box 8a, folder 2, CHBC Archives.

59   "Crusade Begins Sunday 3 P.M.," *Metropolitan Messenger*, January 13, 1952, MS 1740, p. 1, box 8a, folder 3, CHBC Archives.

60   "Hear Billy Graham U.S. Capitol East Steps," *Metropolitan Messenger*, February 3, 1952, MS 1740, p. 1, box 8a, folder 3, CHBC Archives.

61   "Graham Quotes Bible to Warn against Mink Coast 'Influence,'" *Evening Star*, February 2, 1952, 5.

"at any cost," stiffer legislation to combat crime, policies to promote economic stability, national solidarity across differences ("race with race, creed with creed, color with color"), and "lastly and not least," moral and spiritual regeneration. From beneath Thomas Ustick Walter's dome, Graham urged Congress to follow Lincoln's example and institute a National Day of Prayer. Highlighting the ongoing war in Korea against communism, Graham predicted "that we would immediately see things take a turn for the better in world affairs if such a day of prayer were proclaimed." He warned, "If we refuse, I predict nothing but defeat and judgment."[62]

Congress wasted no time in heeding Graham's words. The very next day, Representative Percy Priest introduced legislation calling for a National Day of Prayer.[63] On April 17, 1952, Congress passed the bill into law, establishing a practice that continues to this day.[64]

Figure 9.10. Thousands crowded the US Capitol steps for Billy Graham's historic meeting, including over a hundred members of Congress.

62 "Graham Takes Evangelistic Crusade to the Capitol," *Evening Star*, February 4, 1952, 4.
63 National Day of Prayer, H.J. Res. 382, 82nd Cong. (1952).
64 National Day of Prayer, Pub. L. No. 82-324, 66 Stat. 64 (1952).

For Metropolitan no less than the nation, the crusade was a roaring success. An estimated 308,000 had attended Graham's thirty-one rallies in the capital, and 6,115 had made professions of faith.[65] Beginning in January 1952, Dawson E. Trotman, the head of Graham's follow-up team, began training churches in following up with seekers. Over the course of the crusade, Metropolitan saw seventy-five new members join by baptism.[66] One of those was a seventeen-year-old senior at McKinley Technology High School named Doris Faber.

Doris had grown up attending a Methodist church but stopped after her father died in 1945. "I remember when the war was over in August, everybody was outside cheering and jumping up and down. I was glad it was over too, but I sure missed my father," she explained. When Billy Graham came to Washington in 1952, a friend invited Doris to the meetings. "There wasn't an empty seat in the place," she recalled. "It was so real to me. Billy Graham made it so plain that you could know Jesus, and how he loves you. It changed my life." Doris attended multiple nights and was directed to Metropolitan Baptist Church where she was baptized into membership a few months later. Not long after, Doris met another woman her same age who had likewise found her way to Metropolitan despite growing up Methodist.[67]

Jane Maxine Walker was nineteen, reserved, and new to Washington, DC, where she had come—like thousands of others in the postwar years—to work as a telephone operator for the FBI. The nation's capital was a far cry from the rural town of Littleton, North Carolina, where she had grown up in a house without electricity. On her own in a strange city without many friends, she had by chance turned the

65 "15,000 Crowd Armory to Hear Billy Graham Preach Final Sermon," *Evening Star*, February 18, 1952, 2.
66 Numbers calculated from Membership Book (1949–1953), MS 1630, box 7, folder 4, CHBC Archives.
67 Doris Faber, interview with the author, August 16, 2022, Washington, DC.

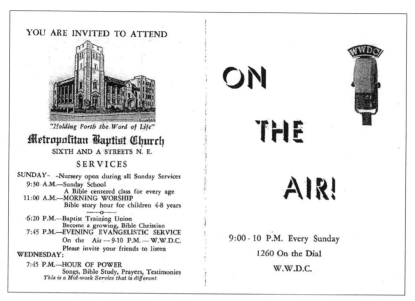

Figure 9.11. Advertisement for Metropolitan Baptist Church's radio ministry in 1952 encouraged newcomers to Washington to tune in to the church's evening evangelistic service broadcast on Sundays at 9:10 p.m. The radio broadcast always began with the choir singing "All Hail the Power of Jesus' Name."

dial of her radio to WWDC 1260 around 9:00 p.m. to hear a choir singing "All Hail the Power of Jesus' Name." Alone in her room in the boarding house, she listened for an hour to the beautiful singing and biblical preaching, noting at the end of the broadcast the name and address of the sponsoring church: Metropolitan Baptist Church at Sixth and A Streets NE.

Walker had never been to a Baptist church before, having grown up Methodist, but was determined to visit. As she disembarked the streetcar at East Capitol and Sixth Street NE, she joined the throngs making their way to church. She later recounted that what she encountered was "a little bit of heaven." Her faith grew under the preaching of J. Walter Carpenter, whom she came to regard as "a father figure," and through a women's Sunday school class taught by Pearl Carneal.

On May 14, 1954, Jane Maxine Walker—later Maxine Zopf—was baptized into membership at Metropolitan Baptist Church.[68]

———

There is no doubt that the fires of the Billy Graham Crusade of 1952 burned long and deep in the hearts of the members of Metropolitan Baptist Church. As Billy Graham wrote to Carpenter a year later in 1953, "Words cannot express the deep gratitude that there is in my heart for all of your many kindnesses to me and to our Team during the Washington campaign." He continued, "Eternity alone can reveal the important part you played in the campaign and the great contribution you made to the winning of souls in our nation's Capital."[69]

How much of this work would have been possible apart from Agnes Shankle? Throughout history, God has worked remarkably through women like Shankle who, although they did not have seminary degrees, knew their Bibles and could tell the difference between faith-undermining liberalism and Bible-affirming orthodoxy. Churches should affirm the goodness of the Bible's teaching on the roles of men and women in the church. But they should never stop praying that, if church leaders ever bring a pastoral candidate who compromises on any of the fundamentals of the faith, they have an Agnes Shankle in their midst who is willing to stand up and say, "Not in my house!" That's what it means to be a congregationally governed church: men and women, brothers and sisters, are equally charged with stewarding the keys of the kingdom and protecting the church's life and doctrine through their congregational vote.

---

68 Maxine Zopf, interview with Mark Dever, February 5, 2002, Washington, DC. For date of baptism, see Membership Book (1953–1965), MS 1625, box 7, folder 1, CHBC Archives. Cf. Maxine Zopf, CHBC Radio History, July 12, 1998, box 12, folder 8, CHBC Archives.

69 Billy Graham to J. Walter Carpenter, May 12, 1953, CN4 Montreat Office, box 233, folder 19. Courtesy Billy Graham Archive & Research Center. © Billy Graham Literary Foundation. All Rights Reserved.

Figure 9.12. Agnes Shankle's Ask-Seek-Knock Sunday school class, photographed on the occasion of her twenty-fifth year as a teacher in 1944. Shankle is seated second from the right. Also seated are K. Owen White (first from the left) and John Compton Ball (third from the right).

By the end of Carpenter's pastorate, the membership of Metropolitan Baptist Church reached its numerical peak at 3,684 members.[70] The church had cemented itself as the leading conservative evangelical church in Washington, DC, and was living up to its motto of "holding forth the Word of Life." For evangelicals, the Greater Washington Crusade of 1952 was a rare moment of triumph. A new era had begun. The question was this: Would they make the most of it, or would it be squandered?

---

70 A. Blanchete, "History: Capitol Hill Metropolitan Baptist Church," February 1, 1993, MS 1287, box 5, folder 20, CHBC Archives.

10

"A Beachhead for Evangelical Christianity"

1956–1960

"ABOUT TWO O'CLOCK one night in 1953," Billy Graham later wrote, "an idea raced through my mind, freshly connecting all the things I had seen and pondered about reaching a broader audience. Trying not to disturb Ruth, I slipped out of bed and into my study upstairs to write. A couple of hours later, the concept of a new magazine was complete." The idea of *Christianity Today* was born.[1]

Ever since the publication of Carl F. H. Henry's *The Uneasy Conscience of Modern Fundamentalism* in 1947, evangelicals had been scrambling to present a cohesive vision of social and moral reform for American culture.[2] While evangelical Christianity had all of the answers, the problem was that mainline Protestantism had all the attention. Whenever *Time* or *Newsweek* needed a comment on Christianity and world affairs, they turned to the

1 Billy Graham, *Just as I Am: The Autobiography of Billy Graham* (New York: Harper Collins, 1997), 286. Cf. Carl F. H. Henry, *Confessions of a Theologian: An Autobiography* (Dallas, TX: Word Books, 1986), 145.
2 Carl F. H. Henry, *The Uneasy Conscience of Modern Fundamentalism* (Grand Rapids, MI: Eerdmans, 1947).

National Council of Churches rather than conservative evangelicals. With the growing war with communism in the East and racial unrest at home, evangelicals knew that they had the message America needed; they simply lacked the mechanism to deliver it. But with the organization of the National Association of Evangelicals (NAE) in 1949 and the election of Dwight D. Eisenhower to the White House in 1952—thanks in no small part to their growth as a core component of the Republican Party's constituency—evangelicals were ready to convey their message to the American people. As Henry wrote in the introductory brochure to *Christianity Today*, the magazine would serve as a vehicle "to apply the Biblical revelation vigorously to the contemporary social crisis, by presenting the implications of the total Gospel message in every area of life."[3]

With the financial backing of oil magnate J. Howard Pew, the editorial skills of Carl F. H. Henry, and a first issue date set for October 1, 1956, *Christianity Today* opened its Washington office on the tenth floor of the famous Washington Building at Fifteenth Street and New York Avenue NW in November 1955. Henry's office, overlooking the White House below, reminded him of the importance of his work and the mission that had brought him from sunny California to dreary Washington.[4]

Carl F. H. Henry and the Hilltoppers Sunday School Class

When he arrived in Washington, ready to bring the Christian worldview to the top echelons of political power, Henry looked for a church that stood unabashedly on the fundamentals of the Christian faith. Billy Graham encouraged Henry to join Calvary Baptist Church because that was where he would "make connections."[5] Henry, however, quickly settled at Metropolitan Baptist Church, where the doctrinally rich preaching better suited his theological convictions than the ecumenism of Clarence Cranford at Calvary. He joined Metropolitan by letter on September 2, 1956.

---

3   "Statement of Policy and Purpose," *Christianity Today*, October 13, 1958, 20–21.
4   Henry, *Confessions of a Theologian*, 149.
5   Mark Dever, interview with the author, December 18, 2023, Washington, DC.

Metropolitan had just called a new pastor, and Henry was impressed by his preaching. J. Walter Carpenter had announced his decision on November 13, 1955, to leave Metropolitan to become the associate pastor of Bellevue Baptist Church in Memphis, Tennessee, under Robert G. Lee.[6] In his final message as pastor on January 1, 1956, Carpenter encouraged the congregation, with the help of their new pastor, to "make Metropolitan an even greater Lighthouse on Capitol Hill."[7]

Metropolitan's new pastor, Walter A. Pegg, arrived in Washington just months before Henry, having previously pastored First Baptist Church of Huntington Park, California—the largest Southern Baptist Church on the West Coast.[8] As Metropolitan's new pastor, he immediately began a series of expositions through the book of Galatians. "Bring a Bible and do not hesitate to mark it as the series progresses," Pegg urged the congregation, printing a sermon card in the bulletin to allow members to study the passage in advance.[9]

A graduate of W. B. Riley's Northwestern Bible Institute in Minneapolis and recommended to the congregation by former pastor K. Owen White, Pegg believed in the power of the word of God and was determined to build his ministry on the assumption that God's word alone would build the church.[10] "We are certainly agreed that a major responsibility of a church is to engage in teaching the Bible, not only as history, as doctrine, but as a guide for everyday living," Pegg wrote. "Do we need anything more desperately than this?"[11] Henry was impressed.

---

6   Minutes of the Metropolitan Baptist Church, November 13, 1955, MS 1610, box 6, folder 10, CHBC Archives, Washington, DC (hereafter, CHBC Archives).

7   J. Walter Carpenter, "Across the Pastor's Desk," *Metropolitan Messenger*, November 20, 1955, MS 1743, p. 2, box 8a, folder 6, CHBC Archives.

8   "Dr. W. A. Pegg Gets Call to Pulpit Here," *Washington Post*, June 8, 1956, 47.

9   Walter A. Pegg, "Sermon Subjects Announced," *Metropolitan Messenger*, October 9, 1956, MS 1744, p. 1, box 8a, folder 7, CHBC Archives.

10 Deacons' Meeting Minutes, January 10, 1956, MS 33, box 1, folder 10b, CHBC Archives.

11 Walter A. Pegg, "From the Pastor's Pen," *Metropolitan Messenger*, January 13, 1958, MS 1746, p. 2, box 8a, folder 9, CHBC Archives.

Figure 10.1. Walter Pegg announced his expositional sermon series in advance in the church bulletin. Pictured is his series through Galatians during the fall of 1956.

Henry immediately wrote to Metropolitan's new pastor, encouraging his fellow California transplant that "something significant for evangelical Christianity may be in the making in the Washington area." With a nod to the Billy Graham crusade a few years earlier, the preaching of Richard Halverson at Fourth Presbyterian in Bethesda, and the work of fellow Metropolitan member Clyde W. Taylor with the NAE, Henry thought that something of a "beachhead for evangelical Christianity" had been established in Washington during the past years. Now with the establishment of *Christianity Today* and Pegg assuming the pastorate of Metropolitan, Henry could not but feel that "something significant is in the making."[12] The time was right for exerting influence on the nation's capital, and through the capital, the nation, and through the nation, the world.

12   Carl F. H. Henry to Walter A. Pegg, September 3, 1956, MS 1150, box 5, folder 11, CHBC Archives.

Soon after arriving in Washington, Henry wrote to Pegg about an idea for assembling a group of influential evangelicals in Congress.[13] "We have tried to get a list of the religious preferences of the 85th Congress," Henry explained, "but have been told that the National Council [of Churches] has the only list which has been compiled, and it has refused to release it as yet." Henry speculated that the National Council might only release the list to "preferential circles," before getting to his point: "The point of my letter is that some organization ought to be set up, it seems to me, by a church the stature of Metropolitan."[14]

By 1962, Henry had his responsibilities at *Christianity Today* sufficiently under control to make his dream a reality. He launched an invitation only Sunday school class called Hilltoppers on January 28, 1962.[15] Regular participants included Senators A. T. Robertson and Strom Thurmond, military generals Charles R. Landon and Paul C. Watson, lobbyists like National Right to Work president Reed Larson, and public intellectuals like NAE secretary for public affairs Clyde W. Taylor. As Doug Coe of the Christian Coalition wrote to Henry, "I think what you are doing is most outstanding. Our prayers are certainly with you."[16] If Henry wanted to reshape evangelical political engagement in Washington, he had picked the right people.

Each class followed the same hour-long format. The moderator—usually Henry—assigned passages of Scripture to be read, followed by fifteen minutes of discussion of the text and its implications by a previously selected panel. The dialogue then opened to the larger group, after which the moderator provided concluding comments on the most significant points.[17]

---

13 For further discussion of Henry's Sunday school class, see Caleb Morell, "Carl F. H. Henry's Anti-Communist Worldview: Insights From Unpublished Notes, 1962–1964," *Journal of the Evangelical Theological Society* 66, no. 2 (June, 2023): 301–13.

14 Carl F. H. Henry to Walter A. Pegg, January 7, 1957, MS 1870, box 11, folder 2, CHBC Archives.

15 Carl F. H. Henry, Reasons for Founding Hilltoppers, October 1956, MS 1830, box 11, folder 1, CHBC Archives.

16 Douglas Coe to Carl F. H. Henry, February 15, 1962, MS 1851, box 11, folder 1, CHBC Archives.

17 Carl F. H. Henry to William H. Stevens, January 30, 1962, MS 1847, box 11, folder 1, CHBC Archives.

For Henry, who missed his teaching opportunities at Fuller Theological Seminary in Pasadena, California, the group seems to have served as a substitute classroom and as a sounding board for ideas that eventually found their way into *Christianity Today* editorials.[18] For instance, in his December 21, 1962, editorial for *Christianity Today*, "On the Brink of a New Order," Henry explicitly referenced the Hilltoppers class and directly quoted some of the class comments.[19] As Henry wrote to his class in a letter on December 13, 1962, "You will enjoy the main editorial in the December 21 Issue of *Christianity Today*, in the shaping of which you had a hand."[20]

Figure 10.2. Carl F. H. Henry (1913–2003), pictured in his early days as editor of *Christianity Today* magazine.

18 Several editorials by Henry critical of communism appeared in 1962, including "Christianity and Communism," *Christianity Today*, March 16, 1962, 26–27; "Has America Awakened At Last?," *Christianity Today*, November 9, 1962, 28–29.

19 Carl F. H. Henry, "On the Brink of a New Order," *Christianity Today*, December 21, 1962, 24. Cf. "On the Brink of a New Order," MS 1881, box 11, folder 3, CHBC Archives.

20 Carl F. H. Henry to Hilltoppers, December 12, 1962, MS 1837, box 11, folder 1, CHBC Archives.

Walter A. Pegg and the Challenges of Suburbanization

Despite the presence of prominent figures, Walter Pegg was fighting an uphill battle to retain church members. During the 1950s, the population of Washington, DC, was shifting dramatically to the suburbs as neighboring counties in Virginia and Maryland grew by as much as 116 percent.[21] The church experienced the same shifts. In 1941, 83 percent of church families resided in the District of Columbia. By 1951 that number had dropped to 74 percent and would continue to drop until levelling out at 39 percent in 1970. As members moved farther from the church, many retained their membership but attended less frequently or stopped coming altogether.

During the first year of his pastorate, Pegg enlisted the deacons to visit and contact non-attending members. At the end of this ten-month process, the deacons and deaconesses reported a combined total of 1,422 visits, 611 phone calls, and 339 cards and letters.[22] Although they saw some fruit from these efforts, the results were mostly discouraging. Pegg pointedly articulated his thoughts and concerns in a 1958 article in the *Metropolitan Messenger* entitled "What Constitutes Church Membership?" Insisting that "every Christian should be a member of a church," he urged members that this must mean more than having one's "name upon some church roll." Over the course of their investigation, Pegg reported the sorry results of their efforts. "In scores of cases no interest in Metropolitan Church has been found at all." In other cases, "thinly veiled hostility has been frequently evidenced." Pegg quoted excerpts from the deacons' report in his letter to the congregation. "She has not attended here for 12 years, but she did not want us to drop her name," read one report. "Have called on her and her husband numbers of times, but they attend another church regularly. They give no promise

---

21 Crosby S. Noyes, "D.C. Population of 279,234 is Half Area Total," *Evening Star*, July 2, 1950, 1–2.

22 "Deacons Elect," *Metropolitan Messenger*, October 1, 1957, MS 1745, p. 2, box 8a, folder 8, CHBC Archives.

to return here at any time, but do not wish to be taken off the roll" read another. Other cases seemed to evince a growing indifference about the obligations of church membership. "Has not been to Metropolitan since he was 20 years old, is now 54."[23]

In light of these responses, Pegg pressed the church to consider, "What does church membership mean? What should it involve? A place where the name is inscribed? A place associated with pleasant memories?" Instead of these options, Pegg turned his congregants' attention to Hebrews 10:25. "The Epistle to the Hebrews urges," he wrote, "'Not forsaking the assembling of yourselves together, as the manner of some is; but exhorting one another: and so much the more as ye see the day approaching.'" Pegg called church members to consider the oath they had taken upon joining the church. "The Church Covenant," he explained, "declares [that responsibility for the church] rests squarely upon each individual member. Surely it is God who is offended and deeply hurt by the indifferent or rebellious attitude of those who once walked with Him."[24]

Toward the end of December 1956, Metropolitan published hundreds of names of members for whom it had no record of addresses or attendance, asking members to help ascertain their whereabouts. The result of this effort was that on May 15, 1957, Metropolitan dropped 995 names—one third of its membership—from the church roll, going overnight from 3,641 to 2,646 members.[25] Pegg took the same action again in 1959, bringing a list to the deacons of non-attenders to recommend to the church that "the list of names be removed from the church roll."[26]

Where had all these non-attending members come from? An astonishing 1,940 members had been brought in under J. Walter Carpenter's

23 Walter A. Pegg, "From the Pastor's Pen: What Constitutes Church Membership?," *Metropolitan Messenger*, March 3, 1958, MS 1746, p. 2, box 8a, folder 9, CHBC Archives.

24 Pegg, "What Constitutes Church Membership?," CHBC Archives.

25 Clerk's Report, May 15, 1957, MS 1633, box 7, folder 6, CHBC Archives.

26 Deacons 'Meeting Minutes, November 24, 1959, MS 33, box 1, folder 10b, CHBC Archives.

PAGE FOUR   METROPOLITAN MESSENGER   DECEMBER 31, 1956

REVISION OF CHURCH ROLL

A committee has been appointed by the board of deacons to revise the church membership roll inasmuch as it has been discovered that we have so many names without addresses. The last issue of the Messenger carried a portion of this list and the remainder is found herewith. Please furnish any information you may have concerning any of these persons and inform the church office as soon as possible.

Mrs. Mildred R. Robinson
Miss Nellie Ruth Robinson
Mrs. Clarney Rockhold
Mr. Thos. M. Roddy
Jerome Rode
Pamela Rode
Perry Rode
Pedro J. Rodriguez
Mrs. E. S. Rogers
Mr. & Mrs. Floyd V. Rose
Mr. & Mrs. Malcolm Ross
Miss Patricia Rothgeb
Miss Isabelle Routh
Mr. George Rowcamp
Robert Rowe
Mrs. Robert Rowe
Mrs. George Rowehamp
Miss Eleanor Rowles
Jimmie Anne Royal
Mrs. Ola F. Royal
Miss Shirley Ruark
Betty Rucker
Miss Eva Rucker
Mrs. Estyleene Lawson Rued
Miss Mattie Rushing
Mrs. Carthy Ryals
Mr. Earl L. Ryan
Jesse Ross Safley
Mr. Wm, N. St. Clair
Mr. Walter E. Simpson
Mrs. E. B. Sams
Kenneth Sanders
Mr. & Mrs. Louis Sanders
Mrs. Samuel G. Sanders
Miss Jimmy Sandy
Miss Ellen Sanford
Mr. Lloyd C. Sanford
Mr. & Mrs. T. L. Samsom
Mrs. Earl F. Scheuring
Mrs. Juanita K. Schull
Mrs. Dorothy Schwarz
Elgin W. Scott, Jr.
Miss Evelyn Scott
Mr. Otis D. Scott
Miss Patricia Lee Scott
Mr. & Mrs. Oren Scruggs
William Scruggs
Mrs. Patricia Scruggs
Mrs. William L. Selin
Mrs. Novia Sessions
Mr. Ralph S. Shackleford
Mr. & Mrs. Marshall Shannon
Mrs. R. E. Shaw
Raymond Edward Shaw
Miss Betty Shears
Mrs. Otis Sheets
David E. Shelton
Mrs. John Shenos
Mr. & Mrs. W. H. Shepherd
Mr. Samuel J. Sherman
Mrs. J. B. Shiflett
Mr. Wm. L. Shiflett
Mr. Kenneth G. Shipley
Mrs. Wilma F. Shorter
Mr. Warren Shuey
Mr. & Mrs. Ernest L. Silber
Mr. William Arley Silver
Mrs. Robert Simkins
Mrs. Horace P. Simmons
Mrs. Mildred G. Simmons
Miss Lillian Sims
Miss Mary E. Singleton
Miss Odetta Sizemore
Mr. & Mrs. Emory Sloan
Miss Betty Sue Smith

Miss Frances E. Smith
Miss Gloria Smith
Miss Harold Smith
Hardy Smith
Mr. & Mrs. Herman Smith
Miss Irene Smith
James G. Smith
Mrs. John Smith
Mary Smith
Mr. & Mrs. Walter Smith
Mr. William Thomas Smith
Mrs. H. D. Smothers
Mrs. Helen M. Smyth
Carl Snead
Mrs. Robert Snook
Miss Bettie V. Speiden
Mrs. William Speiden
Mr. & Mrs. Bruce Speight
Mr. Chas. Daniel Springston
Mr. G. G. Springston
Mrs. Shannon Sproufiske
Mr. Hollis Sprouse
Miss Dorothy M. Stancell
James Stancell
Harold L. Stancil
Miss Ruth Stanley
Mr. Lindell Steel
Mr. Kenneth Steen
Pfc. Rexford Steeves
Mrs. Nina Knight Steinberg
Mr. Gertrude J. Stephena
Mr. Harrison Stephens
Mrs. Jasie Stewart
Mrs. John Stickney
Mrs. Mildred M. Stocks
Mr. C. H. Stodghill
Mr. Charles H. Stone
Miss Virginia Stone
Alva Stout
Kenneth Stout
Robert Strain
Mr. & Mrs. R. F. Stressenger
Miss Elizabeth Stressenger
Miss Ruth Stressenger
Mrs. James Sturgis
Mr. Ernest D. Sturkie
Mr. & Mrs. Howard S. Styles
Miss Marion Sublette
Miss Annie Neal Suges
Miss Ida Mae Sumler
Holten Summers
Miss Earline Suttle
Mr. George Swackhammer
Miss Zelpha Swafford
Mrs. Alan Sweeney
Mr. & Mrs. Charles Sweet
Mr. Leon Sykes
Mrs. William T. Tadlock
Mr. Eugene Talbent
Mr. R. N. Tatum
Mrs. Ernest Taylor
Miss Leota Taylor
Mrs. Lucille M. Taylor
Mr. Milton Taylor
Mr. & Mrs. Harry Tedder
Miss Ramona Terrell
Mr. Robert S. Thirles
Mr. John Haywood Thomas
Miss Nell Thomas
Diana Thompson
Miss Marjorie Thompson
Miss Elizabeth Thompson
Miss Evelyn Thornton
Mr. William R. Tillery
Miss Betty Joe Tiner

Edna Tino
Miss Lottie Ellen Todd
Mr. Woodrow Tolson
Mrs. Carolyn Tompkins
Mrs. H. M. Topham
Mr. Cecil Tribble
Miss May Trimble
Mrs. Juliet D. Troy
Miss Jean Truxall
Mrs. Helen Tucker
Mrs. William D. Tucker
Mrs. Ralph Turner, Sr.
Miss June Marie Umphlet
Mrs. Claude K. VanValkenberg
VanValkenburg
Mr. Lloyd Vaughn
Mrs. Lloyd Vaughn
Mr. Lloyd E. Vaughn
Miss Roslyn Vereen
Mr. Raymond L. Vermillion
Mr. Donald W. Vineyard
Mrs. Minerva G. Vinson
Mrs. Lucile Voegler
Mr. Walter Wade
Mrs. Wm. F. Wagner
Mr. Ernest Waldorf
Miss Jean Walker
Mrs. Lillian Tutt Walker
Miss Rose Walker
Mrs. Beulah Wallace
Miss Marion Walters
Mrs. C. E. Wantland
Mrs. Sarah Ward
Mr. T. E. Ward
Mrs. Thomas M. Warrell
Mr. William R. Waters
Mr. Jack Weatherman
Mr. Newton Weathersby
Mrs. Hazel Weaver
Mrs. William James Weaver
Mr. Phillip J. Webb
Miss Elisabeth Mary Weber
Miss Margaret M. Weedon
Mr. Kennon S. Weeks, Jr.
Mrs. Ruby Marguerite Weeks
Mrs. Dorotha Wells
Mr. Edward Wells
Miss June Wells
Marchant Wentworth
Mrs. W. C. Wheeler
Mr. Joseph Whetzel

Miss Lillie F. Whitacre
Mrs. Buchanon White
Miss Eleanor White
Mr. Henry White
Miss Joyce White
Lee Roy White
Mrs. S. White
Mr. Chauncey Whitecraft
Mrs. Helen Whitmore
Mr. & Mrs. Ward R. Whitmore
Miss Mary Willard
Mrs. Monroe Willey
Miss Faye Williams
Mr. Fred Williams
Miss Geraldine Williams
Miss Mary Virginia Williams
Miss Nancy Williams
Mrs. Norma June Williams
Mr. Paul Willoughby
Mrs. Roxie Willoughby
Miss Florence M. Wilson
Mrs. John Lennie Wilson
Mr. Omar L. Wilson
Mr. Wm. H. Windsor
Mrs. John W. Winner
Mrs. Caryl C. Wold
Miss Dorothy Womack
Miss Louise Womack
Mr. Alton Wood
Mr. & Mrs. Charles R. Wood
Miss Mary Wood
Miss Rachael Wood
Mr. John W. Woodall
Mrs. Mollie Woodnll
Miss Mary Louise Woodard
Robert Woodward
Miss Betty Woody
Mr. James Edmond Worsham
Mr. Thomas B. Worsham
Mr. David L. Wright
Flora Lee Wright
Mrs. C. S. Wright
Mr. Vester Wright
Mr. Lawrence David Yeo
Miss Bobby Jean Young
Mr. Richard Young
Mrs. Richard Young
Mr. William Youngson
Mr. Thomas Zieran

The Metropolitan Messenger

Sixth and A Streets, N.E.
Washington 2, D. C.

Published bi-weekly by the Metropolitan Baptist Church. Subscription 50¢ a year. Entered as second class matter October 9, 1956, at the Post Office at Washington, D. C., under the act of March 3, 1879.

Figure 10.3. Under Walter Pegg, the church revised its membership roll significantly, dropping 995 non-attenders in 1957. In December 1956 the deacons printed in the church newsletter the names of those whose whereabouts were unknown.

five years as pastor of Metropolitan, and 957 of these were by baptism.[27] A significant part of a pastor's responsibilities includes overseeing membership additions and departures. Both steps require careful instruction

27 J. C. Hatfield, "Factual Information concerning the Ministry of Dr. Carpenter as Pastor of Metropolitan," *Metropolitan Messenger*, November 20, 1955, MS 1743, p. 3, box 8a, folder 6, CHBC Archives.

in the meaning of church membership and the necessity of resigning membership upon moving or leaving to join another church. Clearly both aspects were lacking, at least since K. Owen White's departure.

Still, despite Pegg's efforts to clean up the church's membership rolls and preach the Bible, the church's membership continued to decline. Pegg was a faithful preacher and godly pastor, but some circumstances were out of his hands. He knew that the Bible did not provide a formula guaranteeing church growth that was both numerical and spiritual. Still, having previously pastored a large church on the West Coast, he was understandably discouraged by the absence of visible fruit. When Pegg wrote to Carl Henry, informing him of his impending departure for more promising fields as pastor of Magnolia Avenue Baptist Church of Riverside, California, Pegg acknowledged, "I had not expected that our stay in Washington would be so comparatively brief as I have not been accustomed to making frequent moves, but in our work, the unexpected happens."[28] Henry wrote to Pegg acknowledging the challenges of ministering in Washington and the "frustrating experience—as it must be for any minister—of a constant turnover in the faces of the people to whom you are ministering."[29] Henry's Sunday school class meanwhile, whether due to lack of interest or to Henry's ever-demanding travel schedule, petered out by 1964 with little evident lasting fruit.

The pastors of Metropolitan during the second half of the twentieth century tended to alternate between revivalists and reformers. The revivalists tended to increase membership but often left disorder that the next pastor had to address. The reformers tended to revise the membership processes, clean up the membership rolls, and focus on the basics. Thus, the church's experience of preaching and mem-

28 Walter A. Pegg to Carl F. H. Henry, March 2, 1961, MS 1858, box 11, folder 2, CHBC Archives. Cf. "Pegg Resigns From Metropolitan," *Capital Baptist*, March 9, 1961.
29 Carl F. H. Henry to Walter A. Pegg, February 27, 1961, MS 1858, box 11, folder 2, CHBC Archives.

bership differed drastically between the pastorates of John Compton Ball, K. Owen White, J. Walter Carpenter, and Walter A. Pegg. White found the church membership rolls bloated, introduced a membership class, removed nonattending members, and preached expositionally. Carpenter grew the church to its numerical peak, but this proved a pyrrhic victory at best, as Pegg soon discovered.

Pegg meanwhile, like White, focused on the basics, with a focus on expositional preaching. Despite cleaning up the church's membership rolls and faithfully preaching the Bible, Pegg saw the church experience unprecedented decline during his tenure. By 1961, Metropolitan's membership was down to its lowest in twenty-one years.

———

Underneath our professed trust in the ordinary means of grace is the subtle assumption that if we do things right success will follow. We often assume—even unconsciously—that numerical fruitfulness will inevitably follow faithfulness. But if you compare the pastorates of White and Pegg, the similarities are remarkable. While both prioritized expositional preaching and careful membership practices, the results could not have been more different. White saw 848 baptisms in five years, and the church budget more than doubled. Pegg saw the church's membership decline from its all-time high of 3,692 in 1956 to 2,208 in 1961—it's lowest number since 1940. Was Pegg less successful? Was he less faithful?

According to the Bible the measure of a church's faithfulness is not the number of people on its membership roll but the extent of its fidelity to God's word. A church should never mistake God's temporal blessings for a formula. There are lean years, and there are years of plenty, but God's instruction to his church is the same: "Preach the word; be ready in season and out of season; reprove, rebuke, and exhort, with complete patience and teaching" (2 Tim. 4:2).

Both Carl Henry and Walter Pegg had come to Washington, DC, in the middle of the 1950s while evangelicals were riding high on the waves of post-World War II economic growth and evangelistic fervor. By the 1960s, America was hitting choppier waters. The Korean War was quickly followed by the Vietnam War, the sexual revolution began to undermine the plausibility of the church's message, and the Civil Rights Movement began to expose evangelicals' longstanding indifference to racial injustice. In one sense, Metropolitan's emerging difficulties in the 1960s serve as a microcosm of evangelicalism's problems. How could Metropolitan influence the city if it could not even discipline its own congregation? How could evangelicals have the impact they desired on the nation without reckoning with complex dynamics of race? Those were the questions that kept Pegg and Henry awake at night. If evangelicals' influence was to be felt in the national capital, such questions could no longer go ignored. As it turned out, the members of Metropolitan were woefully unprepared for the reckoning on race about to deluge the nation.

11

"Jesus Doesn't Need a Parking Lot"

1961–1980

THE NEIGHBORHOOD was up in arms. For weeks in 1972, Capitol
Hill Metropolitan Baptist Church (the church changed its name in
1967[1]) had planned to bulldoze two historic townhouses on East
Capitol Street, galvanizing the neighborhood into militant protest. As
church members tried to leave the service on Sunday morning, August
6, 1972, a crowd of angry, placard-carrying protesters barred their way.
A child later recalled how his father and a burly plumber nearly came to
blows in the fray. Some elderly women at the church were so horrified
by the profanity-laced screeds that the protesters later issued a public
apology. Once the standoff ended, with church members retreating to
the safety of their suburban homes, a solitary sign remained tacked to
the construction barrier on the corner of Fifth and East Capitol Street
NE: "Jesus doesn't need a parking lot."[2]

For four consecutive days (August 4–7), hundreds of placard-
carrying Hill residents physically blocked construction crews from

---

1   "Church Votes to Alter Name," *Capitol Hill Metropolitan Messenger*, February 15, 1967, MS 1755, p. 1,
    box 8a, folder 18, Capitol Hill Baptist Church Archives, Washington, DC (hereafter, CHBC Archives).
2   Ron Shaffer, "300 Protest Parking Plan," *Washington Post*, August 7 1972, C1.

demolishing the buildings.[3] "We had a big battle. We got out and picketed," one of the protesters, recalled. "I stood in front of the bull-dozer at 6:30 in the morning!"[4] The Victorian-style building at 500 East Capitol Street, which previously housed the Steinle Ice Cream Parlor, had become a restaurant known as Mary's Blue Room.[5] While it was beloved by many in the neighborhood, members of Metropolitan regarded the restaurant as "a place of prostitution and alcohol and drug addicts."[6] "If you ask me," one member explained, "We were doing the neighborhood a service."[7]

The property had been purchased by the church trustees in the 1960s. By 1972, the church owned nearly every square inch of the block. After the tenant of Mary's Blue Room defaulted on rent payments and a fire damaged the building in 1972, the trustees agreed that the time had come to raze the building.[8] For the church, demolishing Mary's Blue Room served two functions. First, it would temporarily provide additional parking spaces for Sunday commuters. Second, it would rid the neighborhood of a disreputable bar, which was fast becoming a liability for the teetotalling congregation.

Early in the morning on August 8, 1972—while even the most vigilant Hill residents were asleep—a crane brought the argument to an end. Neighbors woke to the sound of a wrecking ball demolishing the nineteenth-century house. By midmorning a sizeable crowd had gathered. Many were angry. "The Capitol Hill Metropolitan Baptist Church has declared war on this community," shouted the Reverend Rodney Shaw, pastor of Petworth Methodist Church. "Don't mince

3   "Protesters Again Delay Hill House Demolition," *Evening Star*, August 7, 1972, 20; "Protesters Fail to Stop House Razing," *Washington Post*, August 5, 1972, 4; "Residents, Church Debate Plans to Raze Town Houses: Church, Residents Disagree," *Washington Post*, August 4, 1972, 1.

4   Florine Walker Walther, interview by Ruth Ann Perez and Hazel Kreinheder, November 11, 1974, Capitol Hill History Project, www.capitolhillhistory.org/interviews/florene-walker-walther.

5   Florine Walker Walther, interview

6   John McJilton, interview with the author, May 18, 2022, Washington, DC.

7   Wes Ousley, interview with the author, June 6, 2022, Washington, DC.

8   Minutes of Church Business Meeting, August 9, 1972, MS 1042, box 4, folder 15, CHBC Archives.

words," said Libby Sangster, another protestor and operator of a local antique store. "They deliberately lied to us."[9]

Figure 11.1. A photograph in the *Evening Star* depicts protesters blocking construction crews from demolishing Mary's Blue Room, a historic diner on Capitol Hill. Protesters' signs included statements such as "The church lies," "Our history is being demolished," and "Jesus doesn't need a parking lot."

While the church advertised itself as "A Southern Baptist Witness on the Hill," this raised a question: What kind of a witness was the church?[10] Neighbors felt that the mostly suburban church was increasingly out of touch with the sentiments of the community. More than half of the church's membership—and most of its officers—lived outside of the District of Columbia.[11] From 1963 onward, even the pastor lived in a parsonage in northern Virginia rather than in a town house on Capitol Hill.[12] In a letter to the editor of the *Washington Post*, one

9 "Crane Ends Argument," *Evening Star*, August 8, 1972, 15.
10 "Advertisements," *Washington Post*, November 24, 1971, D12.
11 Only the church treasurer, Claude Dicks, lived on Capitol Hill. District of Columbia Baptist Convention Directory, January 1, 1972, MS 1346, box 5, folder 23, CHBC Archives.
12 Steve Cobb, interview with the author, May 10, 2022, Washington, DC. "When he [Dr. Culbreth] came [in 1963] that's when they bought the parsonage in Virginia. . . . my mom told me the parsonage used to be on Texas Avenue over in Southeast by Fort DuPont Park. And I think that area was getting a little sketchy maybe. So they bought the parsonage in Virginia. . . . Dr. Culbreth was the first one to live there."

resident accused the church of engaging in "visual rape of our neighborhoods and their architectural character."[13] Another Hill resident called
the church's actions "a blitzkrieg bulldozer attack." "Unwittingly," the
writer continued, "the only real service the Baptist Church may have
performed for Capitol Hill, is to make a group of quiet normally law-
abiding citizens into urban guerillas."[14] Even the editorial board of the
Washington Post responded with a long reflection on "Landmarks and
Parking Lots." After summarizing the conflict and the church's stance,
the editors offered this word of censure: "The church might, more
specifically, ponder the question, whether it is possible to love your
neighborhood any less than you love your neighbor. We think that the
two go hand in hand."[15] Where had the church gone wrong?

White Flight to the Suburbs

Parking lots stand front and center in Metropolitan Baptist Church's
story in the 1960s and 1970s. They represent much more than paved
asphalt and yellow paint. They stand for complex dynamics of suburbanization, white flight, and racial prejudice. They represent the growing distance—physically and relationally—between Metropolitan and
its neighbors. They represent the possibilities and pitfalls provided by
the automobile: the power of choice and the accompanying shift toward
a consumer mentality, even when it came to church involvement and
membership. At the same time, they also represent the members who
faithfully continued attending and giving, even while living farther and
farther away, without whom the church would not exist today. Did
Jesus need a parking lot? The neighbors certainly did not think so, but
the members of Metropolitan Baptist Church did.

The story of the parking lots of Metropolitan Baptist Church tracks
with three demographic trends in Washington, DC, following World

---

13 John J. G. Blumenson, "Wrecking Capitol Hill," *Washington Post*, August 10, 1972, A23.
14 Martin R. Ganzglass, "Destruction of Capitol Hill," *Washington Post*, August 19, 1972, A15.
15 "Landmarks and Parking Lots," *Washington Post*, August 12, 1972, A14.

Figure 11.2. Mary's Blue Room, a historic Victorian-era townhouse turned into a diner, was at the center of the church's controversy with the neighborhood in the 1960s.

War II. First, rising housing prices in DC drove members southeast to Anacostia, where housing developments were booming. Second, a little over a decade later, the urban redevelopment of Southwest Washington in the 1950s forced thousands of poor African Americans out of their homes and into the majority-White neighborhood of Anacostia. Third and simultaneously, the 1954 Supreme Court decision in *Brown v. Board of Education* that integrated public schools, along with a rise in racial violence and crime, led Whites to flee Anacostia to Prince George's County, Maryland, or Arlington, Virginia.[16] All three factors played a

16   "Smooth Start Is Disrupted by Hundreds in Capital," *New York Times*, October 5, 1954, 1; "Integration Resistance in Schools Seen Ebbing: Sterner Attitudes of Police, Parents, Teachers Lead

direct role in the downward spiral experienced by Metropolitan Baptist Church in the 1960s and 1970s as the church fought to survive amid peace protests, racial unrest, and rising crime.

When R. B. Culbreth arrived at Metropolitan in 1961 to succeed Walter A. Pegg as pastor, he was pleased with many aspects of the church's life. He commended its "deep-rooted spiritual life," its Training Union, prayer meetings, and youth and music programs. Only one aspect gave him pause about the church's long-term viability. "I would like to see provision for off-street parking," he wrote one month into his pastorate of Metropolitan. "What was sufficient years ago when there were not many cars is not adequate today."[17]

Since the late nineteenth century, motorized streetcars provided easy, safe, and affordable transportation throughout the city. Members and visitors like Maxine Walker had only to hop on a streetcar and pull the rope to signal the driver to stop at East Capitol Street and Sixth Street NE to make the easy commute to Metropolitan. In 1945, Washington's Capital Transit had America's third-largest streetcar fleet. As a result, before 1961, Metropolitan provided no parking for the congregation of well over a thousand. Each Sunday morning and evening, hundreds descended on the building on foot and especially by streetcar.

As buses replaced streetcars, everything began to change in the 1950s. In 1959, the *Metropolitan Messenger* mentioned parking as its primary budgetary appeal for 1960.

Again, what of parking space? Faithful members will doubtlessly continue to come regardless of this inadequacy. Many, indeed have learned to arrive early to find a niche within three or four blocks, but

to End of Protest," *Washington Post*, October 6, 1954, 17; Chris Myers Asch and George Derek Musgrove, *Chocolate City: A History of Race and Democracy in the Nation's Capital* (Chapel Hill, NC: University of North Carolina Press, 2017), 316.

17   R. B. Culbreth, "The Pastor's Pen," *Metropolitan Messenger*, August 30, 1961, MS 1749, p. 2, box 8a, folder 12, CHBC Archives.

how about the visitor, the prospective member, easily discouraged after driving around block after block.[18]

The solution to the parking problem lay in buying up additional properties. In 1961, Metropolitan purchased two homes on Fifth Street. "This makes possible a parking lot for at least 50 cars off-street," Culbreth explained on September 27, 1961. "Work will begin soon on this project of removing those old houses and pouring this much needed parking lot."[19] This was followed in 1962 with the construction of the second, larger parking lot.[20] Together, these provided parking spaces for one hundred automobiles.[21]

Figure 11.3. Metropolitan's first parking lot was completed in 1961.

18 "Why Subscribe the 1960 Budget," *Metropolitan Messenger*, December 16, 1959, MS 1747, p. 1, box 8a, folder 10, CHBC Archives.
19 "The Pastor Writes" *Metropolitan Messenger*, September 27, 1961, MS 1749, p. 2, box 8a, folder 12, CHBC Archives.
20 Minutes of Church Council, March 27, 1962, MS 672, box 2, folder 10, CHBC Archives.
21 "Our Heritage," Capitol Hill Metropolitan Baptist Church, February 28, 1988, MS 1285, box 5, folder 20, CHBC Archives.

DC was already facing a severe housing shortage in the 1940s. World War II only made the problem worse. In 1930, Washington had 468,869 residents. By 1950 this had increased to 802,178. Many of Washington's new residents found cheap housing readily available in the growing portion of Southeast DC just across the river in an area today known as Anacostia. In 1950, 82 percent of Anacostia's population was White. Just 18 percent was Black.[22]

An example of the changing makeup of Southeast Washington is exhibited by one member of Metropolitan Baptist Church. Roy Wyne was the youngest of six siblings who all grew up on Capitol Hill. His father—a policeman—died when Wyne was only thirteen, leaving him and his other siblings to care for the family. They moved around Capitol Hill, with a new address nearly every year. "Whenever the rents went up, they got chased out to the next place," his daughter Susan explained.[23] Working as a government employee during the war, Wyne married Marvis Cox, a fellow member of Metropolitan, in 1942. They settled into their new home just across the Anacostia River.[24] In 1951, they purchased their first home, a three bedroom house, farther southeast.[25] At that time, the predominantly White, working-class neighborhood was safe. Susan Wyne rode the public bus to elementary school by herself each day, free of worry.

In keeping with the pattern set by the Wynes and countless others, the percentage of Metropolitan's members that resided in Southeast Washington doubled from 16 percent to almost 30 percent between 1930 and 1950.[26] Of course, most members still resided in the Capitol Hill area. But younger members—and families in particular—found

22 Eddie Dean, "A Brief History of White People in Southeast," *Washington City Paper*, October 16, 1998, http://washingtoncitypaper.com/. Cf. Asch and Musgrove, *Chocolate City*, 285.

23 Bob and Susan Huber, interview with the author, June 8, 2022, Falls Church, Virginia.

24 Metropolitan Baptist Church Membership Directory 1943, MS 1709, box 7a, folder 9, CHBC Archives.

25 Metropolitan Baptist Church Membership Directory 1952, MS 1723, box 7a, folder 9, CHBC Archives.

26 This data has been compiled from church membership directories. See box 7a, folders 7–10, CHBC Archives.

the area across the river to be an attractive escape valve for affordable housing—that is, until the mid-1950s.

After the 1950s, the percentage of Metropolitan's members residing in Southeast plummeted to pre-1930s levels. By 1970 they had fallen to 19 percent. They continued to decline until dropping below 9 percent in 2000. In other words, between 1950 and 1970, Southeast DC ceased to be an option for members of Metropolitan. What happened? The answer is as simple as it is complicated.

In the 1950s, the Redevelopment Land Agency was commissioned by Congress to transform the District of Columbia into "the country's first major slumless city." The chief impediment was the slum-laden area referred to as Southwest Washington, home to 23,000 residents, 70 percent of whom were Black and 90 percent of whom were poor.[27] The bill, authorized by Congress and approved by the Supreme Court, granted authority to the agency to seize and confiscate private property in Southwest Washington as long as the owners were compensated. During the 1950s and 1960s, the Redevelopment Land Agency bulldozed 99 percent of the buildings in Southwest Washington to make room for new developments, forcing fifteen hundred businesses to move, and displacing nearly all of its residents. In just two decades, the racial makeup of Southwest Washington flipped from 70 percent Black to 70 percent White. Where did the displaced Black residents of Southwest go? The largest percentage of them (46.5 percent) moved to Southeast DC.[28] Within a decade, the Southeast area of Anacostia would go from majority White to Black, as the White population shrank from 82 percent in 1950 to just 37 percent in 1967.[29]

---

27 Asch and Musgrove, *Chocolate City*, 320.

28 Asch and Musgrove, *Chocolate City*, 324. Daniel Thursz's study from 1966 found that 42 percent of displaced African American families later resided in Southeast DC, with most of these residing South of the Anacostia River. Daniel Thursz, *Where Are They Now? A Study of the Impact of Relocation on Former Residents of Southwest Washington, Who Were Served in an HWC Demonstration Project* (Washington, DC: Health and Welfare Council of the National Capital Area, 1966), 26.

29 Dean, "A Brief History of White People in Southeast."

Figure 11.4. Jeanette Devlin directs the children's choir in this picture from 1962.

At Metropolitan, the possibility of integrating public schools led members to consider the possibility of starting a private Christian school. In November of 1952, J. Walter Carpenter "gave a brief outline of a church school with special reference to the church school of the First Baptist Church of Charleston, South Carolina," and explained that he intended to provide further information in the spring.[30] In March 1953, Carpenter wrote in the *Metropolitan Messenger*, discussing the challenges parents faced in the public school system in Washington, DC, which were leading some to consider establishing a Christian day school connected to Metropolitan. Among the challenges in public schooling, Carpenter specifically mentioned evolution and racial integration: "Added to these problems in Washington is the determined effort of the minority to force integration in our public school system. Certainly no Christian would deny any of the good things of life to any race. But the problem of integration forces us as parents to face our problems." Carpenter explained

---

30 Deacons' Meeting Minutes, October 29, 1951, MS 33, box 1, folder 10b, CHBC Archives.

that John Hamrick of First Baptist Church Charleston, South Carolina, would be speaking at Metropolitan on how to establish a successful Christian day school, but "whether or not Metropolitan undertakes a Christian day school and Kindergarten will largely depend upon the interest of you parents."[31] Despite John Hamrick's presentation, the proposal did not move forward, because on March 30, 1953, the board of deacons voted narrowly (ten to nine) against appointing a special committee to "investigate the desirability of a Church Day School."[32]

As Metropolitan continued to navigate the issue of race, the board of deacons discussed "the problems which are confronting Calvary and Centennial churches" on June 27, 1955. The minutes do not record the nature of these "problems," but the timing is telling. Two days later, after a two-hour debate, Calvary Baptist Church admitted its first Black member on June 29, 1955.[33] It would take Metropolitan nearly fifteen years to follow suit.

In addition to the integration of public schools, many members were disturbed by the trend of rising violent crime in the District. Every day, newspapers enthralled readers with stories of murder, robbery, and rape—occurring at all hours of the day, in all parts of the city, to the least suspecting people. A congressional staffer was stabbed nine times and killed while praying in St. Peter's Catholic Church on Capitol Hill. The wife of former SBC president turned presidential aide Brooks Hays was robbed in her home and had her wrist broken. But the crime that most shook the members of Metropolitan Baptist happened to someone they knew. On February 1, 1963, a fifty-five-year-old pastor's wife was attacked in her home, bound, raped, and robbed by a knife-wielding intruder.[34] As R. B. Culbreth explained to Metropolitan, "The minister's

---

31 J. Walter Carpenter, "Across the Pastor's Desk" in *Metropolitan Messenger*, March 8, 1953, MS 1741, p. 2, box 8a, folder 4, CHBC Archives.

32 Deacons' Meeting Minutes, March 30, 1953, MS 33, box 1, folder 10b, CHBC Archives.

33 "Calvary Baptists Admit First Negro," *Evening Star*, June 30, 1955, 33.

34 "Clergyman's Wife Raped in Her Home," *Evening Star*, February 2, 1963, 16.

Across the Pastor's Desk

Christian parents face many problems in rearing their children for the Lord. Worldly attractions take their toll, but even more crucial is the secularism in our public schools which leaves God out of education, which teaches evolution and often scoffs at the Bible.

Added to these problems in Washington is the determined effort of the minority to force integration in our public school system. Certainly no Christian would deny any of the good things of life to any race. But the problem of integration forces us as parents to face our problems.

What a blessing it would be to have born again Christian teachers instruct our children in all of their studies. God can be reverenced and Christ can be honored even in the teaching of history, geography and arithmetic.

Whether or not Metropolitan undertakes a Christian day school and Kindergarten will largely depend upon the interest of you parents. Keep Monday, March 23, 8:00 P.M. open. Plan to be present to hear a discussion of this problem led by Dr. John Hamrick of Charleston, S. C. who has demonstrated a successful Christian day school in the historic First Baptist Church.

This Week At

Metropolitan

SUNDAY
9:30 A.M.—Sunday School
11:00 A.M.—Morning Worship
        Junior Church
12:30 P.M.—Baptist Hour
5:00 P.M.—Youth Council
6:20 P.M.—Training Union
7:45 P.M.—Evening Worship
9:00 P.M.—Youth Fellowship
MONDAY
3:30 P.M.—G.A.'s meet
6:30 P.M.—Brotherhood
7:00 P.M.—R. A. Basketball Playoff.
TUESDAY
10:00 A.M. - 2:00 P.M. - 7:00 P.M.—
        Church Wide Visitation
WEDNESDAY
7:15 P.M.—Deacons meeting
7:45 P.M.—Hour of Power
9:00 P.M.—S. S. Cabinet meeting
THURSDAY
6:30 P.M.—Junior choir
6:45 P.M.—Teen Age choir
7:45 P.M.—Sanctuary choir
FRIDAY
6:30 P.M.—S. S. Workers Conf.
SATURDAY
7:00 P.M.—Bowling (Ft. Davis)

INVITE YOUR SHUT-IN FRIENDS TO WORSHIP WITH US EVERY SUNDAY
8 TO 9 P.M. WMAL

Brotherhood Meeting

Mr. Leon H. Sullivan, converted Roman Catholic and Christian business man, will be the guest speaker at the men's Brotherhood meeting Monday, March 9, 6:30 p.m. Mr. Sullivan has a challenging message. Be sure and get your ticket by Sunday night.

New Radio Folders

Those desiring to help distribute folders announcing our radio broadcast over station WMAL, and inviting people to our church services are asked to meet at the church Monday afternoon at 3:00 p.m.

IN MEMORIAM

Miss Cora Lee Ogle
Died Feb. 26, 1953
"Blessed are the dead which die in the Lord."

Figure 11.5. J. Walter Carpenter acknowledged that the effort to "force integration" was a factor leading the church to consider whether to establish a private Christian school in 1953.

wife that you read about in the paper who was raped by a negro was one of our Baptist pastors' wives."[35] Stories like these—and personal experiences of violence—drove members of Metropolitan to the suburbs in droves.

Families like the Wynes were reluctant to leave the homes they had purchased in the 1950s. But by the 1960s, the neighborhood was

---

35 "The Pastor Writes," *Metropolitan Messenger*, February 6, 1963, MS 1751, p. 2, box 8a, folder 14, CHBC Archives.

rapidly changing. "Crime was starting to ramp up somewhat," Susan Wyne later explained. So in 1964 the Wynes moved like countless others across the Maryland border into Prince George's County. "That was just the place to go," she explained.[36]

Like the Wynes, Frances Brown first moved to the Hill in the 1930s before moving to Anacostia and then out to the suburbs. "We moved up from the south into the Southeast part of the city and then out to Prince George's County," she recalled. After marrying Bill Brown, she moved across the Anacostia River to settle into their first family home. But by the 1950s, the "neighborhood was getting blacker," so they moved to Bethesda, Maryland. Nevertheless, they continued to make the commute to Metropolitan because that was where "the Bible was being taught."[37] For the Wynes, the Browns, and countless others, reasons for moving were numerous—rising crime, school integration, housing costs—but they all came down to the issue of race. And rather than resisting the trends, Metropolitan's members seemed resigned to follow them.

The Johenning Center and Segregated Services

One member who resisted the racial trends of her day was a widow named Anna Johenning. A graduate of the Southern Baptist Theological Seminary, Johenning moved to Washington with her husband in 1923. After his death, she became a missionary of the Women's Missionary Baptist Association, delivering aid and preaching the gospel to the destitute. In 1942, she helped organize "a Christian Center for under privileged children" in Southeast Washington where she taught Bible studies and provided for the material needs of poor families.[38]

---

36 Bob and Susan Huber, interview. Cf. List of Deacon's Addresses and Telephone Numbers, October 28, 1969, MS 56, box 1, folder 11, CHBC Archives.
37 Frances Brown, interview with Sandra S. Howard, June 12, 1994, Washington, DC. Quoted in Sandra S. Howard, Capitol Hill Metropolitan Baptist Church, June 21, 1994, 2, MS 1286, box 5, folder 20, CHBC Archives.
38 "Metropolitan's Activities for This Week," *Metropolitan Messenger*, February 10, 1952, MS 1740, p. 3, box 8a, folder 3, CHBC Archives. "Through their city missionary, Mrs. Carl Johenning,

Anna Johenning was following in the footsteps of Celestia A. Ferris, who died the year after Johenning arrived in Washington. When the Home Mission Board of the Southern Baptist Convention and the DC Baptist Convention raised funds to build a brand new Baptist Center in Anacostia in 1958, there was no question of its name: the Anna B. Johenning Baptist Center.[39]

Starting in 1956, Metropolitan ran a weekly bus to and from the center, picking up and dropping off kids.[40] Its location? Condon Terrace, which by 1980 would be known as the "meanest street in Washington" for its gang-related violence.[41] Through the success of the center, Metropolitan began to consider the possibility of establishing a Sunday school there. In August 1959 the board of deacons and the church approved the motion, "That the Metropolitan Baptist Church start a Mission Sunday school at Condon Terrace, S.E., in the Johenning Christian Center as soon as possible."[42] In July 1960, under the leadership of Martin L. Pratt, services began at what was known as the Southeast Baptist Chapel.[43] By December 1960, Sunday school attendance had grown to eighty, with fifty-six staying to attend chapel services.[44] All the while, Metropolitan contributed members as volunteers, funds to support Pratt's salary, and the credibility of its name as the sponsoring church of the chapel. Practically, this meant that anyone who wanted to join the chapel had to become a member of Metropolitan. There was only one problem. The racial makeup of

---

they operate a Christian Center for under privileged children." District of Columbia Baptist Convention Overview, MS 917, box 3, folder 3, CHBC Archives.

39 "From the Pastor's Pen," *Metropolitan Messenger*, September 10, 1958, MS 1746, p. 2, box 8a, folder 9, CHBC Archives.

40 "Bus to Condon Terrace," *Metropolitan Messenger*, April 1, 1956, 4, MS 1744, p. 4, box 8a, folder 7, CHBC Archives.

41 Courtland Milloy, "The Meanest Street in Washington," *Washington Post*, January 28, 1980, https://www.washingtonpost.com/.

42 Business Meeting Minutes, August 5, 1959, MS 1030, box 4, folder 3, CHBC Archives.

43 Minutes of Church Business Meetings, July 6, 1960, MS 1031, box 4, folder 4, CHBC Archives

44 Report of Southeast Baptist Chapel, November 1960, MS 1031, box 4, folder 4, CHBC Archives.

Figure 11.6. A sketch of the Johenning Baptist Center's new building in Southeast Washington, built through cooperation with the Southern Baptist Convention's Home Mission Board.

Anacostia was rapidly changing, and along with it, the racial makeup of the chapel.[45]

During preliminary discussions over sponsoring the chapel, Metropolitan's pastor and deacons had recognized the sensitivity of—to use their words—handling "racially mixed areas." To their credit, Metropolitan moved forward with sponsoring the chapel, fully aware that either

---

45 Dean, "A Brief History of White People in Southeast."

option would bring opposition. To their shame, Metropolitan opted to follow the "Southern Baptist policy" concerning "Negro attendance at Sunday School in other goodwill centers operating in racially mixed areas." Namely, by segregating its Sunday services.[46]

While sources are lacking on the specifics, the Southeast Baptist Chapel seems to have combined racially segregated Sunday services with integrated activities throughout the week.[47] As Metropolitan's pastor, R. B. Culbreth, explained in a private letter in 1962,

> As to our southeast Chapel, they follow the same practice at the morning worship service but encourage them to attend the afternoon service which is strictly for colored. However their weekday activities for Primaries and Juniors are completely integrated with the ratio of approximately sixty percent white and forty percent colored.[48]

In other words, African Americans would not be barred from attending the morning service at the chapel but encouraged to attend the afternoon service.

Soon, however, the Christian Life Commission—the precursor to the Ethics and Religious Liberty Commission of the Southern Baptist Convention—began to "criticize the practice of segregated services at the center" and instead suggested "integrated services at the center."[49] With pressures from integrationists and segregationists mounting, Metropolitan had to take a stand.

46 Deacons' Meeting Minutes, January 26, 1960, MS 33, box 1, folder 10b, CHBC Archives. For an overview of the Southern Baptist Convention and race relations during the Civil Rights Era, see David Roach, *The Southern Baptist Convention & Civil Rights, 1954–1995* (Eugene, OR: Wipf and Stock, 2021).

47 In January 1964, Martin Pratt, the chapel's pastor, raised the issue of segregated services during a church council meeting of Metropolitan Baptist. He stated that "a problem has arisen due to the fact that the program of the Center during the week is integrated and the Chapel program on Sunday is not." Minutes of Church Council, January 21, 1964, MS 674, box 2, folder 10, CHBC Archives.

48 R. B. Culbreth to Samuel Southard, November 8, 1962, MS 1169, box 5, folder 12, CHBC Archives.

49 Deacons' Meeting Minutes, October 23, 1963, MS 93, box 1, folder 11, CHBC Archives.

Culbreth claimed to neither be an advocate or opponent of racial integration. He was a man stuck in the middle. As he explained in a 1962 letter to Samuel Southard, a professor at the Southern Baptist Theological Seminary who had grown up at Metropolitan,

> We are not seeking to integrate, neither are we making an issue of it to remain a segregated church as such. As you know, Washington has very capable colored ministers and one of their strong churches, Mount Zion, is within two blocks of Metropolitan. I know, however, that many of our members would vote against integration of membership if the decision were left entirely to them.[50]

Six months later, however, Culbreth would change his mind.

On Good Friday, April 12, 1963, Martin Luther King Jr. was arrested in Culbreth's hometown of Birmingham, Alabama. Day after day, newspapers and television networks broadcast the videos and images of police brutality toward peaceful protesters, pricking the conscience of the nation. On April 16, 1963, King wrote his Letter from Birmingham Jail. Though an open letter, it could have been personally directed to Metropolitan Baptist Church. "I must confess," King wrote, "that over the past few years I have been gravely disappointed with the white moderate." King continued,

> I have almost reached the regrettable conclusion that the Negro's great stumbling block in his stride toward freedom is not the White Citizen's Counciler or the Ku Klux Klanner, but the white moderate, who is more devoted to "order" than to justice; who prefers a negative peace which is the absence of tension to a positive peace which is the presence of justice; who constantly says: "I agree with you in the goal you seek, but I cannot agree with your methods of direct action";

---

50 R. B. Culbreth to Samuel Southard, November 8, 1962.

who paternalistically believes he can set the timetable for another man's freedom; who lives by a mythical concept of time and who constantly advises the Negro to wait for a "more convenient season." Shallow understanding from people of good will is more frustrating than absolute misunderstanding from people of ill will. Lukewarm acceptance is much more bewildering than outright rejection.[51]

Culbreth was cut to the heart.

On May 26, 1963, Culbreth preached a sermon at Metropolitan entitled "The Musts of Jesus," in which he came down decisively in favor of desegregation. While we do not have a copy of the sermon, we know about it through a letter Carl F. H. Henry wrote to Culbreth that evening. "It took a lot of courage to come down as hard as you did for acceptance of the Negro this morning," Henry wrote to his pastor,

> and that's to your credit. If you can post a copy of your comments about being a Birmingham native, about the need for assisting the Negro to get his rights, about the failure of the Birmingham ministers to respond, and about Martin Luther King (about whom I don't share your enthusiasm), I'd be glad to use some comments in an upcoming editorial.[52]

Given Culbreth's comments six months earlier—"many of our members would vote against integration of membership if the decision were left entirely to them"[53]—one can understand why Henry commended Culbreth for his courage.

Later that year, Culbreth led the church to sponsor Shiloh Baptist Church's request to join the DC Baptist Churches—the very same

---

51 Martin Luther King Jr., "Letter from Birmingham Jail," April 16, 1963, box 6623, folder 4, University of Alabama Libraries Special Collections, http://purl.lib.ua.edu/181702.

52 Carl F. H. Henry to R. B. Culbreth, May 26, 1963, MS 1869, box 11, folder 2, CHBC Archives.

53 R. B. Culbreth to Samuel Southard, November 8, 1962.

African American congregation that had withdrawn its application in 1879 despite Joseph W. Parker's efforts to integrate the convention.[54] Not long after, services at the Southeast Baptist Chapel were finally fully integrated. Though detailed discussion in its records is lacking, the chapel's pastor wrote in 1966 as if segregated services were a relic of the past. He commended Metropolitan's "Christ-like Spirit which prevailed when integration became apparent and for your continued support and prayers as our colored friends came to accept the Lord Jesus Christ as Saviour and to unite with our fellowship by baptism and letter."[55]

Still, though publicly preaching against racism, Culbreth opposed direct church involvement into what he considered "political questions." When a quarter million gathered for the March on Washington later that year on August 28, 1963, Culbreth insisted that the church steer clear. "The church has tax exemption because it preaches the Gospel, and it does not engage in direct political activities," he told reporters.[56] For Culbreth, the mission of the church lay strictly with preaching the gospel not with political engagement—a distinction that allowed evangelicals to couch inaction in pious language.

While continuing to support the work of the chapel financially until 1974, Metropolitan formally handed off responsibility for the Southeast Baptist Chapel's Sunday programming in 1966, giving greater autonomy to the growing church plant.[57] By October 1969, thirty-nine constituent members were ready to form as an independent congregation. Though largely forgotten by the members of Capitol Hill Metropolitan Baptist Church, the chapel never forgot its debt to Metropolitan, adopting the name Anna Johenning Baptist Church.[58]

---

54 Deacons' Meeting Minutes, October 28, 1963, MS 674, box 2, folder 10, CHBC Archives.
55 Raleigh M. James to Metropolitan Baptist Church, June 22, 1966, MS 1037, box 4, folder 10, CHBC Archives.
56 "Race and Religion: The March on Washington," *Christianity Today*, August 30, 1963, 35.
57 Minutes of Church Business Meetings, May 25, 1966, MS 1037, box 4, folder 10, CHBC Archives.
58 "Rev. Dr. Samuel W. Hale, Jr.—'The History of Anna Johenning Baptist Church,'" YouTube video, August 4, 2012, https://www.youtube.com/.

In the 1960s, Metropolitan was caught between two competing visions for the church. One pushed toward disengagement and suburbanization. The other pushed toward greater community outreach and engagement. The church had a choice. They could choose the path of least resistance and retreat to the suburbs or stay rooted on Capitol Hill and view the changing demographics of the city as an opportunity for the light of the gospel to shine forth.

The tension was not simply a matter of zip codes. There is an inseparable connection between ease and entertainment, between consumerism and complacency. A church that is addicted to ease is not a church that will do hard things. A church that chooses entertainment will not tolerate uncomfortable sermons about racial prejudice. A church built around a consumeristic, attractional model of ministry will not be able to handle hard conversations. Sadly, Metropolitan was choosing the path of least resistance.

Suburbanization and Membership Decline

As members moved to the suburbs, Metropolitan fought to keep them from moving their church membership. They changed the slogan of the *Metropolitan Messenger* to "The Church *DEAREST* to you—Not the church *NEAREST* You!"[59] They printed a map of Metro Washington showing the driving distance from each of the suburbs. "No Home in Greater Washington Is Too Far From Metropolitan Baptist Church" the heading reads. "It all depends on what you want."[60] The efforts did not work. Metropolitan continued to decline.

The church tried to retain members by advertising its programs, talented choir, and rich services. "Where can you find a Training Union like ours, and you will have to look a long time to find a better choir—not to say anything about the Spirit of this church and its

59 *Metropolitan Messenger*, January 14, 1959, MS 1747, p. 3, box 8a, folder 10, CHBC Archives (emphasis in original). The church newsletter attributes this slogan to J. Conally Evans.
60 *Metropolitan Messenger*, October 18, 1961, MS 1749, p. 1, box 8a, folder 12, CHBC Archives.

great fellowship," Culbreth appealed.[61] It was true, Metropolitan had a thriving Training Union on Sunday evenings that attracted around 500 weekly. And its choir, which had recorded several LPs, was known across the city and frequently invited to sing elsewhere.[62] But appealing to a consumer mentality only exacerbated the underlying problem.

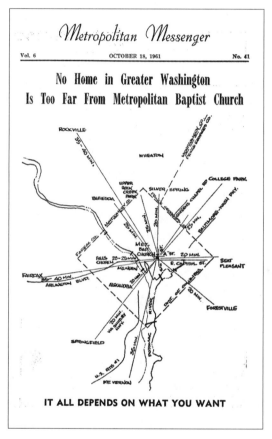

Figure 11.7. The front cover of the *Metropolitan Messenger* in 1961 depicts a map of the commuting times from neighboring suburbs.

61 "The Pastor Writes," *Metropolitan Messenger*, October 18, 1961, MS 1749, p. 2, box 8a, folder 12, CHBC Archives.
62 For instance, the Metropolitan church choir had been invited to sing for the pastor's conference of the Southern Baptist Convention at Atlantic City, New Jersey, in 1964. Minutes of Church Council, March 17, 1964, MS 674, box 2, folder 10, CHBC Archives.

Culbreth recognized the trends but thought revival would stem the tide of decline. He brought in pastors of national reputation, including Merv Rosell and Clyde Fransisco, hoping for a "time of rebirth for many people." But as Culbreth acknowledged at a church council meeting in 1963, the "visible results had not been what we had hoped they would be."[63]

By 1969, Sunday school attendance, which had averaged around 900 when Culbreth arrived,[64] dropped below 500.[65] "What can we do?" Sunday school superintendent Raymond Ryan asked. He had four ideas. Set ambitious goals, practice visitation, take weekly attendance, and hold a revival.[66] It didn't work. Attendance continued to decline, reaching 312 by 1971.[67]

And while Metropolitan continued to boast a membership of over 2,000, the strength of the congregation was superficial. By 1966, over 300 members were considered "non-residential." Nevertheless, they still appeared on the membership rolls.[68] For instance, when Caroline J. Lamson of Manhasset, New York, who had joined Metropolitan in the year 1900, wrote to the church secretary requesting to be "removed from the mailing list," she received a telling reply:

> Dear Miss Lamson:
> I received your card a few days ago. If it is all right with you we should like to continue to send you the Metropolitan Messenger and to keep your name on our church roll. You have been a member of long standing at Metropolitan and we appreciate that.
> Sincerely in Christ,
> Secretary[69]

---

63 Minutes of Church Council, April 23, 1963, MS 674, box 2, folder 10, CHBC Archives.
64 Financial Report, April 27, 1964, MS 87, box 1, folder 11, CHBC Archives.
65 Deacons' Meeting Minutes, September 29, 1969, MS 72, box 1, folder 11, CHBC Archives.
66 Sunday School Cabinet Agenda, March 22, 1963, MS 673, box 2, folder 10, CHBC Archives.
67 Deacons' Meeting Minutes, February 22, 1972, MS 60, box 1, CHBC Archives.
68 "Monthly Report," July 1966, MS 1037, box 4, folder 10, CHBC Archives.
69 Secretary of the Pastor to Caroline T. Lamson, February 26, 1963, MS 1384, box 5, folder 29, CHBC Archives.

Moreover, the church lacked addresses for 390 of its members.[70] All of this raises the question, what was Metropolitan's real strength?

In 1966, Carl Henry summarized the church's predicament under four headings: its downtown location, failure to grapple with changing racial dynamics, need for a powerful pulpit ministry, and need to engage students and universities intellectually. "I think Metropolitan is at the crossroads," Henry wrote. "One of its great assets—and also its liability at the present juncture of history—is that it is a downtown church located only about six blocks from the Capitol."

But what really gnawed at Henry was the church's lack of "creative leadership" in addressing racial problems. "The whole color complex in Washington is changing, so that it is overwhelming Negro, and Metropolitan has shown little creative leadership in facing that problem. That means that there is only one real option for significant survival, as I see it," Henry continued. "Since its membership will more and more move to the suburbs or be confined to government workers in the immediate area: it must have a powerful pulpit and a special ministry to students in the Washington area (on an intellectual level and not merely social). If these two elements were combined, I think it could gain a reputation as a powerful center." Apart from such changes, however, Henry's outlook was bleak. "Without them, I see no really significant future for the church."[71]

Henry was right. Metropolitan was at a crossroads. Washington was a powder keg of racial unrest. The fuse was lit, and the keg was about to burst.

Capitol Hill Metropolitan at the Crossroads

On April 4, 1968, Martin Luther King Jr. was shot at the Lorraine Motel in Memphis, Tennessee. Within hours, grief-stricken crowds in Washington gathered to air their frustration in ways that quickly

---

70 "Members of Metropolitan for Whom We Have No Address," May 27, 1966, MS 1037, box 4, folder 10, CHBC Archives.

71 Carl F. H. Henry to Bob Marsh, December 12, 1966, MS 1862, box 11, folder 2, CHBC Archives.

became violent.[72] Community leaders called for peace and restraint. But the torrent of rage had already been unleashed. The next seventy-two hours were filled with looting, arson, and violence to a degree that the capital had never known. Nearly 3,000 were arrested as 11,500 troops, including the 82nd Airborne, sought to restore order to the capital.[73]

Robert Nordan was eleven years old at the time. He lived about fifteen miles from the church in Maryland, but his father worked for the Metropolitan Police Department in Washington, DC. He recalls standing in the backyard of his house, watching black clouds of smoke rising over Washington. When he asked his mother, "What's happening?" she replied, "Your father won't be home for a few days." "It wasn't long after that," Robert explained, "that we made the decision to leave Capitol Hill Metropolitan and go to a Baptist church in the Maryland suburbs."[74]

Though the building of Capitol Hill Metropolitan Baptist Church remained unscathed, the same could not be said of the church's members. One member, Mrs. Dicicco, lost her restaurant on H Street, which was completely looted and destroyed.[75] Another member's car was pelted with stones. On Palm Sunday, only 338 showed up for church that morning. "All around the Capitol," one member recalled, "soldiers lined the way, forming a perimeter around the Capitol."[76]

On Easter Sunday, April 14, fewer than 600 made the journey through the smoke and rubble to attend the morning service at Capitol Hill Metropolitan. Those who did, however, heard an unusual Easter message. The new pastor, John Stuckey, addressed the racial situation

72 "The City's Turmoil: The Night It Began: How the Violence Began: Chronology of a Night of Turmoil," *Washington Post*, April 14, 1968, A1.
73 "11,500 Troops Confront Rioters; Three-Day Arrest Total at 2686," *Washington Post*, April 7, 1968, A1.
74 Robert Nordan, interview with the author, April 29, 2022, Washington, DC.
75 "From the Pastor's Study" *Metropolitan Messenger*, April 10, 1968, MS 1756, p. 1, box 8a, folder 19, CHBC Archives.
76 Bob and Susan Huber, interview.

in Washington head-on. He addressed the underlying causes of rioting and the need for the church to understand the plight of the Black
community. One member wrote to him after his message:

> I am glad you spoke to our congregation last Sunday about the plight
> of the negro in this community and this country. I know something
> about the hopes, fears and poverty among the Washington negroes
> because I have visited among them over the years.
>
> The average white person just doesn't realize the plight of the poor,
> underprivileged negro in this community and this country. They
> either don't read the newspaper, or do not have contact with them
> in any way. They live modestly and since they have most of their
> needs satisfied they just don't have compassion for the negro, or the
> poor. Well, nothing is more dangerous than a hungry, unemployed,
> homeless man, and when his emotions explode, God help us. . . .
> Negroes are asking for some answers to these questions now. Tomor-
> row may be too late.[77]

Unlike any of the previous pastors, Stuckey saw the changing landscape of Washington as an opportunity. "Our church is in a small
enclave where the population shift in recent years has been from white
to black," he wrote in 1971. "What an opportunity this church has to
create a real fellowship of believers crossing racial and national lines!"[78]
Stuckey challenged the church to engage the community that it had
largely abandoned by retreating to the suburbs. He hired Wayman Jones
as youth minister who energized the youth to see the brokenness of
their community and do something about it. Jones organized summer
youth outreach activities for local children.[79] "We've studied the origin

77 John R. Stuckey, "From the Pastor's Study," *Metropolitan Messenger*, April 24, 1968, MS 1756,
   p. 2, box 8a, folder 19, CHBC Archives.
78 John R. Stuckey, "This Difficult City," *Capitol Hill Metropolitan Messenger*, February 10, 1971,
   MS 1759, p. 2, box 8b, folder 2, CHBC Archives.
79 Minutes of Church Council, MS 678, box 2, folder 11, CHBC Archives.

of the Bible, God as creator, the meaning of worship," one member wrote in 1971. "The response on the part of parents and children has been heartening." Most of the children had not previously experienced any kind of religious instruction. One student later recalled that they would visit the DC General Hospital on Saturday afternoons to rock abandoned babies, who had been born in prison or left on doorsteps.[80]

Figure 11.8. John R. Stuckey officiates over the Lord's Supper at a New Year's Eve Watchnight Service in 1970.

Stuckey described his philosophy of ministry as a "social ministry," combining theological conservatism with progressive activism. In a sermon from 1970 entitled "Ministry in This Decade," Stuckey laid out his approach. "There are three views of social ministries, by and large, in the church today," he explained. One view is that the church engages only in evangelism and soul saving. "I do not think that is

---

80 Barbara Sorrels, interview with the author, May 18, 2022, Washington, DC. Cf. *Metropolitan Messenger*, January 27, 1971, MS 1759, p. 1, box 8b, folder 2, CHBC Archives.

adequate," Stuckey said. On the other hand, some people teach that "the church is to do only social ministry and social action." Stuckey likewise rejected such a view. "But lying between these two," he explained, "is the concept of evangelism through ministry. This is the only real valid kind for today. Jesus did this kind of evangelism."[81]

Certainly, by today's standards, Stuckey was no liberal—politically or theologically. He emphatically preached against the doctrine of evolution.[82] He preached a scarcely veiled endorsement of Richard Nixon on the eve of Nixon's inauguration entitled "The Making of a President."[83] He even condemned the 1967 March on the Pentagon as serving the interests of the Communist movement and called on churches to "align themselves in opposition."[84] But Stuckey challenged the congregation in terms of the church's social and community outreach in ways that made members uncomfortable. The *Washington Post* was not far off when it stated that Stuckey "blended a conservative theological stance with an effort to propel his congregation in the direction of a social-action involvement with the neighborhood."[85]

In 1969, Capitol Hill Metropolitan issued a report of the church's long-range planning committee. The report listed several areas of concern, including the continued net loss in membership, the imbalance of the age distribution among church members, the need to improve the church's reputation in the community, the absence of evangelism in the community, the absence of unsaved persons in the church's Sunday

81 John R. Stuckey, "Ministry in This Decade" (sermon, Capitol Hill Metropolitan Baptist Church, Washington, DC, 1971), box 12, folder 1, CHBC Archives. For more on John R. Stuckey's view of social action, see Kenneth Dole, "Evangelicals Studying Shifts to Social Action," *Washington Post*, November 30, 1968, D7.

82 John R. Stuckey, "The Naked Ape?" (sermon, Capitol Hill Metropolitan Baptist Church, Washington, DC, July 21, 1968), box 12, folder 1, CHBC Archives.

83 John R. Stuckey, "The Making of a President" (sermon, Capitol Hill Metropolitan Baptist Church, Washington, DC, January 19, 1969), box 12, folder 1, CHBC Archives.

84 John R. Stuckey, "The Church and the Peace Marchers" (sermon, Capitol Hill Metropolitan Baptist Church, Washington, DC, October 22, 1967), box 12, folder 1, CHBC Archives.

85 Michael B. Hodge, "'I Leave With Satisfaction, Regret': Capitol Hill Pastor Resigns," *Washington Post*, February 13, 1971, B9, Proquest.

school classes, the community's lack of interest in the Christian message, the church's lack of knowledge and interest in community problems, and the increasing rate of juvenile delinquency in the local area.[86]

The facts were obvious, and the report did not try to conceal them:

1. Since 1965 we have had a steadily declining membership.
2. In the years 1959–1966 we had an average of one baptism per 30 members. During 1967 and 1968 our average has declined to one baptism per 83 members.
3. There is a disproportionately low number of baptisms in the intermediate age group of 13–16 years.
4. A third of our members (521) are 60 years and above; 518 are between 10 and 29 years of age.
5. There is a disproportionately low number of members in the age range of 30 through 59 years.[87]

In terms of understanding and meeting the needs of their community, the report was particularly unforgiving. "We have not yet come to grips with the effort of relating ourselves to the people of our immediate area," it noted. "[W]e feed ourselves and run the danger of becoming bloated . . . [because] we have failed to relate to their needs."[88]

Stuckey's hopes of effectively engaging the community and modeling an interracial witness on the Hill were partially realized in 1969 when the first African American member joined the congregation: Margaret S. Roy. Born on June 17, 1909, in Broad Run, Virginia, Roy came to DC at age ten and worked as a teacher in Prince William County and later as a school principal. Roy explained that she began attending Capitol Hill Metropolitan because she had heard its hymns on the

86 "Report of the Long-Range Planning Committee," May 28, 1969, MS 1040, pp. 1–38, box 4, folder 13, CHBC Archives.
87 "Report of the Long-Range Planning Committee," 21.
88 "Report of the Long-Range Planning Committee," 32.

radio. Her reasons for attending were multifaceted. On the one hand, she wanted to disprove those who thought "it was a church that didn't want Negroes." She explained that she believed that she could go into a White church, and "she wanted whites to know that there were blacks that weren't all bad." There were also worship preferences. "While some blacks like lots of clapping," Roy explained that she preferred "quiet," believing that "it's more important to listen and learn the gospel." One month after she began attending, she received a letter from Stuckey inviting her to join the church, which she did.[89]

Not everyone was pleased at this. Stuckey recounted that four White families left the church when she joined. But despite experiencing some serious unpleasantness, Roy resolved "that she would treat people right regardless of how they may treat her." At a women's Bible study, "one woman [rudely] turned her back on her," but through her persistent efforts, "that woman later became a friend." Another way she built friendships in a nearly exclusively White church was by making a point of visiting elderly women who were members of the church. They were often surprised to be visited by Roy, but she "didn't think it mattered what color they were."[90]

In February 1971, Stuckey resigned from the pastorate of Capitol Hill Metropolitan Baptist Church. As the *Capitol Hill Metropolitan Messenger* explained his departure, "John R. Stuckey sought to challenge us in these difficult days—of inner city turmoil, of a shifting population, and of decline in inner city churches—preaching that programs rooted in the gospel was the only way in which our church would continue to proclaim the word on Capitol Hill."[91] Stuckey had

89 Margaret S. Roy joined the church in March 1969 and was a member until her death on November 7, 2001. Thankfully, a former member conducted an interview with Roy, otherwise we would know little about her. Margaret Roy, interview with Bernard Myers, September 22, 1996, MS 1310, box 5, folder 21, CHBC Archives.

90 Roy, interview.

91 "Dr. John R. Stuckey," *Capitol Hill Metropolitan Messenger*, February 10, 1971, MS 1759, p. 1, box 8b, folder 2, CHBC Archives.

led the church through navigating the riots of 1968, welcoming its first African American member in 1969, and finding new avenues of engaging the community. While he acknowledged encountering little open resistance, he admitted to receiving little support.[92] In his last entry in the church newsletter, Stuckey wrote, "God demands more . . . of us. And we have not met the demand. It is my hope and prayer that you will in the future, under new leadership."[93]

Figure 11.9. Margaret Roy (right), Luella Dicks (center), and Jessie Reichard (left) are pictured together at a reception in 1983.

No Rocking the Boat

The next pastor, C. Wade Freeman, came to a declining downtown congregation from one of the largest churches in Tulsa, Oklahoma. He had heard about the opportunity through Raymond Burnley, the minister for youth at Capitol Hill Metropolitan, who had previously

92   Hodge, " 'I Leave with Satisfaction, Regret': Capitol Hill Pastor Resigns," B9.
93   John R. Stuckey, "Do Something for Your Pastor," *Capitol Hill Metropolitan Messenger*, February 17, 1971, MS 1759, p. 2, box 8b, folder 2, CHBC Archives.

served under Freeman in Tulsa. One of the trustees, C. Vinton Koons, had apparently told Burnley, "The church is going to die in thirty years. We're not going to have anybody because there's not going to be anybody alive." He asked, "Do you have any suggestions?" Burnley replied, "Call Wade Freeman."[94]

Freeman hoped to turn the dwindling church around. He identified non-attendance as the primary problem plaguing the church. "This church cannot thrive and grow when the majority of her members simply do not attend," he wrote on September 27, 1971.[95] The attendance at morning worship the previous day had been a measly 413—less than a third of the church's boasted membership of 1,436.[96]

To correct the problem of non-attendance, Freeman introduced a visitation plan. He divided the membership into twenty-seven geographical areas and assigned workers to each area as visitors.[97] Each deacon or deaconess would be responsible to fill out and return visitation forms indicating the number of visits, phone calls, and cards to those in their area. At the joint meeting of deacons and deaconesses, Freeman told them that "a spirit of enthusiasm appears to be evident."[98] However, perception could hardly be further from reality. Ever since John Compton Ball, each new pastor had insisted on visitation as the solution to the church's non-attendance woes, but it had never worked. The only visitation forms on hand indicate that the deacons averaged about five telephone calls per month and no in person visits.[99] Enthusiasm was far from evident.

94 Wadonna Freeman Duncan, interview with the author, June 2, 2022, Fredericksburg, Virginia.

95 "From the Pastor's Pen," *Capitol Hill Metropolitan Messenger*, September 27, 1971, MS 1759, p. 2, box 8b, folder 2, CHBC Archives.

96 "The Record Speaks" *Capitol Hill Metropolitan Messenger*, September 27, 1971, MS 1759, p. 4, box 8b, folder 2, CHBC Archives.

97 Little Flock Visitation, n.d., MS 59, box 1, folder 11, CHBC Archives.

98 Deacons' Meeting Minutes, January 25, 1971, MS 60, box 1, folder 11, CHBC Archives.

99 Guide for the Administration of the Fellowship Fund by the Deacons, March 1, 1958, MS 58, box 1, folder 11, CHBC Archives.

Freeman's typical Southern Baptist approach to ministry "didn't rock the boat," as one member later put it, but it also didn't stop the leaks.[100] While Freeman proposed establishing a new members' class, he resisted the idea of making it a prerequisite to membership.[101] Freeman encouraged the deacons to begin moving toward the rear of the sanctuary during the end of the sermon when an "invitation" to come forward and receive Christ was customarily given. When one deacon expressed his concern about this practice, Freeman cited the Billy Graham meetings as an example "of using pre-planned movement to encourage people to come forward."[102] Freeman stated that it did "not hurt the invitation, but probably helped because the movement encouraged people to move out and come forward." Freeman's plan was not without effect. The church saw several baptisms that year—the median age being eleven.[103] Still the church continued to decline.

Figure 11.10. Wade Freeman pictured at the church's centennial celebration in 1978.

100 Sorrels, interview.
101 Deacons' Meeting Minutes, May 30, 1972, MS 41, box 1, folder 11, CHBC Archives.
102 Deacons' Meeting Minutes, March 26, 1973, MS 138, box 1, folder 12, CHBC Archives.
103 Church Directory, n.d., MS 146, box 1, folder 12, CHBC Archives.

When the crowds surrounded Capitol Hill Metropolitan Baptist Church in the early morning of August 6, 1972, they were channeling anger that had been building for over a decade. While the church had been contracting numerically, it had been expanding its footprint locally. As members moved out of the area, the church grew more programmatic. All the while, the gap between church and community grew and, along with it, the gap between the church and the Christ it proclaimed.

"I used to hear this phrase a lot," one former member recalled in an interview, "We're the lighthouse on Capitol Hill. And they took great pride in that. . . . They were very proud of being on Capitol Hill." At the same time,

> we thought that the reason the church was dying is because we didn't have enough parking. But I was like, no, that's not the reason. It wasn't parking that stopped people from coming when we had a thousand [attending]. . . . It's seeking that quick fix, or the next gimmick to get people into the church versus just teaching the word of God.[104]

———

Today, Anna Johenning Baptist Church—now called The Temple of Praise—and Capitol Hill Baptist Church remain separated by the Anacostia River, the historic boundary marker dividing Washington along racial lines. Nevertheless, a shared history unites them into one story, and a shared Spirit unites them into one body. Capitol Hill Baptist Church exists because Celestia Ferris started a prayer meeting in her home on Capitol Hill. The Temple of Praise exists because a widow named Anna Johenning similarly started a Sunday school in Anacostia.

To this day, those churches remain divided by a river. But one day, a river will unite them. Revelation 22 paints a picture of the saints

104 Sorrels, interview.

gathered around the river of the water of life, flowing from the throne of God. On either side of the river are the branches of the tree of life, whose leaves are "for the healing of the nations" (Rev. 22:2). One day all the saints throughout the ages will join Ferris and Johenning at the foot of *that* river to worship the Lamb. On that day, every wound of sin and strife and every tear of injustice will be wiped away because we will see his face (Rev. 22:4). The question is this: What does it look like to live now in light of that day? Johenning showed us what it looks like: choosing self-sacrifice over comfort and choosing love over self-protection.

In Revelation, Jesus warns the Ephesian church that unless they repent, he would remove their lampstand (Rev. 2:5). The light may have been still burning on Capitol Hill, but it was a light hidden under a basket not set on a stand. In its racial attitudes, ministry methods, and political sensibilities, the church prided itself as a Southern Baptist witness on Capitol Hill. That they certainly were. But were they a *Christian* witness on Capitol Hill?

In one sense, the neighbors were right. Jesus didn't need a parking lot. In fact, he didn't even need Capitol Hill Metropolitan Baptist Church. What Jesus needed was for the church to be the church and to radiate the purity of their Savior to a watching world. The question was, would they repent, or would he remove their lampstand?

12

"When a Christian Leader Falls"

1981–1993

Disclaimer: This chapter contains sensitive content related to sexual misconduct. To protect the privacy of the offended party, her name is not mentioned in this chapter.

IN DECEMBER 1992, Capitol Hill Metropolitan Baptist Church was at a crossroads. The church, which had been in numerical decline since the 1970s, had recently hired a gifted pastor who was finally beginning to turn things around. But just as the church was growing and young people were returning, a credible accusation of sexual immorality called into question his qualification for ministry. How would the church respond? To answer this question, and to understand how it came to this point, we need to go back to the 1970s when two best friends from Oklahoma moved to Washington, DC.

Everyone at Capitol Hill Metropolitan Baptist Church knew and loved Bob Sorrels. He was funny, hardworking, and charismatic. He had a lucrative job and a large circle of friends. He had graduated from the University of Oklahoma in 1974 and moved to Washington, DC, to work for a bank on Capitol Hill. Later that year, Sorrels joined Capitol Hill Metropolitan after being invited by a coworker. A year later, his college friend Bill V. followed his footsteps to DC and joined the church.[1] Best friends and college fraternity brothers, Sorrels and Bill were pillars of the church's young professionals' group and often had people over to the home they shared in Kingman Park.

One Sunday, Sorrels announced to the church that he was quitting his job at the bank to become a missionary. As part of the Southern Baptist Convention's "Bold Mission Thrust" emphasis, Sorrels planned to raise funds to volunteer for one year with the Foreign Mission Board (FMB), known today as the International Mission Board.[2] There he would use his skills as an accountant to support the work of the Nigerian Baptist mission for a year.[3] As Sorrels explained to the church, he had always known, even as a boy growing up in Oklahoma, that God wanted him to do something out of the ordinary. "I told God that whatever he wanted me to do in my life I would do."[4] He had dedicated his life toward that purpose and was ready to go.[5]

Only days after Sorrels left the United States for Nigeria, tragedy struck. On April 16, 1980, he was riding in the backseat of a car with local Nigerian seminary professor Titus Oluwafemi and longtime missionary William Bender when they were hit head-on by a drunk driver. Oluwafemi was killed instantly. Bender died five days later. Sorrels survived the accident but was paralyzed from the neck down due to injuries to his vertebra. "God was kind to me and saved my life," Sorrels

1   Bill V. Membership Card, Capitol Hill Baptist Church Archives, Washington, DC (hereafter, CHBC Archives).

2   "Pastor's Pen," *Metropolitan Messenger*, April 8, 1980, MS 1768, box 8b, folder 11, CHBC Archives.

3   "Foreign Missionary Dies in Nigeria Auto Crash, MSC Volunteer Paralyzed," *Word and Way*, May 1, 1980, 5.

4   "Bob and Barbara: A Legacy of Love, Loss and Perseverance," Vimeo video, November 26, 2017, https://vimeo.com/.

5   "Pastor's Pen," *Metropolitan Messenger*, February 12, 1980, MS 1768, p. 1, box 8b, folder 11, CHBC Archives.

wrote in a dictated letter a week later. "I praise the Lord in all things and I have trust and faith and hope that God's will be done."[6]

Church secretary Mary Lou Cobb received the telegram from the FMB on April 16, 1980, that Sorrels had been in a car accident and was in critical condition. His church family poured out prayers on his behalf as he was flown back to the United States in a Stryker frame to be treated at Baylor University Medical Center. His friend Bill drove a group from church down to Dallas to celebrate Sorrels's twenty-ninth birthday in the hospital.[7] In a note to the congregation, Sorrels thanked them for their prayers and support, writing, "If God would let me choose my time schedule for recovery, it would be less than a week, but since we walk by faith and wait on God's timing, I'll have to be patient, work hard and always remember to glorify our Lord and Savior Jesus Christ each day in everything I do."[8]

When Sorrels's recovery began to appear doubtful, questions of providing for his ongoing medical and long-term care began to drive a wedge between the Capitol Hill congregation and the FMB. The FMB pointed out that Sorrels had signed a waiver before going on the field, absolving the entity of responsibility in case of "loss of property, damage to same, personal harm or injury that may come."[9] Simply put, they would not be responsible for any additional support for Bob Sorrels.

The church was shocked by the abrupt announcement. The church had previously raised thousands of dollars for Sorrels's support but diverted them to other FMB programs after being informed that the FMB

---

6   Bob Sorrels to Capitol Hill Metropolitan Baptist Church, April 22, 1980, box 12, folder 7, CHBC Archives.

7   *Metropolitan Messenger*, July 1, 1980, MS 1768, box 8b, folder 11, CHBC Archives; Bill V. to "Friends of Bob Sorrels," June 13, 1980, box 12, folder 7, CHBC Archives.

8   "Excerpts from a Letter from Bob Sorrels," *Metropolitan Messenger*, July 22, 1980, MS 1768, box 8b, folder 11, CHBC Archives.

9   "Volunteer Missionary Says Board Has Abandoned and Betrayed Him," *Richmond Times-Dispatch*, November 20, 1981, 44.

would be taking care of him.[10] Now the FMB appeared to be reneging on its word. Sorrels felt abandoned and betrayed by the FMB, which he characterized as a group of "very cold businessmen."[11]

In response, a group led by Bill organized a letter-writing campaign on Sorrels's behalf. As an article in the *Richmond Times-Dispatch* explained, a group that called itself "Friends of Bob Sorrels" challenged Southern Baptist trustees and entity heads to take "remedial action to prevent the suffering" of disabled volunteers such as Sorrels.[12] They hoped the FMB would change its policies to "implement a plan that would enable all Mission Volunteers to have disability coverage regardless of who would be responsible for the payments."[13] "Let's stuff Keith Parks' mailbox with letters from CHMBC," Bill wrote in October 1981, referring to the president of the FMB as the target of his letter-writing campaign.[14] This controversy, which exploded across denominational newspapers and even the popular press, placed Capitol Hill Metropolitan Baptist Church at loggerheads with the Southern Baptist Convention and placed the church's new pastor in an uncomfortable situation.

Walt Tomme Jr.

Walt Tomme Jr. had become Capitol Hill Metropolitan's pastor after C. Wade Freeman suddenly resigned in November 1981 to take a job with the Reagan administration.[15] "My first day in the office," Tomme recounted, "Wade Freeman told me Reagan had appointed him to become the liaison to the evangelical community."[16] With that, Tomme,

10 Deacons' Meeting Minutes, December 7, 1981, MS 256, box 1, folder 15, CHBC Archives.

11 "Volunteer Missionary Says Board Has Abandoned and Betrayed Him," 44.

12 "Volunteer Missionary Says Board Has Abandoned and Betrayed Him," 44.

13 Deacons' Meeting Minutes, December 7, 1981.

14 Bill V. and Barbara Cobb to "Friends of Bob Sorrels," October 23, 1981, box 12, folder 7, CHBC Archives.

15 Wade Freeman had been aided in this endeavor by a member of the church, Becky Norton Dunlop, who was Reagan's deputy assistant for presidential personnel. C. Wade Freeman Jr. to CHMBC, November 8, 1981, MS 1052, box 4, folder 22, CHBC Archives.

16 Walt Tomme Jr., interview with the author, July 13, 2022, part 1, Gainesville, Virginia.

who had just been hired to serve as Freeman's associate, found himself thrust into the pastorate of a once-prominent church at age thirty-three without significant previous pastoral experience.

Born in Beaumont, Texas, on October 20, 1947, Tomme was a marine and a freshly minted graduate of Southwestern Baptist Theological Seminary in Fort Worth, Texas. In a word, he was a fighter, ready to reform Capitol Hill Metropolitan, whatever the cost. Tomme did not find the church in a flourishing condition and wasted no time in diagnosing its problems and introducing changes. Though there were approximately 1,200 names in the membership directory, only 280 attended on Sundays.[17] He found church structures, committees, and classes all "calcified" in unhealthy ways. When he proposed changes, he was simply told, "We never did it that way before."[18] Tomme knew that Capitol Hill Metropolitan needed to be turned around, so he challenged the church to engage in a process of church growth.

For Tomme, church growth combined two critical aspects of ministry: evangelism and meeting felt needs in the community. First, "church growth," Tomme wrote, "implies that people who are outside the church are being introduced to Christ," and second, "Christians who are not involved in a local church . . . are being drawn in where their needs are being met."[19] In Tomme's view, both evangelism and meeting felt needs were the only way the flagging church could reestablish itself among its increasingly alienated neighbors.[20]

---

17 Financial Report, October 1, 1980, MS 263, box 1, folder 15, CHBC Archives. Tomme estimated that around 175 attended on Sundays when he arrived. Tomme, interview, part 1.

18 Walt Tomme Jr., "A Word From Your Pastor," *Metropolitan Messenger*, June 4, 1985, MS 1775, p. 2, box 8b, folder 16, CHBC Archives.

19 "From the Associate Pastor," *Metropolitan Messenger*, February 23, 1982, MS 1771, box 8b, folder 13, CHBC Archives.

20 In working toward church growth, Tomme was not falling into the so-called homogeneous unit principle of the Church Growth Movement. See Donald A. McGavran, *Understanding Church Growth* (Grand Rapids, MI: Eerdmans, 1970), 190–211. On the contrary, he insisted that "the mature church is a heterogeneous church." Like John Stuckey in the 1960s, Tomme was committed to seeing Metropolitan grow as an interracial and diverse community on Capitol Hill. "The gospel is for all people. Here in Washington that means that Jesus is the need of blacks, whites,

The main way the church sought to meet the needs of the surrounding community was through its child development center (CDC), an initiative led by Barbara Cobb. The CDC provided quality childcare for members of the community, created opportuntities for evangelism, and helped heal the rifts that had grown between the church and its neighbors.[21] When the CDC formally opened on September 1, 1983, providing services for children aged three to five, every spot was taken.[22] Tomme relished the opportunity to witness to nonbelieving parents, leading parenting workshops where he found neighbors surprisingly open to the Bible's instructions for parents.[23]

As the church sought to build bridges to the community, Tomme also sought to reconcile Bob Sorrels and the FMB. "Y'all just need to forgive the Foreign Mission Board," Tomme told the "Friends of Bob Sorrels."[24] On January 5, 1982, Tomme, Bill, and Barbara Cobb drove Sorrels to the FMB headquarters in Richmond, Virginia, to meet with the president, Keith Parks. Parks explained that the FMB was taking steps to develop a disability package for Southern Baptist volunteers. He agreed to personally contribute toward the fund established by the District of Columbia Baptist Convention to provide for Sorrels's ongoing needs. "It doesn't bring glory to God for Christians to have bitterness and conflict over a difference of opinion," Sorrels told Parks at the meeting. "The hurt is gone, I feel like a great burden has been lifted off of me."[25]

---

orientals, chicanos, street people, straight people, democrats, republicans, northerners, southerners, blue collar, white collar, rich, poor, married, single, divorced, remarried, skeptical, open and on and on and on. We must never be guilty of giving our message to just those like us." Tomme, "A Word From Your Pastor," 2.

21 Deacons' Meeting Minutes, April 5, 1982, MS 249, box 1, folder 15, CHBC Archives.

22 "Child Development Center," *Metropolitan Messenger*, May 10, 1983, MS 1772, p. 3, box 8b, folder 14, CHBC Archives.

23 Tomme, interview, part 3. Cf. Deacons' Meeting Minutes, June 27, 1985, MS 165, box 1, folder 14, CHBC Archives: "Pastor Tomme stated that there is a real opportunity to reach parents with children attending the Child Development Center. The pastor has the opportunity to counsel these parents."

24 Barbara Sorrels, interview with the author, May 18, 2022, part 3, Washington, DC.

25 Robert O'Brien, "Sorrels, FMB Reconciled; Foundation Launches Fund," *Arkansas Baptist Newsmagazine*, January 28, 1982, 10.

Sorrels married Barbara Cobb and moved to Texas to enroll in classes at Southwestern Baptist Theological Seminary.[26] But even as the conflict with the FMB came to a close, problems within the church were beginning to spell the end of Tomme's ministry at Capitol Hill Metropolitan.

Figure 12.1. Walt Tomme Jr. served as pastor of Capitol Hill Metropolitan Baptist Church from 1981 to 1988.

Many factors contributed to Tomme's resignation in 1988. The cause might be described as "irreconcilable differences." For an elderly congregation, used to doing things a certain way, Tomme's frequent innovations simply proved too much. "I was doing things different," he later explained. For instance, after attending a spiritual awakening conference led by Stephen Olford, Tomme had a new idea. "To inspire

26 "New Address for Bob Sorrels," *Metropolitan Messenger*, December 13, 1983, MS 1773, p. 3, box 8b, folder 14, CHBC Archives.

us to experience unity," he explained, "I would have us stand up at the end of service and hold hands across the aisles."[27] Such practices did not go over well with many members.

More than anyone, however, Tomme consistently found himself at odds with one member named Bland Wright. Wright was a longtime member, a deacon, and head of the building committee. Any step taken by Tomme was opposed by Wright, who felt defensive of his control of the building. When the church began to experience a series of nighttime robberies, Tomme hired a recently converted homeless man to serve as the night watchman. They met at Stanton Park in 1986 during an evangelistic event and began meeting daily for discipleship. Doing so solved two problems at once. It protected the building and provided a place for the newly converted homeless man to sleep. "I took a little heat for it," Tomme later recounted, "but he just became one of my favorite people."[28]

Wright, however, was not pleased and made sure the church knew about it. He brought a report from the house committee to the church at a members' meeting, expressing his "disapproval of the action taken by church staff and deacons to allow the 'so-called' night watchman to reside in the church without notifying the House Committee in advance."[29] But that was just the beginning.

When Tomme's sermons began to run too long for the taste of some, Wright installed a clock on the balcony in direct line of sight from the pulpit. When that failed, on several occasions during the humid summer months, Wright turned off the church's air conditioning midway through the service. Tomme could only bear so much, and finally the church had had enough. At a special meeting of the board of deacons on August 30, 1987, Tomme brought a report of Wright's actions to the deacons, asking them to initiate a disciplinary

27 Tomme, interview, part 2.
28 Tomme, interview, part 3.
29 Church Business Meeting, January 14, 1987, MS 1066, box 4, folder 29, 1987, CHBC Archives.

process.[30] A letter drafted by Bob Huber on behalf of the board of deacons requested that Wright step down from all leadership positions for several reasons, including "shutting off the air conditioning system during worship" and his "continual open and harmful discussions concerning the pastor's leadership."[31] In his reply the following week, Wright refused to step down until "at such time the church membership votes me out."[32]

With rising tensions between Tomme and Wright, the deacon board found itself divided within. The younger deacons rallied around Tomme while the older deacons supported Wright.[33] By this time, however, Tomme had grown disenchanted with the ministry on Capitol Hill. Increasingly attracted to the methods of Bill Hybels at Willow Creek Community Church in northwestern Chicago and eager to try something new, Tomme resigned as pastor on Sunday, August 14, 1988.[34] As Tomme wrote to the church, "The difficult times have been times of growing and maturing for us. We have come to understand the strength and the power of God even in the midst of great pain and disappointment."[35]

---

30 Deacons' Meeting Minutes, August 30, 1987, MS 158, box 1, folder 13, CHBC Archives.

31 Robert Huber to Bland Wright, n.d., Deacons' Meeting Minutes, August 30, 1987.

32 Bland W. Wright to Board of Deacons, September 4, 1987, Deacons' Meeting Minutes, August 30, 1987.

33 Jeffrey G. Nutt, interview with the author, May 25, 2022, Washington, DC; Wes Ousley, interview with the author, June 6, 2022, Washington, DC.

34 Special Business Meeting, August 14, 1988, box 4, folder 30, CHBC Archives. Andrea Blanchette summarized the causes of Walt Tomme's departure: "In an [sic] dramatic effort to 'modernize' the traditional worship services in hopes of offering greater appeal to church-goers, Tomme subsequently alienated the large elderly congregation who were still the faithful saints who kept Metropolitan afloat. Many of these retirees had been members of CHMBC for over half a century. The results were tragic. The rift between the traditionalists and the modernists widened until at last the church split in 1988, with Tomme taking a majority of the young adults and young families with him to the Virginia suburbs to begin a new church. So dramatic was the split that even families were torn apart as some stayed at Metropolitan and others, usually the second generation, left with Tomme or went in search of other congregations." Andrea Blanchete, "History: Capitol Hill Metropolitan Baptist Church," February 1, 1993, MS 1287, box 5, folder 20, CHBC Archives.

35 Walter S. Tomme Jr. to Capitol Hill Metropolitan Baptist Church, July 31, 1988, MS 1067, box 4, folder 30, CHBC Archives.

During Tomme's ministry, over 250 new members had joined the church, many of them residents of Capitol Hill, singles, and young parents with children.[36] To the great disappointment of the church, many of those young people who joined under Tomme's ministry left with him when he started Tysons Community Church in the suburbs. Families split as older parents—who had been at Capitol Hill Metropolitan for generations—stayed while their children left. To those who stayed, this felt like a betrayal. After Tomme's resignation, one of the older deacons, Charlie Trainum, approached a younger man named Jim Sims and said, "I don't know what the problem was. We let you guys do whatever you wanted." To this Sims replied, "That's the problem. It was always 'we' versus 'you.'"[37]

By 1988 Tomme was gone, and Metropolitan was again without a pastor. Bob and Barbara Sorrels were in Texas, struggling to make ends meet as Bob, still wheelchair bound, searched for pastoral positions. Most of the church's young people had left. But of all the deacons from the younger generation, one stayed: Bob Sorrels's good friend Bill.

Bill stayed out of loyalty to the church. As one member later explained, "Bill was the young, dynamic version of how we were going to recover from Walt leaving."[38] Capitol Hill Metropolitan was where he had grown spiritually, met his wife, and started a family. When many of the older deacons were talking of disbanding the church and distributing its assets to missions, Bill fought for the church. Bill told the deacon board that his fraternity in college had almost gone bankrupt. But because they had a shared vision, they were able to pull through. He was confident that the church would pull through as well. Through Bill's youthful zeal and financial savvy, the church kept going.[39]

36 "A Word From Your Pastor," *Metropolitan Messenger*, January 13, 1987, MS 1778, p. 2, box 8b, folder 18, CHBC Archives.
37 Jim Sims, interview with the author, December 7, 2022, Washington, DC.
38 Ousley, interview.
39 Ousley, interview.

Figure 12.2. Bill, the young man and deacon who stayed and fought for the church.

Bill quickly became chairman of the board of deacons. It was his idea to sell the parsonage and move the pastor to the block. He said, "This is a local church, we should give them the option to be local."[40] So with renewed vision, the church began looking for a new pastor.

Harry Kilbride

Toward the end of 1989, Carl F. H. Henry was receiving medical treatment at the Mayo Clinic in Minnesota when he shared with a pastor friend about the need for a pastor at Capitol Hill Metropolitan. His friend, John Steer, had just become personally acquainted with a fellow Englishman named Harry Kilbride who was presently searching for

---

40 Ousley, interview, quoting Bill V.

a new pastorate.[41] "I was surprised and honored when Dr. Carl Henry telephoned me toward the close of 1990," Kilbride later recounted, "and asked me to consider seriously the pulpit and pastorate of Capitol Hill Metropolitan Baptist Church." As Kilbride explained, "The rest is history!"[42]

For the weak and weary Capitol Hill congregation, everything about Harry Kilbride seemed too good to be true. He had previously pastored Lansdowne Baptist Church, one of the largest and most influential evangelical churches in England. His current church—Brandywine Baptist in Wilmington, Delaware—boasted two services, a 10 percent growth rate, and a missions budget of $250,000 a year. His radio ministry, Kerygma, had a wide following across the East Coast. He came to Capitol Hill Metropolitan with glowing recommendations from Stephen Olford, James Montgomery Boice, and R. T. Kendall of Westminster Chapel, who called Kilbride the "best preacher in England."[43] Moreover, Kilbride presented himself as a personal disciple of Martyn Lloyd-Jones in England and had connections in high places.[44] If that wasn't enough, his wife June was a gifted musician and could readily fill the need for a music minister.

Most importantly for the Capitol Hill church, Kilbride was in nearly every respect the opposite of Walt Tomme. Tomme was a Texan and a marine; Kilbride was British and a former schoolteacher. Tomme had never thought of himself as a gifted student. Kilbride glistened with degrees and accomplishments. Tomme had virtually no previous pastoral experience. Kilbride had been senior pastor of three churches. Yet despite these qualifications, Kilbride was willing to take the pastorate of a diminished church, with a small budget, and virtually no staff.

41 John C. Steer, interview with the author, January 17, 2023, Washington, DC.
42 "From the Pastor's Desk," *The Capitol Hill Metropolitan Messenger*, October 4, 1992, MS 1784, box 8b, folder 23, CHBC Archives.
43 Special Business Meeting, June 13, 1990, MS 1069, box 4, folder 32, CHBC Archives.
44 Matt Schmucker, interview with the author, September 7, 2022, part 1, Washington, DC.

As chairman of the board of deacons, Bill did everything he could to get the Kilbrides settled on Capitol Hill. In order to make up for a meager compensation, the cash poor but land rich church agreed to sell one of the church-owned houses to the Kilbrides. The idea was Bill's, a lucrative deal that would vest the Kilbrides with an increasing share in any appreciation in the value of the house after each year.[45]

Figure 12.3. Harry Kilbride (1934–2022), pastor of Capitol Hill Metropolitan Baptist Church, 1991–1993.

When Kilbride preached his first sermon as pastor on October 7, 1990, less than 150 were attending the church's Sunday school classes on average. He chose Psalm 127:1 for his text:

45 Special Business Meeting, June 13, 1990, CHBC Archives. As Herb Carlson explained, "As part of his calling, CHMBC agreed to sell him a townhouse as a type of retirement account with funding up to $150,000. CHMBC would sell '516' to Dr. Kilbride at market accessed value, and allow him a loan with no interest. CHMBC would give Dr. Kilbride $15,000/year to build up equity in the house." Regular Business Meeting, March 6, 1991, MS 1071, box 4, folder 34, CHBC Archives. Cf. Bill V., interview with the author, August 10, 2022, Washington, DC.

Unless the LORD builds the house,
> those who build it labor in vain.

Alongside the hope of growth, Kilbride warned the church to fear the Lord and not labor in vain. "How awful if all that effort was 'in vain' because the Lord was not the builder and disowned it. So let *us* be warned!" he told them. "This is the greatest work in the world. I have never been so full of vision and expectancy," Kilbride explained.

> I believe God has been preparing me for this call all my life. . . . Will you labor with me, alongside me? Will you support me? Please give yourself afresh to the Lord and may it please Him that we see great and mighty things in the very center of the city which can change the nation which can change the world.[46]

As a preacher, Kilbride insisted that growth and revitalization was God's work, not man's. "The kind of preaching I was bringing to you this morning on the cost of discipleship is not going to fill the church," he said. "If you want this church filled you better fire me and get one of these guys in who will just turn it into an entertainment complex." The older members wanted the church to grow, but as Kilbride explained, he was committed to preaching, not gimmicks.

As a theologian, Kilbride recommended the works of J. I. Packer, R. C. Sproul, Carl Henry, Iain Murray, and above all "the Doctor"— Martyn Lloyd-Jones. "'The Doctor' was my mentor," he liked to remind the church, "and perhaps the greatest preacher this century."[47] A cherished photograph showed Lloyd-Jones preaching at Kilbride's installation as pastor of Lansdowne Baptist Church in 1976. Like

---

46 "A Digest of Dr. Kilbride's First Message to CHMBC, October 7, 1990," *Metropolitan Messenger*, October 30, 1990, MS 1782, p. 2, box 8b, folder 21, CHBC Archives (emphasis in original).

47 "Pastor's Desk," *Metropolitan Messenger*, February 14, 1991, MS 1783, p. 2, box 8b, folder 22, CHBC Archives.

Lloyd-Jones, Kilbride was unafraid of stepping on toes when it came to matters of theological conviction. He put an end to the practice of holding an "invitational" after the service, much to the anger and dismay of some members. He likewise opposed the practice of baptizing children of eight years or younger, upon profession of faith, convincing the deacons to approve a baptismal policy that would reserve baptism for children who had reached adolescence.[48]

Yet for all these qualifications and accomplishments, something was deeply wrong with Harry Kilbride. What later came to light was that he was guilty of serious sexual immorality. Whether Kilbride engaged in such immorality at a prior church is difficult to know, but this sin would come into the light at Capitol Hill.[49]

Matt and Elizabeth (Eli) Schmucker first met Kilbride on November 13, 1990, just one month after his installation, at the funeral of Eli's grandmother, Madeline Dunmire, a longtime member of Capitol Hill Metropolitan. "It was raining," Matt Schmucker recalled. "We were knocking on the door. We weren't even sure the building was Metropolitan because the exterior signs were all missing," he laughed. "When we got inside, everything was old. The carpet was worn out, some of the ceiling lights had fallen down, there was a spot in the ceiling of the sanctuary where water dripped every time it rained." Even the smell of the church—a combination of mold and mothballs—gave off a sinister aroma of death. Nevertheless, when Schmucker moved his family to Washington, DC, later that year, they decided to join "grandma's church."[50]

The church was in dire straits financially, so when Kilbride learned that Schmucker had a background in finance, he asked him to help

---

48 "From the Pastor's Desk," *Metropolitan Messenger*, March 13, 1991, MS 1783, p. 1, box 8b, folder 22, CHBC Archives.

49 Trevor Archer, interview with the author, August 11, 2022, part 1, Washington, DC; Gordon Showell-Rogers, interview with the author, September 30, 2022, Washington, DC; Howard Gerlach, interview with the author, December 7, 2022, Washington, DC.

50 Schmucker, interview, part 1.

part-time as church administrator.[51] Soon, however, Schmucker began to notice that something was wrong.

When Kilbride gave Schmucker a tour of the building, part of that tour involved showing his corner office on the first floor at Fifth and A Street. "There was a phone on his desk," Schmucker explained, "and there was a second phone behind his desk." The phone on his desk was connected to the church office, but the phone behind his desk was on a separate line. It wasn't a published number, and no one was allowed to answer it. Kilbride was particularly sensitive on this point. "No one can answer this phone but me." When Schmucker asked why, Kilbride became defensive and explained that it was for "special counselees who needed privacy."

One day, while working in the office, Schmucker heard the phone behind the desk ring while Kilbride was out of the office. Forgetting Kilbride's warning, Schmucker answered the phone only to hear the sharp intake of a woman's voice as she hung up quickly. When Schmucker told Kilbride that someone had called but did not give her name, Kilbride went ballistic and reproved Schmucker sternly for answering the phone.[52]

On the same tour of the church building, Schmucker noticed something else that confused him. Kilbride showed him his second office on the fourth floor of the educational building. Kilbride was clear with Schmucker that this was his private office. Only he had a key to it. That's where he would write his sermons. And since his first-floor office was not "one-hundred percent soundproof," this fourth-floor office was where he conducted his most sensitive counseling sessions. Schmucker thought it strange for Kilbride to occupy an office in the far recesses of the church but did not think much of it until other things began to happen.

Early one morning Schmucker noticed Kilbride's car parked across two parking spaces in the main lot, pulled all the way up to the back of the church. When he asked Kilbride about it and why he had not

51 Clerk and Treasurer's Report, January 6, 1991, CHBC Archives.
52 Schmucker, interview, part 1.

parked in his usual spot behind his house, Kilbride explained that he had been counseling a young woman the previous evening and speaking to her in his car. It was pouring rain, so he had pulled his car up as close as he could to the awning. "But Harry," Schmucker asked, "It didn't start raining until late last night."

"I know that" Kilbride replied. "What of it?"

"Why were you with her so late at night?" Schmucker pressed.

Kilbride became furious. Normally a reserved and quiet man, he stood up and chased Schmucker out of his office, shouting, "What are you suggesting? I would never do anything of the kind!"[53] Rather than seeing Schmucker's concern as a desire to protect the pastor's reputation and the safety of the flock, Kilbride was living as if such rules did not apply to him.

Though Schmucker did not know it at the time, Kilbride had another counselee: the wife of Bill V., the chairman of the board of deacons. For over a year, she had been seeing Kilbride for counseling because she "had wanted to learn about grace." But instead of receiving help, she experienced horrific pastoral abuse at the hands of one who ought to have been a protector. During the pastoral counseling relationship, Kilbride began acting inappropriately toward her, and he later escalated the conduct to sexual immorality.[54]

The Truth Comes to Light

For months Bill had been suspicious that something was going on but could not figure out what. "I think my wife's having an affair with somebody," he confided with a friend. "I can't figure out how. She's here with the kids all the time. The only time she's out of the house is to see Kilbride for counseling."[55]

53 Schmucker, interview, part 1.
54 Bill V., interview. See Harry Kilbride to Herb Carlson and Members of CHMBC, January 18, 1993, MS 1925, box 24, folder 1, CHBC Archives.
55 Steve Cobb, interview with the author, May 10, 2022, Washington, DC.

Bill first learned the truth standing beside his wife's bed at the intensive care unit of a local hospital on November 10, 1992, after she had attempted to take her own life. Tearfully asking her why, he was unprepared for her answer. "I didn't believe her when she told me what was going on," Bill said. "It didn't make sense. I couldn't imagine that she would have that relationship with anybody, let alone him."[56]

As is common in cases of pastoral misconduct, the counselee did not at first appear to be a credible witness. The pastor, on the other hand, was entirely believable.[57] "I would have believed him," Bill reflected.[58] And therein lay the problem. As Barbara Sorrels later recounted, "Harry had pretty much told [Bill's wife], 'Nobody's going to believe you. So you can go tell who you want.'" "And that," Barbara explained, "is why she tried to commit suicide."[59]

Bill did not know what to do, so he prayed. "I remember praying harder than I have ever prayed before or since. 'Cause at that point I was desperate for the truth." After a night of anguished prayer on November 15, 1992, Bill became convinced that his wife's allegations were true.[60] "I remember falling to the ground thinking, 'Oh my God, it's true.'" Though Bill did not yet know the extent or duration of Kilbride's misconduct, he knew enough to escalate the matter.[61]

On November 19, 1992, Bill resigned as chairman of the board of deacons in order to allow them to carry out an investigation without any conflict of interest.[62] The deacons found themselves in a difficult position. On the one hand, they had a skilled and celebrated pastor who was in the process of turning the church around. On the other

56 Bill V., interview.
57 Cobb, interview.
58 Bill V., interview.
59 Barbara Sorrels, interview, May 18, 2022, part 1.
60 Bill V. to Herb Carlson, December 7, 1992, MS 1919, box 24, folder 1, CHBC Archives.
61 Bill V., interview.
62 Deacons' Meeting Minutes, November 19, 1992, MS 312, box 1, folder 16, CHBC Archives.

hand, they had received serious allegations against his character, and Bill believed his wife and stood unflinchingly by her side. Moreover, Bill was the one who had fought for the church in 1988 when the deacons were considering disbanding. What is more, Bill was the one who had fought for Kilbride and done everything in his power to get him settled at the church. Bill was a godly and earnest man, who made his appeal to the deacons but then prayerfully recused himself from the investigative process, trusting that the board would do the right thing. He embodied David's words in Psalm 37:5:

> Commit your way to the LORD;
>   trust in him, and he will act.

God answered Bill's prayers.

On December 3, 1992, Herb Carlson, Paul Huber, and Bill met privately with Kilbride to ask him about the allegations. At the meeting, Kilbride confessed that "unspecified sexual activities had occurred during the 'counseling sessions' that clearly were against scriptural mandate and all ethical codes related to counselor/counselee relationships."[63] What had prompted his confession? "You know, I don't think there was any hard evidence," Bill later recalled. "I think God caused him to admit."[64]

On Tuesday evening, January 19, 1993, a special church-wide meeting was held. As then college student and church member Wendi Reedy later recalled, "I think I missed class to be there."[65] At the members' meeting, the deacons read a resignation letter from Kilbride where he confessed openly to "serious sexual immorality with a woman member of our church. . . . I was given a position of trust and leadership," he wrote, "and have betrayed it. I am so sorry to you all." Though neither

63 Bill V. to Herb Carlson, December 7, 1992.
64 Bill V., interview.
65 Wendi Reedy, interview by the author, March 23, 2023, Washington, DC.

Harry nor June were present at the meeting, the letter was forthright and unsparing. "The worst thing of all is I have brought shame to the Name of Christ. I do not deserve to continue as your pastor and preacher, or ever to preach again."[66] By unanimous vote, Kilbride's resignation was accepted by the church.[67]

After Kilbride's letter, Bill asked to read a letter on behalf of his family. Without any malice, he offered his heartfelt forgiveness to the Kilbrides. "June and Harry—we love you. Harry—we forgive you." For Bill, Kilbride's sin was great, but his confession was evidence of God's grace. "People have been praying that Dr. Kilbride would be delivered and God would be glorified by it. I believe God clearly answered that prayer."[68]

Before coming to Metropolitan, Kilbride had been pastor of Brandywine Valley Baptist Church where he had written a booklet entitled "When A Christian Leader Falls."[69] "It is devastating when a Christian leader falls, and the wider, greater and more public his ministry, the more devastating it is." Why this happens to the leaders of God's people was one of the questions probed in Kilbride's booklet. "Leaders are special targets of the enemy," Kilbride wrote.[70] Some find themselves, like David, with time on their hands. Some live constantly near the edge of nervous exhaustion and turn to "some immoral diversion" as an escape from pressure. Some "neglect the means of grace."[71] In all of this, Kilbride wrote, "We, too, must not put our trust in men. Men will fail us. We must not put preachers and leaders on a pedestal. We will find that they have feet of clay."[72]

---

66 Harry Kilbride to Herb Carlson and Members of CHMBC, January 18, 1993, CHBC Archives.

67 Deacons' Meeting Minutes, January 19, 1993, MS 309, box 1, folder 16, CHBC Archives.

68 Bill V. to CHMBC, January 14, 1993, MS 1923, box 24, folder 1, CHBC Archives.

69 Harry Kilbride, "When A Christian Leader Falls" (unpublished booklet, n.d.), MS 1241, box 5, folder 16, CHBC Archives.

70 Kilbride, "When A Christian Leader Falls," 7.

71 Kilbride, "When A Christian Leader Falls," 8.

72 Kilbride, "When A Christian Leader Falls," 13.

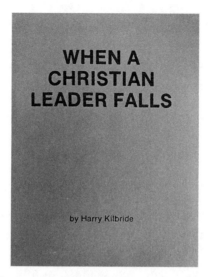

Figure 12.4. Before coming to Capitol Hill Metropolitan, Harry Kilbride authored a booklet entitled "When a Christian Leader Falls."

Harry Kilbride died on July 30, 2022, at his family home in Bournemouth, England. On hearing of his passing, Bill responded just as he had done on first hearing the allegations against him: by praying. "Thank you for letting me know," Bill wrote. "He is truly in our Lord's hands now. I'll pray for his wife and kids."[73]

A little over a year later, after forty-three years in a wheelchair, Bob Sorrels, who had left behind a lucrative career in banking to serve as a missionary, went to be with the Lord. He never walked again. But through pain and suffering, he continued to follow Jesus his entire life. And as his wife Barbara wrote on announcing his passing, "Bob has finally been healed!"[74]

Bill had come to Capitol Hill Metropolitan in 1975, following the path blazed by his best friend Bob. More than anyone else during those difficult decades, Bill was responsible for keeping the church from going under. He had given it his all but seemingly lost everything as a result.

73 Bill V., personal communication to the author, August 2, 2022.
74 Barbara Sorrels, Facebook post, April 23, 2023.

Schmucker never forgot the warning of Kilbride's life and fall. "A man can be all Harry was, and more," Schmucker wrote on hearing of his death. "But the Lord looks on the heart. It's hard to know what really happened to Harry when he stood at the judgment seat. I can only hope he received the mercy he once preached."[75]

———

By requiring Kilbride's resignation, the church took a stand and said that faithfulness to Scripture matters more than expedience. There was nothing convenient about rejecting any option to keep Kilbride at the church. He was an incredibly gifted preacher. Losing him seemed like the nail in the coffin for the ailing church. But it was what Scripture demanded, because Kilbride had disqualified himself biblically from serving as an elder. Though it was the right decision, it was a costly one—as most right decisions are. At that time no one knew whether the church would survive. No one knew who the next pastor would be or even if the church would be able to find another pastor. In hindsight, the decision seems obvious, but it did not seem so at the moment.

If there is a secret sin in the life of a person or in the life of a church, doing the right thing by unveiling and dealing with the sin will be painful. It will often seem to cost *everything* in the moment. It feels like a death of sorts because it *is* a death of sorts. But it is always the right thing to do—even when it hurts. This is why churches need leaders with courage.

Many of the most important things in life depend on displaying courage to do the right thing at a crucial turning point. What if Bill had not been willing to prayerfully listen to his wife when no one else would have believed her? What if the deacons had not confronted Kilbride? What if they had swept his actions under the rug in an effort

75 Matt Schmucker, personal communication to the author, August 2, 2022.

to protect his or their reputation? How many churches could have been affected if the church had refused to do the right thing? C. S. Lewis said that "courage is not simply *one* of the virtues, but the form of every virtue at the testing point, which means at the point of highest reality."[76] How you respond in those moments of crisis—those critical decision points—is the test of character. And character isn't cultivated in a moment but over the course of a lifetime. That is why character matters—because it shows up in crucial moments in the form of courage.

Churches and their pastors must never value giftedness over godliness. Kilbride was unbelievably gifted. R. T. Kendall, called him "the best preacher in England." Nevertheless, a pastor is not qualified for ministry by his giftedness but by meeting the qualifications for elders laid out in 1 Timothy 3:1–7 and Titus 1:5–9.

God's ways are mysterious. But all things are ordained for good. It certainly seemed like the devil had gotten the upper hand of this church. But God, who is sovereign over all things, works even the most difficult circumstances according to his plan. Despite how things appeared, the Lord was not yet finished with this church on Capitol Hill.

---

76 C. S. Lewis, *The Screwtape Letters*, in *The Complete C. S. Lewis Signature Classics* (New York: Harper Collins, 2007), 270.

13

"Preach, Pray, Love, and Stay"

1994–2000

MARK DEVER was residing happily in Cambridge, England, with his wife Connie and their two children when he received a letter from Carl F. H. Henry in January 1993, hand delivered by New Testament scholar D. A. Carson. It was not unusual for Dever to get letters from Henry. They had maintained a consistent correspondence since meeting in January 1987 while Dever was studying at the Southern Baptist Theological Seminary in Louisville, Kentucky. Southern Seminary was also where Dever's lifelong friendship began with his classmate R. Albert Mohler Jr., as they exchanged books and bonded over what Mohler called "a shared fanaticism" for Calvinism, evangelicalism, Baptist polity, and the quest for what it meant to be an evangelical Southern Baptist. "Carl Henry was always looking for younger leaders, particularly younger men who he thought would be the vanguard of the new evangelical leadership," Mohler later recounted. "I think he kind of saw both of us as that and gave us an incredible amount of attention."[1]

---

1   R. Albert Mohler Jr., interview with the author, March 27, 2023, Washington, DC.

Having finished his doctorate in ecclesiastical history on the Puritan Richard Sibbes at the University of Cambridge the year before, Dever had stayed at Cambridge to teach while continuing to serve as associate pastor at Eden Baptist Church. Henry, meanwhile, kept Dever apprised of events at Capitol Hill Metropolitan Baptist Church and offered choice advice regarding Dever's future. "You are one of the bright spots in the future of Southern Baptists," Henry wrote in 1988.[2] "Your big decision, post-Cambridge," he wrote in 1992, "it seems to me is between academics and pastoring."[3]

Writing in January of 1993, however, Henry asked Dever to consider the now vacant pulpit of Capitol Hill Metropolitan. "The church . . . urgently needs a pastor with preaching ability, intelligence and passion, both for the lost and for integrity," Henry wrote. "If there's the slightest interest (you won't play with their need I know) write to Mr. Paul Huber / Mr. Herb Carlson at the church address."[4]

Dever, who had been preparing to teach, was intrigued by Henry's suggestion. Since college he had considered planting himself in a strategic city. "[The apostle] Paul always strategized about trying to choose crossroads cities," Dever recounted in 1993. "My wife and I had talked and prayed, even before we were married, in college about where would be a strategic place for the gospel in America. And we thought Washington." As his model, Dever considered the example of three preachers—Richard Sibbes, Charles Simeon, and John Stott—each of whom planted themselves at a strategic crossroads for a lifelong ministry of preaching and raising up leaders. Could Washington be that kind of city?[5]

---

2 Carl Henry to Mark Dever, March 15, 1988, Dever personal collection.

3 Carl Henry to Mark Dever, May 14, 1992, Dever personal collection.

4 Carl Henry to Mark Dever, January 1993, Dever personal collection.

5 Mark Dever Pastoral Candidate Interview, November 29, 1993, CD-ROM, Capitol Hill Baptist Church Archives, Washington, DC (hereafter, CHBC Archives). As Dever explained in a letter to Schmucker, "My wife and I had always considered Washington a strategic place for the gospel, but were fairly certain that I should be teaching." Mark Dever to Matt Schmucker, February 3, 1994, box 12, folder 9, CHBC Archives.

Mark Dever's Pastoral Candidacy

Writing to the pulpit committee in February 1993, Dever expressed a willingness to preach in July while in the United States to teach a class at Beeson Divinity School in Birmingham, Alabama. He noted in his letter that he was committed to Eden Baptist Church for another year and a half. He said that he would understand if "this unavailability would remove me from consideration for the position."[6] On the contrary, the newly formed pulpit committee assured Dever that his letter and resume had elicited significant interest. "Obviously we place considerable stock in Carl Henry's opinions," they wrote on March 30, 1993.[7] As one member later recounted, "Carl Henry was the theological mind of Capitol Hill Baptist Church. And if Carl Henry said, 'This is the guy, and I vouch for him,' no one was going to gainsay Carl Henry."[8] The date was set. Dever would preach on July 25, 1993.

Meanwhile, another development was underway. At 6:00 a.m. on February 20, 1993, Dever's home phone in Cambridge rang. It was Mohler, calling at 1:00 a.m. from Atlanta to let Dever know that Mohler was being nominated as the next president of the Southern Baptist Theological Seminary. Dever was stunned. This changed everything. After a few moments of silence, Mohler pressed, "Mark, are you still there? What do you think?"[9]

Flying to Washington to preach on July 25, 1993, Dever now also planned to visit Louisville where Mohler had an offer letter ready for Dever to sign to teach at Southern Seminary. Wearing khaki pants, Top-Siders, and a green and blue plaid shirt, he arrived in Washington on Saturday, July 24, 1993, as the perfect picture of a fast-talking, fast-walking academic. After preaching on Sunday and meeting with the

6 Mark Dever to Matt Schmucker, February 3, 1994, CHBC Archives.
7 Bob Anderson to Mark Dever, March 30, 1993, Dever personal collection.
8 Ethan Reedy, interview with the author, March 23, 2023, Washington, DC.
9 Mohler, interview. Cf. Mary K. Mohler, "Recovering Faithfulness: A Family Perspective," *Southern Seminary Magazine*, Spring 2023, 28; Gayle White, "Georgian Tapped by a Search Panel to lead Southern Baptist Seminary," *Atlanta Constitution*, 23 February 23, 1993, 8D.

pulpit committee for further discussion, Dever and Schmucker stayed up late into the night talking about the church's needs and Dever's desires. Dever laid out three options and asked Schmucker for advice. He could stay at Cambridge where he was happy teaching and seeing good fruit from his ministry to students. He could accept Mohler's offer to teach and help reform Southern Seminary. Or he could come to Washington. "Do you really think Capitol Hill is one of the options?" Schmucker asked incredulously. Dever affirmed that it was. "About mid-night," Schmucker later wrote to Dever, "you had me convinced that you should go to Southern." But as Schmucker shared about the history of the church, what had happened with Harry Kilbride, and their present needs, something in Dever began to soften.[10]

The next morning, Schmucker gave Dever a ride to Reagan National Airport. As they drove past the US Capitol building on I–395, Dever suddenly announced, "I think the Lord has moved my heart here." "I almost drove off the side of the road," Schmucker later recalled laughing.[11] What had changed? Dever gave the answer a few months later at his Q&A session with Capitol Hill Metropolitan's members on November 29, 1993. During his quiet time on Monday the Lord turned his heart towards the congregation.[12] In subsequent years Dever would refer to that moment as one of only a few times in his life when he felt the Lord subjectively but unmistakably telling him to do something.[13] "I have had much time to pray and reflect," Dever wrote to the pulpit committee the next day. "I feel a continued, not diminished, excitement about the possibilities for ministry there."[14]

To give the pulpit committee a taste of his philosophy of ministry, Dever sent them a copy of a letter he had written two years earlier laying out what would eventually become known as the "nine marks"—that

10 Matt Schmucker to Mark Dever, September 17, 1993, box 12, folder 10, CHBC Archives.
11 Matt Schmucker, interview with the author, March 13, 2023, part 1 of 2.
12 Mark Dever Pastoral Candidate Interview November 29, 1993, CHBC Archives.
13 Mark Dever, interview with the author, July 7, 2023, Washington, DC.
14 Mark Dever to Pulpit Committee, July 27, 1993, box 12, folder 10, CHBC Archives.

is, nine characteristics that made them distinct as a church, which they should also be looking for in a pastor.[15] "I point these out after much thought and prayer, because, unfortunately, they are rarely prized among those who profess themselves called to be pastors and shepherds today," Dever wrote. The nine marks included:

1. A Commitment to Expositional Preaching
2. A Sound Theological System (i.e., reformed theology)
3. A Biblical Understanding of the Gospel
4. A Biblical Understanding of Conversion
5. A Biblical Understanding of Evangelism
6. A Biblical Understanding of Church Membership
7. A Plurality of Elders
8. Biblical Church Discipline
9. Promotion of Christian Discipleship and Growth

The letter came to summarize Dever's understanding of what was wrong with contemporary evangelical churches, and how they could be restored to health.[16]

The next few days at Southern Seminary were exciting and tense. "We were brothers who had a lot to talk about," Mohler recalled. He had the offer letter ready for Dever to sign, but Dever was not ready. After discussing it for a few days, Mohler leaned over and said to Dever, "I don't think you're going to take this job. You're going to go pastor that church in DC, aren't you?" Dever had to choose.[17]

As Dever continued to wrestle with how to respond to the offer to teach at Southern Seminary, the pulpit committee began investigating Dever's references in earnest. Determined not to repeat the mistake

---

15 For the original letter, see Mark Dever to New Meadows Baptist Church, October 30, 1991, MS 269, box 1, folder 16, CHBC Archives. The letter is reprinted as appendix 3 in Mark Dever, *Nine Marks of a Healthy Church*, 4th ed. (Wheaton, IL: Crossway, 2021), 283–90.

16 Mark Dever to Matt Schmucker, July 27, 1993, box 12, folder 10, CHBC Archives.

17 Mohler, interview.

they had made with Kilbride, the pulpit committee was nothing if not exhaustive. Dever provided sixteen references, including Timothy George, Don Carson, and Roger Nicole.[18]

Above all, Dever's references commended him as a disciple maker and evangelist. Carson commended Dever's "gift of friendship" and "fearless evangelism" but noted that his preaching had room to grow. "He is a good and growing preacher," he wrote, "though not in this area utterly outstanding." Carson continued, "If you're looking for a 'glitzy' person, Mark is not your man. If you are looking for a pastor with traditional biblical virtues, but certainly cast in contemporary mold, go no further." "If I had to emphasize one gift above others," Carson went on, "it is his continuing ability to challenge others, in the context of genuine friendship."[19] In a word, Dever was a "man for the long-haul—not flashy."[20]

Others, such as Roger Nicole, commended Dever's character but did not conceal their belief that he was destined for the professorship—not the pastorate.[21] One exception in this regard was Timothy George. As Dever's mentor at Southern Seminary, George commended Dever's academic credentials and love for students but explained that he saw Dever first and foremost as a pastor.[22] While even some of Dever's recommenders questioned whether his pulpit gifts were sufficiently strong to hold an urban pulpit, George remained insistent: "I can't think of a better person to assume the challenge that you've described than Mark Dever."[23]

As the official candidate of the pulpit committee, Dever flew to Washington in November to preach, to meet with the committee, and

---

18 Mark Dever to Pulpit Committee, n.d, box 12, folder 9, CHBC Archives.
19 Don Carson to Bruce Fleming, September 29, 1993, box 12, folder 9, CHBC Archives.
20 Handwritten Notes from Telephone Call with Don Carson, September 14, 1993, box 12, folder 9, CHBC Archives.
21 Roger Nicole, Reference Questionnaire, box 12, folder 9, CHBC Archives.
22 Timothy George to Matthew Schmucker, September 27, 1993, box 12, folder 9, CHBC Archives.
23 Transcribed Notes from Phone Interviews, September 14, 1993, box 12, folder 9, CHBC Archives.

to conduct a church-wide Q&A.[24] Asked about the kind of ministry he hoped to have on Capitol Hill, he gave an answer that has become a staple of his ministry: preach, pray, love, and stay. "Preaching," Dever explained, "I really do think that's central to the pastoral ministry. A lot of churches in America don't think that. I think they're wrong." Prayer, Dever continued, means "realizing that everything we do is dependent upon God." Love means "trying to, slowly but surely, build good relationships with people individually. Trying to encourage them to grow as Christians, trying to befriend non-Christians as you have the opportunity, and try to tell them the gospel faithfully and pray that they come to know the Lord." And finally, he discussed the patience needed to stay: "I wouldn't want to necessarily see something happen quickly. I think, often, things that happen quickly don't last very well."[25]

To those looking for a quick fix, Dever offered no promises as to the future of Capitol Hill Metropolitan Baptist Church. Instead, he encouraged the church to trust God's ordinary means of grace for whatever results he saw fit to sovereignly bestow. "God's kingdom could get on without this church," he told them. "It wouldn't be the end of the world without this local church. But no, I think if the Lord wants a people here, he'll provide. And I don't think I would lose too much sleep over that."[26]

On December 8, 1993, in agreement with the recommendations of the pulpit committee and the board of deacons, the church voted sixty-nine to three (with one abstention) to extend a call to Dever.[27]

While encouraged by the vote, Dever had previously committed to take a week to pray before giving the church his final decision. As he had told the church a few weeks earlier, accepting the call was no light

---

24 Pulpit Committee Minutes, October 3, 1993, MS 276, box 1, folder 16, CHBC Archives.
25 Mark Dever, Pastoral Candidate Interview, November 29, 1993, CHBC Archives.
26 Mark Dever, Pastoral Candidate Interview, November 29, 1993, CHBC Archives.
27 Pulpit Committee Minutes, December 2, 1993, MS 275, box 1, folder 16; "Mark Dever Accepts Call to CHMBC," *Capitol Hill Metropolitan Messenger*, December 19, 1993, MS 1785, p. 1, box 8b, folder 24; R. V. Anderson to Mark Dever, December 9, 1993, box 12, folder 9, CHBC Archives.

matter. "As Connie and I've prayed about it, if you do indeed think the Lord is calling us here, our intention is to be here a long, long time." Capitol Hill Metropolitan was not a steppingstone toward a more attractive ministry. "Our assumption is we should come here and just buy cemetery plots. This is what we should do with our lives."[28] After a week of prayer, he sent a handwritten letter on December 15, 1993, to Matt Schmucker, which Schmucker typed up to give to the church. Dever told them,

> The notification last week that the church there thought it was the mind of the Spirit that I should come and serve as your pastor was the final confirmation I desired. Thinking it wise to pray knowing the church's mind, I've waited a further week. This has been out of no uncertainty on my part, but simply in a desire to hear any correcting word the Lord may have, should I be moving in the wrong direction. But in prayer over the last week, I have known only further confirmation. It is therefore with a mixture of amazement at God's providence, a true sense of awe at the responsibility I am accepting under God, and a great sense of joy at the prospect of labouring with you, that I accept the call to Capitol Hill Metropolitan Baptist Church.[29]

The decision was made. Mark Dever was moving to Washington.

Cleaning the Aquarium

As Dever settled in as pastor in mid-August 1994, he sought first to take control of the services and membership. He engaged in "cleaning the aquarium," as he later put it, installing a filter (membership) and introducing good food (preaching). One member who was serving as a

28 Mark Dever, Pastoral Candidate Interview, November 29, 1993, CHBC Archives.
29 "Dr. Mark Dever's Letter of Acceptance," *Capitol Hill Metropolitan Messenger*, December 19, 1993, MS 1785, box 8b, folder 24, CHBC Archives. Cf. Letters, Minutes, and Financial Report, July 22, 1993, MS 328, box 1, folder 17, CHBC Archives. For the original letter, see box 12, folder 9, CHBC Archives.

deacon at the time recalled that Dever never seemed in a hurry. "Mark really took his time to make sure the church was with him. As he was teaching these new things, and trying to encourage us in a particular direction, it never felt rushed."[30] On December 7, 1994, the church voted to drop "Metropolitan"—which had developed different connotations by the 1990s—so as to simply be known as Capitol Hill Baptist Church.[31]

Figure 13.1. Pictured (left to right) at Mark Dever's installation service on September 25, 1994, are Roger Nicole, R. Albert Mohler Jr., Timothy George, and Harold J. Purdy (Mark Dever's boyhood pastor). Carl F. H. Henry can be seen on the left just over Nicole's shoulder.

"The Spirit is blessing Mark's preaching," Carl Henry wrote to a friend at the church on January 21, 1995. "So I hear from every source—and new spiritual opportunities will soon be evident."[32] What neither Henry nor Dever foresaw, however, was that his first challenge was just around the corner.

30 Reedy, interview.
31 *Messenger*, January 29, 1995, 1, box 18, folder 15, CHBC Archives.
32 Farewell Service Bulletin for Henrys, October 4, 1992, MS 1855, box 11, folder 1, CHBC Archives.

Figure 13.2. Mark Dever, early in his ministry at CHBC, pictured on his balcony with the Capitol in the background.

When Dever arrived, church membership consisted of a massive rolodex that sat in the church office. The church secretary maintained the list that amounted to around 483 namcs.[33] Of these, only 199 were considered "active members."[34] For Dever, that was a problem.

Dever was not simply aiming to clean the rolls. He was concerned about the hundreds of members whom no one had seen in decades. Soon after arriving he began conducting what he privately referred to as "reverse-membership interviews" with current members. He met with them and asked them about their testimony, their experience at the church, and their understanding of the gospel. It was a form of pastoral visitation and soul care for those God had called him to shepherd.

33 Capitol Hill Metropolitan Baptist Church, Membership Report, February 1995.
34 Memorandum, "Members: Where Are They Now? As of January 17, 1999," box 16, folder 14, CHBC Archives.

As he met with regularly attending members, Jeannette Devlin and Maxine Zopf began working tirelessly to locate and establish contact with nonattending members. They mailed letters along with the church's statement of faith and church covenant for each member. They were asked to either sign the documents or resign their membership. Otherwise, they would be removed from the membership roll.[35]

Dozens replied, notifying Capitol Hill Baptist of having joined another church and requesting to resign. Others did not appreciate being contacted and simply wished to be dropped from membership. Many sent no response.

Gradually some progress was made. Devlin and Zopf discovered that some members on file had died long before, such as Nora Geddings who was born in 1892![36] Others had simply never formally severed ties. In total, 227 regularly attending members signed the statement of faith and church covenant. A handful of others signed the documents but could not attend regularly for various reasons. A few others attended regularly but refused to sign. But 256 members gave no response or could not be located.

Throughout the process of revising the membership, Dever had been steadily teaching the church about what membership meant. At Schmucker's suggestion, Dever published a series of nine articles in the church newsletter called "Nine Marks of the Healthy Church" between May 7, 1995, and May 5, 1996. These articles, which provided the basis for his subsequent book *Nine Marks of a Healthy Church*[37] allowed him to speak pastorally into the present church transitions. "It should mean something to be a member of the church," Dever wrote on April 7, 1996. "Church discipline is one of the things which gives meaning to being a member of the church."[38]

---

35 Schmucker, interview, part 2, March 13, 2023.

36 Covenants Returned, April 16, 1996, box 12, folder 6; Members Removed since February 1996, box 12, folder 6, CHBC Archives. Cf. Matt Schmucker, "Cleaning Up the Rolls," *9Marks*, February 26, 2010, https://www.9marks.org/.

37 Mark Dever, *Nine Marks of a Healthy Church* (Wheaton, IL: Crossway, 2000).

38 Mark Dever, "A Biblical Understanding of Church Discipline," *Messenger*, April 7, 1996, 1, 4.

At a church business meeting on May 12, 1996, Dever brought the following motion, "It is recommended that the following members be dropped from CHBC rolls because (a) they have not responded to the letter requesting a signed covenant; (b) the church has been unable to locate a current address."[39] The list included Bob and Barbara Sorrels. It also included Bill's wife.

By motion, the wording of the membership report was amended to "256 members dropped because they were inactive and who did not sign the church covenant."[40] When someone asked, "Can't we do this all as one motion?" Dever replied, "No. We took them all in individually and we'll see them all out individually."[41]

When the first name was read—a young man who had grown up in the church with his twin brother—one older member raised her hand and said, "But we know where those boys are!" To which, Bruce Keisling, the chair of the meeting, responded adroitly, "The problem isn't that we don't know where they are but that they don't seem to know where we are."[42]

What followed was 256 motions, 256 seconds, 256 requests for questions, and 256 votes. "It would be a kind of water torture," Dever later recounted. "We would all be reminded of the significance of church membership."[43]

At the close of 1996, Dever presented his annual report to the church. Church membership was down to 229, its lowest number since 1892![44] Nevertheless, Dever was not discouraged. He highlighted the thirteen baptisms they had witnessed, the readoption of the church covenant in February, and the multiple "Explaining Christianity" classes through which people were being converted. The next step, he explained, would

---

39 Covenants Returned, April 16, 1996, box 12, folder 6, CHBC Archives.
40 Capitol Hill Baptist Church Business Meeting, July 14, 1996, Dever personal collection.
41 Capitol Hill Baptist Church Business Meeting, May 12, 1996, Dever personal collection.
42 Mark Dever, "Why We Disciplined Half Our Church," *Christianity Today*, October 1, 2000, https://www.christianitytoday.com/.
43 Mark Dever, "Why We Disciplined Half Our Church."
44 Capitol Hill Baptist Church Report for month of August, 1996, Dever personal collection.

be passing a new church constitution, which would soon be brought to the church for a vote.[45]

Revising the Constitution and Recognizing Elders

For over a year, the rough draft for a new church constitution had been working its way through committees. After an initial draft started by Dever and Schmucker in 1995, a constitution subcommittee composed of Pete Rathbun, Ethan Reedy, Eric Pelletier, and Bruce Keisling spent over half a year on it until they could unanimously affirm it. On April 23, 1997, Dever sent the subcommittee's completed draft constitution to the deacons for discussion and approval before a congregational vote.

The most significant change proposed in the new constitution was the recognition of a plurality of elders. From the church's organization in 1878 until 1998, the church had always operated with a single pastor and a plurality of deacons. Dever, however, was convinced from Scripture and sought to convince the church that the Bible called for a plurality of elders to oversee the church's teaching ministry, membership, and discipline.[46] "He started preaching and teaching on elders and meaningful membership," Schmucker recalled. "It felt like almost immediately, whenever he came across it, he would camp on it."[47]

Once the language of the constitution was largely settled, the deacons adopted a five-month process to conclude with a congregational vote in May 1998. By that point, the church had hosted half-a-dozen meetings for various groups to ask questions and discuss the changes to the constitution. On May 17, 1998, the congregation voted overwhelmingly to approve the new constitution.[48] Only one member voted no.

The entire process of devising and passing the constitution took over a year and ten months.[49] One neighbor on Capitol Hill even joked that

45 Capitol Hill Baptist Church Business Meeting, September 8, 1996, Dever personal collection.
46 Mark Dever to Board of Deacons, November 20, 1997, box 16, folder 14, CHBC Archives.
47 Schmucker, interview, part 2, March 13, 2023.
48 Capitol Hill Baptist Church Members' Meeting, May 17, 1998, Dever personal collection.
49 Capitol Hill Baptist Church Special Business Meeting, April 5, 1998, Dever personal collection.

the US Constitution was written faster than CHBC's![50] But Dever was not in a hurry.

The transition plan called on the pastor to nominate a slate of elders to the congregation in August 1998, to be voted on at the members' meeting in October.[51] Dever requested that each member of the church send a signed list of those men in the church they considered meeting the biblical qualifications of an elder.[52]

After prayer and consideration of the congregation's suggestions, Dever nominated five men to the congregation to serve as elders: Chris Bruce, Andy Johnson, Aaron Menikoff, Eric Pelletier, and Matt Schmucker.[53] "These men have already shown great commitment to God's work here in this place, and in the lives of many of our number," Dever wrote. "If recognized by the congregation, these five men will join me in bringing prayerful, spiritual oversight to God's work here."[54]

Many in the church were surprised by the relative youth and apparent inexperience of some of the nominees. In particular, several members were upset that three of the most respected men in the church had not been nominated. But as one member recounted when he asked Dever about the three, Dever explained his reasoning straightforwardly. One of these men was disagreeable, another believed in women's ordination, and a third would not commit to being at the church other than Sunday mornings.[55]

At the special members' meeting on October 11, 1998, the church met to vote on the nominees. After reading 1 Timothy 3:1–7 and Titus 1:5–9, Dever gave a summary of the life and ministry of each elder.[56] In

50 Schmucker, interview, part 2, March 13, 2023.
51 "Proposed Transition Plan (28 April 1998)," box 16, folder 14. CHBC Archives, Cf. Capitol Hill Baptist Church Members' Meeting, May 17, 1998, 6.
52 Mark Dever to the Congregation, May 19, 1998, box 16, folder 14, CHBC Archives.
53 Mark Dever to the Congregation, August 16, 1998, box 16, folder 14, CHBC Archives.
54 Mark Dever to the Congregation, August 16, 1998.
55 Reedy, interview.
56 Capitol Hill Baptist Church Members' Meeting Minutes, October 11, 1998, Dever personal collection.

the discussion that followed, several people spoke up in favor of each individual, commending evidence of grace in their lives.

Others offered criticism. One member, spoke out against each nominee. Another expressed a "high discomfort level with the inexperience and youth of this slate of nominees." Another frustrated member was upset "with all individuals being nominated by Mark alone" as the "sole elder" and thought the slate was fraught with "biases." He feared that each man was too similar to Dever.[57] Clearly the meeting was not headed in a positive direction.

Before going to a vote, Dever offered a final word in favor of the nominees. He explained that it was his responsibility as pastor to bring these nominees to the church. He said that he had been honest and up front with the church and conducted himself according to Scripture. Voting for these five men as elders was the best way to continue the good work going on at the church.[58]

While the ballots were being counted, Brad Byrd urged the church to pray that they would be united and that the new elders would be strengthened to lead. No one was ready for what happened next.

When the results were read, none of the nominees had reached the constitutional 75 percent threshold. Pelletier had come closest with 73 percent, followed by Schmucker with 72 percent, Aaron Menikoff with 68 percent, Andy Johnson with 67 percent, and Bruce with 65 percent.[59] The meeting closed as the congregation sang the hymn "Only Trust Him." "It was discouraging," Schmucker recalled, "because I saw Mark maybe for the first time discouraged."[60]

For a whole month, Dever thought, prayed, and sought counsel before deciding to put forward the same five names again. In a lengthy letter to the congregation following the October members' meeting, he explained his reasoning. While acknowledging that he could be in the

---

57 Capitol Hill Baptist Church Members' Meeting Minutes, October 11, 1998, Dever personal collection.
58 Capitol Hill Baptist Church Members' Meeting Minutes, October 11, 1998, Dever personal collection.
59 Capitol Hill Baptist Church Members' Meeting Minutes, October 11, 1998, Dever personal collection.
60 Schmucker, interview, part 2, March 13, 2023.

wrong ("I certainly do not believe in pastoral inerrancy!"), he also raised the possibility that the congregation had been wrong ("I certainly do not believe in the inerrancy of congregational votes"). He was nominating the same five men, because "after continuing to pray about it, I cannot see any others to nominate at this time," Dever explained.

> My understanding of God's leading has not changed. God has led me again to the same people. . . . This hasn't been an easy process for me. . . . You would be well within your rights to find another pastor [who could] find those nominees who would get a 75% vote from you. . . . In coming to this church, I knew that I would be coming in to a trust-poor area. . . . I have certainly been frustrated by not being more trusted.

Dever concluded, "I do see this as a clear referendum on the direction of this church, even more clear than when you called me to be your pastor. . . . It is therefore, whether it is recognized as such by those voting, a confidence vote on my pastorate."[61]

The mood was tense at the next members' meeting on November 15, 1998. "In my mind," one deacon recounted, "this was undoubtedly the most controversial moment in the early days of Mark Dever."[62] Dever explained that he would be "renominating [the] same five men." But "this [was] not done lightly." As before, secret ballots were distributed. Aaron Menikoff recalled having no expectation that they would pass.[63]

Nevertheless, this time each nominee received the 75 percent threshold.[64] After reading the results to the congregation, Dever thanked them for their prayer and support during the process, and he asked those who had voted against the candidates to be in prayer for the elders.[65]

61 Mark Dever to the Congregation, October 29, 1998, box 16, folder 14, CHBC Archives.
62 Reedy, interview.
63 Aaron Menikoff, interview with author, March 30, 2023, Washington, DC.
64 Handwritten note, November 15, 1998, Dever personal collection.
65 Capitol Hill Baptist Church Members' Meeting Minutes, November 15, 1998, Dever personal collection.

"That was *the* turning point," Schmucker recalled. With a constitution in place, a church covenant being used, and meaningful membership being practiced, "that's when we become a real church."[66]

———

As noted above, when Dever was asked about his philosophy of ministry in November 1993, he discussed four aspects of pastoral ministry that he aimed to focus on: preaching, prayer, loving relationships, and the patience to stay and persevere.[67] Patience requires knowing what fights are worth fighting. Fred Catherwood had warned Dever, "You may have your name on the letterhead. But for the first five years, it's the last man's church."[68] True to Catherwood's word, it took nearly five years to revise the church membership, readopt the statement of faith and the church covenant, and introduce elders.

Dever did not attempt to change everything overnight. He was committed to the long haul, so many aspects of the church's ministry continued untouched. Elders were another matter. Elder leadership was taught by Scripture, and once adopted as the form of leadership in the church constitution, it was Dever's responsibility to put forward men he believed were qualified by Scripture.

It's easy to be reckless and blow up a church. It's also easy to be cowardly and refuse to challenge a church. Reformation requires the patience that proceeds from courage and wisdom. Dever stood by his convictions under pressure. In the process, the congregation chose to trust their pastor. Dever knew that he was coming to a "trust-poor" congregation that had been burned before. Still they chose to trust him because they trusted the Lord and believed that the Lord was not finished with Capitol Hill Baptist.

66 Schmucker, interview, part 2, March 13, 2023.
67 Mark Dever, Pastoral Candidate Interview, November 29, 1993, CHBC Archives.
68 Schmucker, interview, part 2, March 13, 2023.

14

"Doing Nothing and Church Planting"

2001–Present

THE GOSPEL COALITION (TGC) blog released a video on September 28, 2010, that evoked a firestorm across Reformed evangelicalism. Within hours, the comments—numbering in the hundreds—became so vicious that TGC quickly pulled the video from its site. What was the content? A twelve-minute discussion featuring Mark Dever, Mark Driscoll, and James MacDonald on the topic of multisite churches. At the time, Mark Driscoll pastored Mars Hill Church in Seattle, which boasted ten locations and twenty-four services. James MacDonald pastored Harvest Bible Chapel in Chicago with thirteen services and more than ten thousand in weekly attendance at six different locations where sermons would be broadcast in from the mother-site. Both defended the emerging practice of multisite churches as a legitimate church-planting strategy. Then there was Mark Dever, a longtime critic of the multisite model, whose congregation at Capitol Hill Baptist Church (CHBC) in Washington, DC, had just recently reached nine hundred in regular Sunday morning attendance.

"But you certainly could fill more if you had them with your amazing gift of preaching," pressed MacDonald. Why wouldn't Dever leverage his preaching abilities, embrace a multisite model, and grow as large as possible for the sake of the spread of the gospel?

The disagreement driving the debate was simply this: If planting churches is the goal and raising up pastors is a necessary part of that work, what sort of church best advances the work of raising up pastors? For Driscoll and MacDonald, having personality and influence presented an opportunity to leverage. "If I can in my lifetime cash that influence," said MacDonald, "I believe that people will go and hear me in that region where I've built up hopefully a reputation for being a trustworthy source of spiritual nourishment." For Dever, platform and personality were potential liabilities, risking the long-term health of the church for short-term gains.

"Are you concerned that it builds people too much into you particularly?" Dever asked Driscoll.

"No, actually it does the opposite," Driscoll replied. "They're more addicted to you. They have to come talk to you, shake your hand, be in the same room with you, get around the '*shekinah* glory.' And for me, I'm not even there."

Concerned that streaming his sermons to twenty-four services each week created an unhealthy dependence on Driscoll, Dever continued to probe,

> One of my concerns is that I want to see young men raised up to preach, which I know you both want to see as well and we don't have a debate there, but I would think that particularly for somebody who has pronounced gifts in preaching, that's going to mean sometimes me putting other people up there instead of me doing it. And I would think a church plant in a sort of multisite situation would be a perfect place to do that.[1]

---

1   Collin Hansen, "Multiple Sites: Yea or Nay?" The Gospel Coalition, September 28, 2010, http://thegospelcoalition.org/. Although the video has since been removed from the TGC website, it is available at "The Gospel Coalition—Multi Sites Yay or Nay—Dever Driscoll and MacDonald," Vimeo video, August 31, 2018, accessed April 18, 2024, https://vimeo.com/.

In other words, putting other men in the pulpit—teaching the congregation to give them as much attention as they give the senior pastor—is part of how a church helps its members be addicted to God's word, not simply the personality of the preacher. As Dever would often tell pastors attending a 9Marks weekender in Washington, DC, "If you're gifted, this may mean that you need to sit on your personality—because it will make it harder for others to be raised up as preachers—so that the congregation doesn't get addicted to a particular style of presenting the Bible."[2]

Behind this exchange on multisite churches—which went viral in 2010 and resurfaced again in 2021 during the *Christianity Today* podcast *The Rise and Fall of Mars Hill*—were two different philosophies of ministry driving twenty-first-century evangelicalism.[3] One emphasized outputs (sites, services, attenders) as key markers of church health. The other emphasized inputs (preaching, membership, gathering) as protectors of church health. One centered on finding a gifted man, platforming him, and extending his influence as far as possible. The other focused on raising up a plurality of pastors within a church, and many churches within a region, as the best way to preserve the gospel within a church and across a region.

CHBC's commitment to a single site and a single service was not an accidental outgrowth of Mark Dever's personality or the unique context of pastoring in Washington, DC, but the result of costly and deliberate decisions made by the elders during the mid-2000s as the church was noticeably starting to grow. Rather than becoming as large or as influential as possible, CHBC focused on strengthening its culture of discipling, raising up pastors, planting and revitalizing churches, and supporting other churches through the ministries of 9Marks and Together for the Gospel. Matt Schmucker summarized this vision in 2005 as lighting dozens of candles throughout the region rather than building a furnace.

---

2 Mark Dever, "Raising Up Leaders" (sermon, Capitol Hill Baptist Church, Washington, DC, March 20, 2023).

3 "Red Sky at Morning," October 5, 2021, in *Rise and Fall of Mars Hill*, produced by Mike Cosper, *Christianity Today* podcast, https://www.christianitytoday.com/.

"Mark Dever gives us a useful picture of us *not* building one big furnace in the city," Schmucker wrote, "but perhaps many smaller furnaces around the region."[4] For the light of the gospel to continue to shine in Washington, more than a single light on the Hill was needed. This was never more apparent than in the dark days following the 9/11 attacks.

The Light Shining in the Darkness

On Tuesday morning, September 11, 2001, CHBC's pastoral staff members were preparing for a regular staff meeting in Mark Dever's home office when the news broke just before 9:00 a.m. that a plane had struck the World Trade Center in New York City. Then a second plane struck. As the staff stood silently huddled around the television, they felt the floor shake. "It was significant enough, loud enough, palpable enough in feeling that we thought it was the Capitol," Scott Croft later recounted. Looking out the windows, they could see smoke rising from the southwest. The Pentagon had been hit.[5]

Outside, men and women in suits sprinted from Hill offices. They had been told that a plane was headed toward the Capitol. Meanwhile, Secret Service agents mounted machine guns on top of the White House and strapped tear-gas masks to their belts. Everywhere chaos reigned, as the blare of sirens only temporarily drowned out the roar of low-flying fighter jets. A solitary handwritten sign in the window of Sun Trust Bank at Third Street and Pennsylvania Avenue SE captured the mood: "Bank closed due to circumstances."[6]

Gathered in Mark's study, the staff began to pray. Scott Croft recalled, "We all prayed, including for the terrorists, not solely for them, but including

---

4   Matt Schmucker, "Bull Moose Bed & Breakfast," Elders' Meeting Minutes, February 15, 2005 (emphasis in original). All meeting minutes (elders', members', and business meetings) in this chapter are cited from Mark Dever's personal collection.

5   Recounted in Sarah Eekhoff Zylstra, "Remembering 9/11: The Day the Sky Turned Black," The Gospel Coalition podcast, September 8, 2021, https://www.thegospelcoalition.org/.

6   Steve Twomey, "Security Heightened in D.C.; Government Shuts Down, Employees Sent Home," *Washington Post*, September 11, 2001, A2.

them, which I thought was weird at the time. But I've since realized that was just the right thing."[7] In the days and weeks that followed, letters of condolences and prayers overwhelmed the church from around the world. Future senator Josh Hawley who had attended the church the previous summer as an intern, wrote from Stanford, "Doubtless you're inundated with email and other major concerns at this time, but I wanted to let you know that the prayers of Stanford students are with you, your congregation, and those who are suffering in D.C. . . . Let me know if there is anything specific I can do." Philip Jensen wrote from Sydney, Australia, "We are all shocked and horrified by this latest expression of human sinfulness, and concerned for our friends such as yourselves. We hope you are all safe, and that these events provide you opportunities to bring glory to our Lord."

"I have found the news looming large over the city-folks here of the devastation that has taken place there," Conrad Mbewe wrote from Lusaka, Zambia. "In many ways I feel like the comforters of Job who for seven days failed to utter a word because of the sight of Job's suffering." Iain Murray wrote from Edinburgh, "We really saw almost a glimpse of what the future will be for the world. How few seem to have spoken of the resurrection and the judgment."[8]

Bert Daniel was a twenty-six-year-old student at the Southern Baptist Theological Seminary in Louisville, Kentucky. On September 11, 2001, he stood in a crammed dorm room with his fellow seminarians watching television footage of the Twin Towers falling down. As he watched in horror, it dawned on him, "I'm supposed to preach at CHBC this weekend." He immediately called Dever and offered to step aside. "Mark," he insisted, "seriously, I am happy to bow out and for you to preach this Sunday. It will not hurt my feelings." But Dever refused, pointing to God's providence in planning the sermon series Daniel was scheduled to preach.[9]

7 Zylstra, "Remembering 9/11."
8 These letters were reprinted in *Messenger*, September 2001 and October 2001, box 18, folder 21, Capitol Hill Baptist Church Archives (hereafter, CHBC Archives), Washington, DC.
9 Bert Daniel, email message to the author, December 21, 2023.

Months before, Dever assigned twenty-four-year-old Jamie Dunlop, then serving as a pastoral assistant, to come up with the two-week sermon series to be preached September 9 and 16, 2001. Dunlop was to preach the first sermon on September 9, and Bert Daniel the second sermon on the September 16. Dunlop asked Chris Bruce, one of the elders, what would be a good topic, and he suggested the book of Habakkuk. "It's probably one of the most succinct treatments of the problem of evil in the entire Bible," Dunlop recalled. "It's amazing looking back to see how the Lord used me to prepare this church for what was about to happen across the river and in New York City two days later."[10] Dunlop had titled the two-part series through Habakkuk, "When Bad Things Happen."

Dunlop preached the first of the two sermons, titled "Questions," on September 9, 2001. "Where was God when evil of all sorts and shapes and sizes happens in our world?" he asked in his sermon opening. "If God is all powerful and all good, then why does he permit pain and suffering in our world?" Dunlop then turned to Habakkuk, which addresses the issues of evil and suffering. Habakkuk questions God about why he tolerates evil, and God responds by explaining that he will use the Babylonians to punish Judah for its sin (Hab. 1:5–11). Habakkuk is horrified by this answer (Hab. 1:12–17) but ultimately chooses to trust in God's character and promises (Hab. 2:3–4). In the sermon, Dunlop emphasized the importance of trusting God, even in the face of suffering and unanswered questions. He concluded by pointing to the cross of Christ as the ultimate resolution of God's justice and mercy, before ending with a prayer that proved prophetic: "Father, when these things happen to us, when things happen to our congregation that are too difficult to explain, oh God, we pray that we would hang on to your justice, that we would delight in your glory, and that you would cause us to trust."[11]

10 Jamie Dunlop, interview with the author, December 11, 2023.
11 Jamie Dunlop, "Questions" (sermon, Capitol Hill Baptist Church, Washington, DC, September 9, 2001), https://www.capitolhillbaptist.org/sermon/questions/.

The following Sunday, hundreds packed the Capitol Hill congregation's morning service. Before Bert Daniel's sermon, Dever opened the meeting with a brief word about September 11. "Most of us, if we don't know people who were directly affected by the events on Tuesday, know people who do. Some sitting here this morning do." Dever spoke of the government's responsibility to protect American lives and retaliate proportionally but focused his remarks on the uncertainty of life and the certainty of death.[12]

Then, Daniel preached Habakkuk 3:1–19 in a sermon titled "Confidence." After acknowledging the questions and emotions that arose in the aftermath of 9/11, he explained how the Bible continues to speak even when no one else knows what to say. He pointed to how Habakkuk 3 deals explicitly with evil, war, comfort, and deliverance. He insisted that the answers to questions of suffering and evil lie within Scripture and that God will establish justice and offer salvation to those who hope in him. He emphasized the sovereignty of God and the need to trust in his goodness, even in the face of tragedy. Daniel concluded by encouraging believers to hold onto the hope of salvation through Christ and to proclaim this message to a world in need of answers.[13]

The series in Habakkuk was immediately followed by an eight-week series in the Psalms with titles like "The Quest for Peace," "The Quest for Justice," and "The Quest for Security." Finally, in December, Dever preached five studies in Revelation on the topic "What the Future Holds." In God's providence, the previously planned sermon series provided much-needed guidance from God's word. In subsequent years, Dever often pointed to this as an example of how God's sovereignty extends over planning, not just spontaneity. "I don't know why people think that the Holy Spirit only leads at the last moment," he liked to say. "He also leads through planning."[14]

12 Mark Dever, "A Word on September 11, 2001" (Capitol Hill Baptist Church, September 16, 2001), https://www.capitolhillbaptist.org/sermon/a-word-on-september–11–2001/.

13 Bert Daniel, "Confidence" (sermon, Capitol Hill Baptist Church, September 16, 2001), https://www.capitolhillbaptist.org/sermon/confidence/.

14 Mark Dever, interview with the author, December 13, 2023.

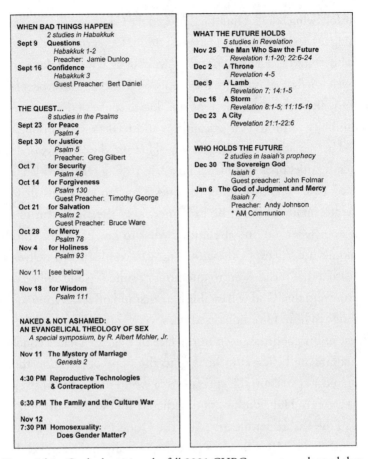

Figure 14.1. Card advertising the fall 2001 CHBC sermons—planned that summer and printed in August—demonstrates how God provided for the church before and after the 9/11 attacks. Series titles included "When Bad Things Happen" and "What the Future Holds."

Most pastors would have insisted on taking the reins and preaching the Sunday following an event like 9/11. But not Mark Dever. Platforming other people, giving them opportunities to preach and lead publicly, taking the spotlight off of himself as the primary preacher was a central aspect of raising up leaders. "Mark is a strong leader," Bert Daniel later recalled. "No one would mistake Mark's leadership for passivity. At the same time, Mark is resolved to not build the church around his personality and to make leadership decisions that will foster the church's maturity and promote the church's flourishing independent of his leadership and long after his departure."[15]

Reflecting over two decades later on the church's willingness to give young men like him opportunities to exercise leadership, Daniel connected the dots between delegating and raising up leaders. He observed,

> Part of Mark's gifting as a discipler is his willingness to take risks on young men, to entrust young men with meaningful ministry opportunities, and then to walk alongside them in those opportunities to provide sincere encouragement and honest critique. Few pastors generously share their pulpit with young men as Mark does[,] and fewer still would have been willing to share their pulpit with a seminary student on the Sunday after 9/11. This humble generosity is one of the reasons Mark has so profoundly impacted so many young pastors.[16]

Trusting God's sovereignty and allowing God's Spirit to work through others is a crucial component of growing a culture of discipling and providing space for other leaders to develop.

The Dilemma of Stewarding Growth

As the nation and the city grappled with responding to the 9/11 attacks, CHBC saw a remarkable surge in spiritual interest. During Dever's first five years at the church, membership had been steady, with only 162 new members joining between 1994 and 1999.[17] After the purge of 256 non-attending members on May 12, 1996, membership was only at 274 by December 1997.[18] By April 1998, Dever estimated that regular attendance at morning services averaged somewhere between 325 and 375.[19]

---

15 Daniel, email message.
16 Daniel, email message.
17 "Summary of Members Joinining CHBC in 1994–1998," box 16, folder 14, CHBC Archives.
18 Capitol Hill Baptist Church Business Meeting, January 11, 1998, 2.
19 "Numerical snapshot of CHBC in April, 1998," box 16, folder 14, CHBC Archives.

But membership in 1999 was still only at 262 members—hardly an extraordinary growth rate in the first five years![20]

In the decade following 9/11, however, subtracting the members who died, resigned, or were excommunicated, CHBC added over 750 members in net growth. In September 2001, CHBC had 329 members.[21] But as figure 14.2 indicates, by 2011 this number had grown to 1095.

As a symbol of the church's growth, the overflow seating in the west hall was opened for the first time on a Sunday in over thirty years. This space had historically been used as the Sunday school auditorium, but the walls separating the sanctuary and west hall could be raised to make more room. In 2001, they were raised for Sunday morning services to accommodate attenders.[22] Elderly members who had witnessed the church decline since the 1960s and were present when the walls were closed looked on in wonder as the walls were once again raised, something they never thought they would live to see.

That fall the church passed its first million-dollar budget. Until 2008, Dever did every membership interview personally. After 2008, there were simply too many new members for him to accomplish this alone, and he reluctantly handed off most of the interviews to other pastoral staff and elders. After years of patient sowing, the church began to enjoy years of reaping. Growth, however, quickly began producing its own challenges.

As the church membership grew and the building began feeling full for the first time in half a century, the elders wrestled with how to respond to the growth. With the current configuration, they had only 700 seats available, not nearly enough for those attending weekly.[23] Architectural drawings contracted by the elders showed possibilities for a sanctuary expansion. But the idea seemed cost prohibitive. A feasibility study showed that expanding the sanctuary to seat 1,600 people would

20 Members' Meeting Minutes, September 26, 1999.
21 Elders' Meeting Minutes, November 18, 2001.
22 Elders' Meeting Minutes, March 13, 2001.
23 Elders' Meeting Minutes, January 29, 2004, 21.

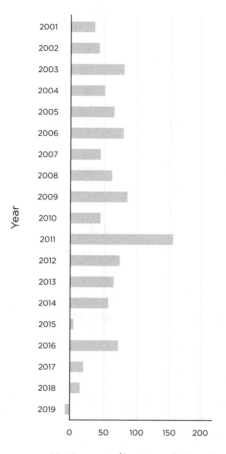

Figure 14.2. CHBC net membership increases and decreases indicates how membership surged in the 2000s, peaking in 2011 when 235 new members joined. Nearby church plants account for lower numbers in 2010 and 2015.

cost $16 million, $7 million of which would go toward constructing underground parking facilities, a project well beyond their current financial means.[24]

More than anything, the elders were feeling the strain of shepherding a growing congregation. In 2004, the church had nine elders overseeing

24 Elders' Meeting Minutes, January 15, 2004, 2.

a congregation of 450.[25] At one point, the elders were tracking nineteen different member care situations that were either possible discipline cases or areas of serious pastoral concern.[26] During 2004, elder meetings were regularly running from 7:00 p.m. until after 1:00 a.m. and occasionally going as late as 2:30 a.m.[27]

Some elders thought that they would be able to raise the needed $16 million in funds to renovate the sanctuary from outside, but others were skeptical. As table 14.1 indicates, the church budget was growing and even outpacing membership growth. But it was not growing enough to fund a massive renovation project. There were other pressing financial needs as well, including renovating staff housing and providing housing for the growing pastoral internship program, which had recently increased to twelve interns annually.[28] In October 2003, Dever shared with the elders that he was "still feeling visionless about the growth of the church."[29] What was the best way forward?

Table 14.1 CHBC membership and budget, 1999–2005

	Membership	Actual revenue	Average giving per member
1999	275	$634,000	$2,305.45
2000	331	$779,000	$2,353.47
2001	348	$900,000	$2,586.21
2002	369	$1,053,000	$2,853.66
2003	448	$1,283,000	$2,863.84
2004	484	$1,573,000	$3,250.00
2005	471	$1,950,000	$4,140.13

25 Church membership passed 400 at the members' meeting on March 16, 2003. Elders' Meeting Minutes, March 13, 2003.

26 Elders' Meeting Minutes, November 16, 2004, 2–3.

27 Michael Lawrence, interview with the author, November 13, 2023, Washington, DC.

28 Members' Meeting Minutes, July 21, 2002, 9.

29 Elders' Meeting Minutes, October 23, 2003, 1.

If the elders of CHBC had listened to church growth consultants, they would have built the church around Mark Dever's personality and preaching abilities, adopted multiple services (and eventually multiple sites), and sought to grow as large as possible, all under the sincere desire for maximal kingdom impact. But would this approach have encouraged the cultivation, formation, and development of pastors and leaders for other churches? Would it have strengthened the gospel witness of other churches in the region? Or would it instead have slowly absorbed them, as transfer growth slowly tapped the strength of the very churches that had helped CHBC get started back in the 1870s? Would it have caused an undue dependence on a single person and a single church in a way inconducive to long-term stability? Would catering toward church growth have caused CHBC to change its message over the years in ways that undermined the church's gospel fidelity?

As the elders were wrestling with these questions, Mark Dever sent around a memo one night entitled "Doing Nothing and Church Planting." The memo, written on October 28, 2003, and sent to the church staff and elders, proposed planting other churches as the solution to the church's building capacity problem. "We should thank God for the growth that He is giving us," Dever wrote. "It is from Him." But Dever had a suggestion for "one thing that we could do" to ensure "years of near-capacity use of this building." The plan? Doing nothing and planting churches. The idea, Dever later recalled, came from Martin Luther's famous reflection on the Reformation in Wittenburg. "I simply taught, preached, and wrote God's Word; otherwise I did nothing," wrote Luther in 1522. "And while I slept, or drank Wittenberg beer with my friends Philip and Amsdorf, the Word so greatly weakened the papacy that no prince or emperor ever inflicted such losses upon it. I did nothing; the Word did everything."[30] By allowing the church to stay at capacity, there would be a consistent pressure to plant churches,

---

30 "The Second Sermon, March 10, 1522, Monday after Invocavit" in Martin Luther, *Luther's Works*, vol. 51, ed. and trans. John W. Doberstein (Philadelphia: Fortress, 1959), 77–78.

with each new plant providing a needed escape valve for members tired of jostling for seats or parking spots. As Dever explained to the elders, "This would have the disadvantage of not following a track to make this church as large as we could, and thereby forfeit opportunities that would come along with that growth." But the long-term fruit would be worth it—that is, the consistent "emphasis this would continue to place on church planting." Dever was committed to God's word doing the work of reforming the church, even if that meant rejecting a path to growing the church as large as possible.[31]

On March 31, 2004, elders Mark Dever, Michael Lawrence, Bill Behrens, Scott Croft, Michael Griffin, Jim Hollenbach, Andy Johnson, Jim Smith, and Steve Boyer piled into the church van at 7:00 a.m. for an hour-long drive to Covenant Life Church in Gaithersburg, Maryland, for an all-day elders retreat to discuss Dever's proposal and the church's growth problems.[32] During Dever's early years on Capitol Hill, he had gotten to know Covenant Life's pastor, C. J. Mahaney. During pivotal moments as CHBC navigated growing pains, Mahaney provided gracious mentorship and friendship, including frequently hosting CHBC's elders meetings.[33]

As they brainstormed options, the elders came up with ten possibilities:

1. Rent a larger space for Sunday mornings;
2. Relocate to the suburbs;
3. Renovate the church for $16 million;
4. Do nothing;
5. Multiple locations (either within the building or at different sites);
6. Multiple services;
7. Video feed;

31 Memorandum by Mark Dever, "Doing Nothing and Church Planting," October 28, 2003; Elders' Meeting Minutes, November 13, 2003, 45.
32 Elders' Meeting Minutes, March 31, 2004, 1.
33 For an example of Mahaney's participation in a CHBC elders' meeting, see Elders' Meeting Minutes, September 15, 2005, 3.

8. Segmented attendance (asking others to pray during service);
9. Church planting;
10. Create a family of congregations.

In light of these options, the elders needed a unified plan. Many in the congregation wanted the church to adopt an ambitious growth plan, following the logic that "the larger it grows, the more people will come."[34] Covenant Life Church offered a compelling example of what a large church could accomplish, including housing a seminary. "You have to remember," Steve Boyer later recalled, "that seeker-sensitive Willow Creek- and Saddleback-type churches were strongly influential in evangelicalism at the time, as they seem to have the special know-how in how to do church growth."[35] The standard script at that time for growing churches was to adopt a second service, start a new campus, and grow as large as possible.

Some of the elders were open to the idea of setting up multiple locations in the church to use as overflow rooms and displaying the service via video. This would allow the church to utilize all its space and increase capacity inexpensively. Other elders had concerns. "The dangers with this option," one noted, "are that it will be close to having multiple congregations and will not allow for the congregation to meet in one place."[36]

For his part, Dever opposed multiple services as a matter of principle. "Two services, to me," he had previously written to the board, "seems almost by principle to be excluded (unless one were developing to be a separate church, and this were a phase of church planting)."[37] Steve Boyer recalled spending an extended amount of time discussing the New Testament word for "church" (Greek, *ekklēsia*). "This one assembly was paramount for how we thought about the biblical structure of the church and how we thought through what to do with the strong

34 Elders' Meeting Minutes, March 31, 2004, 1.
35 Steve and Donna Boyer, email message to the author, November 29, 2023.
36 Elders' Meeting Minutes, March 31, 2004, 2.
37 Dever, "Doing Nothing and Church Planting," 45.

cultural influence of moving to multiple services or separating the church meeting throughout the building."[38]

By the end of the day, God had provided a unified vision for the elders. Jim Hollenbach, chairman of the elder board, remembered that the elders broadly agreed on the importance of one assembly. "We were committed to the principle that a congregation ought to congregate: a single-service in a single location, which excluded the multisite, multi-service option."[39] As the board summed up their conclusion at the end of the day, "Church planting is our number one option of handling growth."[40]

Jamie Dunlop, who began serving as an elder in 2006, recalled Dever envisioning a "donut" around the DC Metro area. "The idea was we have people driving from an hour away, and so let's look for concentrations of people around the DC area and see if we can't find dying Baptist churches who have buildings in the area and try to restart those churches."[41] Since the church had not done this for decades, the elders recognized that revitalizing and planting other churches would go slowly at first, but as they put it, "we will learn and get better at it as time goes on."[42] In the meantime, they would undergo small renovations in the main hall and west hall to expand seating capacity. Instead of a major building renovation, they would focus on church health and strengthening the culture of discipleship while working to raise up leaders and pastors and to send out members to plant churches.

Executing the Plan and Planting Churches

In the summer of 2004, the church began making plans to expand seating in the main hall and west hall.[43] In addition to making the best use of the space already available, CHBC hired three senior pastoral assistants in 2003

38 Steve and Donna Boyer, email message.
39 Jim Hollenbach, interview with the author, November 29, 2023, Washington, DC.
40 Elders' Meeting Minutes, March 31, 2004, 3.
41 Dunlop, interview.
42 Elders' Meeting Minutes, March 31, 2004, 2.
43 Elders' Meeting Minutes, July 8, 2004, 42.

and 2004 to eventually be recognized as elders and then be sent out to pastor area churches: Mike McKinley, John Folmar, and Thabiti Anyabwile.

All three men had come to Washington, DC, before adopting ministry aspirations. Mike McKinley met Mark Dever and began attending CHBC after Dever spoke at an InterVarsity Fellowship event at George Washington University. John Folmar had moved to DC after law school to work as legislative counsel for a senator. While jogging one day in August 1995, Folmar passed CHBC's building and decided to visit. After introducing himself to Dever at the end of a service, they began meeting regularly to study the Gospel of Mark. On December 17, 1995, Folmar returned home from church, read John 3, and placed his trust in Christ for salvation.[44] Thabiti Anyabwile moved to DC with his wife Kristie and their two daughters to work in public policy and to grow spiritually as members of CHBC. All three were part of CHBC's deliberate effort to raise up pastors and to plant and revitalize area churches.

Not everyone thought the idea would work. On one of his first days on staff in 2004, McKinley met John Piper, pastor of Bethlehem Baptist Church in Minneapolis, Minnesota. Dever introduced them and explained the plan for McKinley to plant a church thirty to forty minutes away and siphon off CHBC members who were driving a long distance. "It'll never work," was Piper's reply. "We've tried that. People will go for a year or two, but eventually everyone will just decide they can just drive an extra half-hour to hear you preach. And so no one's going to go listen to him preach when they can just keep driving and hear you preach." Dever disagreed. Thus, McKinley was to be the trial balloon—the guinea pig—of CHBC's church planting efforts.[45]

Soon after, McKinley began talking with a church called Guilford Fellowship that was eager to find a new pastor quickly.[46] Guilford was a

44 John Folmar, membership interview, January 20, 1996, CHBC Archives.

45 Mike McKinley, interview with the author, December 6, 2023, Leesburg, VA.

46 Mike McKinley, *Church Planting Is for Wimps: How God Uses Messed-Up People to Plant Ordinary Churches That Do Extraordinary Things* (Wheaton, IL: Crossway, 2010), 40–41.

Southern Baptist church in Sterling, Virginia, with about sixteen people in attendance and a small chapel that seated one hundred. At first the opportunity seemed unappealing to McKinley, who wanted more time to build a core team before being sent out. Slowly, however, his heart turned. As he explained to CHBC's elders on March 3, 2005, other planters he had spoken with had described the challenges in finding a suitable church building, but Guilford already had one. Moreover, revitalizing an existing church rather than planting "helps to provide a shepherd for the sheep and works to convert a potentially bad witness for Christ into a good one."[47] McKinley was ready to move forward with a CHBC church plant into Guilford in 2005.[48]

On June 1, 2005, Mike McKinley was installed as pastor of Guilford Fellowship. He was joined by eight members from CHBC, which would continue to pay his salary for two years in the hope that the church would soon be self-sustaining. Between 2005 and 2008, Guilford cleaned its membership rolls, adopted a statement of faith and constitution, grew to seventy-five members, and affirmed two additional men to serve the church as elders.[49]

As Guilford grew in health, it began its own church planting. The church worked with Fredy Hernandez to plant a Spanish-speaking congregation, Iglesia Bautista Hispana Guilford, in June 2006. In 2012, Guilford planted Winchester Baptist Church. And in 2013, Guilford—which had already outgrown its building and was meeting in a school—merged with Sterling Park Baptist Church, reclaiming another gospel witness in the greater-DC region.

Other church plants and revitalizations from CHBC soon followed, largely conforming to the pattern set by McKinley and Guilford as CHBC hired staff members and gave them time to develop a shepherding and preaching ministry in the church—especially through Dever sharing

---

47 Elders' Meeting Minutes, March 3, 2005, 5.
48 Elders' Meeting Minutes, March 3, 2005, 45. Cf. McKinley, *Church Planting Is for Wimps*, 44–46.
49 McKinley, *Church Planting*, 68–69.

the pulpit. As of 2023, over four hundred different men have filled the pulpit of CHBC on either a Sunday morning or evening since 1994.[50]

Del Ray Baptist Church was revitalized in 2011 through the work of CHBC and Garrett Kell. Del Ray has since planted or revitalized six churches and trained over twenty-five pastoral interns who are presently serving around the world.[51] Similar things could be said of CHBC's work with nearly a dozen other churches in the greater-DC region, including Anacostia River Church planted in 2015 by Thabiti Anyabwile with Matt Schmucker and Jeremy McClain sent as elders.

Another significant development occurred in 2005 when CHBC sent John Folmar to pastor the Evangelical Christian Church of Dubai (ECCD) in the United Arab Emirates. Longtime CHBC-supported worker Mack Stiles, who brought a Christian student ministry to the Persian Gulf states of the Middle East, approached CHBC in 2004 about sending a pastor to fill the strategic position.[52] A strong pulpit ministry in the Middle East, Stiles maintained, could be a catalyst for church planting and training throughout the Middle East, North Africa, and South Asia. Since taking up the ministry in 2005, John Folmar and the ECCD have seen three churches planted in the Emirates and dozens of pastors trained and sent out to Tanzania, Sudan, Tunisia, Indonesia, Kazakhstan, Afghanistan, Germany, Somalia, Egypt, Jordan, Pakistan, Nepal, Kashmir, Japan, Palestine, Ethiopia, South Africa, Kuwait, India, the Philippines, the United Kingdom, and Syria. As Folmar explained to his congregation in 2010, "Rather than one mega-church, we long to see multiple gospel-centered churches in neighborhoods throughout the city. This is the best way to reach the nations with the gospel. And that's our ultimate goal."[53]

---

50 The number calculated by CHBC deacon of media, Destry Edwards, was 430. Destry Edwards, email message to the author, November 28, 2023.

51 Garrett Kell, personal communication to the author, November 29, 2023.

52 Michael Lawrence, "United Christian Church of Dubai," January 27, 2005, Elders' Meeting Minutes, January 27, 2005, 1–3.

53 John Folmar, "Our Short History: 50 Years of God's Faithfulness," Evangelical Christian Church of Dubai, accessed November 28, 2023, https://www.eccdubai.org/short-history.

Today, many of CHBC's church plants are planting their own churches. When a church in the Washington, DC, area is looking for a pastor, that man is just as likely to be supplied by Sterling Park Baptist Church, Del Ray Baptist Church, or Anacostia River Church as by CHBC. As Steve Boyer shared, "I think the decision of not trying to make CHBC as large as she could be but looking to plant and revitalize elsewhere helped to creating a giving/sending culture in the church (and in those churches we helped)."[54] One candle had become many candles—not just one church, one pulpit, or one pastor but dozens of lights burning bright for the gospel.

All of this happened without broadcasting Mark Dever sermons on Sunday mornings or making Sterling Park Baptist Church, Del Ray Baptist Church, or Anacostia River Church a multisite campus of CHBC. What it took was a long-term investment in raising up leaders and giving them opportunities to preach—like the opportunity given to Bert Daniel after 9/11—and a willingness of the congregation to raise up leaders, send them, and be spent for the sake of the gospel. As McKinley reflected, "Sharing the pulpit with other people and giving room and encouragement for growth builds a culture in the church that serves church planting well."[55]

The Origins of 9Marks and Together for the Gospel

While planting churches locally and even sending out pastors internationally, CHBC also adopted a focus on building up churches more broadly through the ministry today known as 9Marks. The ministry began with Dever's original "nine marks" letter first written to New Meadows Baptist Church in 1991.[56] At Matt Schmucker's suggestion, Dever expanded that letter by writing an article on each of the nine

54 Steve and Donna Boyer, email message.

55 McKinley, interview.

56 See Mark Dever to New Meadows Baptist Church, October 30, 1991, MS 269, box 1, folder 16, Deacons-Pulpit Committee 1991–1998, CHBC Archives. Reprinted as appendix 3 in Mark Dever, *Nine Marks of a Healthy Church*, 4th ed. (Wheaton, IL: Crossway, 2021), 283–90.

marks in CHBC's newsletter between May 7, 1995 and May 5, 1996.[57] In 1997 Dever published an expanded version of the combined nine articles in a booklet for Founders Press entitled *9 Marks of a Healthy Church*, which went through two editions.[58]

Not long after, a neighbor on Capitol Hill approached Schmucker about the church starting a nonprofit to disseminate these ideas more widely. Though he was not a member, the neighbor was impressed with the impact the church was having on the neighborhood. He offered to donate $100,000 to get the organization off the ground and suggested the name Center for Church Reform (CCR).[59]

CCR's ministry consisted in publishing books, making media resources available online, and organizing conferences to promote the ideas that contributed toward church health. In February 2002, CCR hosted its first weekender conference for seventeen pastors and seminarians, which has since become a staple of CHBC's broader ministry to pastors, hosting three such conferences annually. In 2003 CCR's name changed to IX Marks Ministries, and later simply to 9Marks.[60] While initially a ministry of the church, in 2006 CHBC voted to designate 9Marks as an "integrated auxiliary," alongside another ministry that had grown up within the church: Together for the Gospel.[61]

Between 2006 and 2022, Together for the Gospel (T4G) became one of Reformed evangelicalism's most influential conferences, growing

57 For copies of these newsletters, see box 18, folders 15–16, CHBC Archives.

58 Mark Dever, *9 Marks of a Healthy Church* (Cape Coral, FL: Founders, 1997). The original 29-page booklet was expanded as a 255-page volume, comprising nine sermons preached at CHBC on "Nine Marks of a Healthy Church" between January 17 and April 25, 1999, and published as *Nine Marks of a Healthy Church* (Wheaton, IL: Crossway, 2000).

59 Members' Meeting Minutes, January 17, 1999.

60 As CHBC's elders explained, "First, having the word 'reform' in the name makes CCR's audience think that CCR's function is to promote [C]alvinism. The second reason is because having 'church reform' in the name makes church leaders hesitant to subscribe to CCR for fear it would mean their church would need to totally change instead of improving in health." Elders' Meeting Minutes, September 18, 2003, 5.

61 Members' Meeting Minutes, March 19, 2006.

from 2,800 attendees in 2006 to 12,000 in 2022. The idea developed out of the friendships between Mark Dever, Ligon Duncan, Albert Mohler, and C. J. Mahaney. Dever and Mohler had met as students at the Southern Baptist Theological Seminary, and Mahaney had become a friend and mentor to Dever during his early years of pastoring in Washington. Dever and Duncan became friends during their doctoral studies in the United Kingdom in 1988. At age twenty-seven, Duncan had just begun studying at the University of Edinburgh in Scotland when a friend connected him with Dever. "I called Ligon that day and we must have talked for an hour or two on the phone," Dever recalled. "It was just great." The rest was history.[62]

Figure 14.3. T4G speakers, pictured on January 19, 2011, in Louisville, Kentucky. From left to right: Kevin DeYoung, Thabiti Anyabwile, John Piper, Ligon Duncan, Albert Mohler, Mark Dever, David Platt, C. J. Mahaney, and Matt Chandler.

62 Mark Dever, interview with the author, December 18, 2023, Washington, DC.

As early as December 20, 2001, Dever shared with CHBC's elders that he was eager to organize an annual conference with Mohler and Duncan aimed at encouraging pastors and elders.[63] A year later he presented more definite plans to create a "CCR Conference," where "All nine marks will be dissected over nine years, and each year will only concentrate on one of the nine marks (e.g. expositional preaching)." Dever noted that he would be meeting with Mahaney, Mohler, and Duncan to discuss this idea soon.[64]

In April 2005, Schmucker announced to CHBC that with one year to go, 9Marks was partnering with Sovereign Grace Ministries (of which Mahaney was president) to organize the first T4G in Louisville, Kentucky, in April 2006 with space for 2,800 attendees. "Pray that God would use this for His glory," Schmucker told the church, "and in the lives of the pastors and seminarians who attend."[65] As the conference approached, dozens of CHBC members volunteered their time to make the conference possible.[66]

Those who attended were overwhelmed by the preaching, the singing, the warm spirit of evangelical catholicity, and the fellowship between pastors, as R. C. Sproul, John MacArthur, and John Piper joined Dever, Duncan, Mohler, and Mahaney as conference speakers. Among the 2,800 in the audience were future speakers Matt Chandler, David Platt, and Kevin DeYoung.

The second T4G in 2008 brought 5,000 to Louisville. The third and fourth conferences in 2010 and 2012 grew to 7,000. Soon T4G had outgrown the Kentucky International Convention Center and moved to the Yum Center, home of the University of Louisville Cardinals, where 12,000 gathered in 2014.

By 2014 T4G was experiencing challenges. Mahaney voluntarily withdrew from his speaking slot so as not to be a hindrance, though

63 Elders' Meeting Minutes, December 20, 2001, 3.
64 Elders' Meeting Minutes, December 5, 2002, 4.
65 Members' Meeting Minutes, March 20, 2005, 3.
66 Members' Meeting Minutes, November 20, 2005.

he still attended the 2014 gathering. In 2012 a lawsuit had been filed (and was later dismissed) regarding Sovereign Grace Ministries and an abuse case that had occurred in Covenant Life Church decades earlier. The firestorm of public criticism tested the limits of what it meant to be "together for the gospel."[67] Although Mahaney returned to T4G in 2016, that proved to be his final conference, as he withdrew from the 2018 conference to avoid being a distraction. This perhaps served as the first sign of the impending implosions within Reformed evangelicalism, as disagreements over how to respond to the #MeToo movement, the election of Donald Trump in 2016, and protests over police shootings of African Americans engulfed the evangelical world. Moreover, as additional speakers were added to the lineup year by year, every invitation or disinvitation seemed like a political statement as the T4G speakers list seemed to become a bellwether of sorts for status and respectability.

Some were surprised and disappointed when Dever and Duncan announced that 2022 would be the final T4G.[68] But to those who were paying attention, something seemed appropriate about holding only nine T4G conferences. In fact, as Dever had told CHBC's elders in 2002, "All nine marks will be dissected over nine years, and each year will only concentrate on one of the nine marks." As it turned out, there proved to be a remarkable degree of similarity between the themes addressed by the conferences and the nine marks.

Hugging the Parade

Through the pastoral internship program, its pastoral staff posi-tions, and supporting 9Marks and T4G, the church has constantly put helping other churches ahead of its own immediate interests.

---

67 Sarah Eekhoff Zylstra, "Final Call for T4G," The Gospel Coalition podcast, November 17, 2021, https://www.thegospelcoalition.org/podcasts/recorded/final-call-for-t4g/.

68 Kate Shellnutt, "T4G Conference Will End in 2022," *Christianity Today*, October 21, 2021, https://www.christianitytoday.com/.

"CHBC is and should be characterized by a 10th mark of a healthy church," Dever wrote to the elders in 2005, "a biblical investment in the church universal."[69] But such a radical investment in the health of other churches rarely comes without cost. For the members who work, stay, support, and pray, the phrase "hugging the parade" emerged as a summary of the church's commitment to love the "parade" of those who would come to CHBC—either as members or as pastors—for only a short while before being sent out into ministry. For example, in a period of less than a year, between March 2015 and January 2016, CHBC sent out eight elders to pastor six different churches.[70]

Beginning in 2010, Jamie Dunlop delivered a sermon to CHBC members every few years on the subject "Life in a Transient Church" to encourage those who stay. He acknowledged the benefits of being a transient congregation, such as the ability to expose more people to the good things God is doing. But he also addressed the challenges, including the exhaustion and isolation that can come from constantly building new relationships and—to use the expression of one longtime member—being "pastored by a parade." Dunlop offered five strategies for navigating these challenges. First, he suggested taking advantage of the church's culture of deep, transparent relationships by being open and vulnerable with new acquaintances. Second, he emphasized the importance of living near other church members to facilitate regular interaction and connection. Third, he advised members to be strategic about relationships by investing in people who can teach and mentor, who can benefit from their experiences, and who are different from them. Fourth, he encouraged building friendships with others who

69 Elders' Meeting Minutes, February 15, 2005, 4.
70 Thabiti Anyabwile, Matt Schmucker, and Jeremy McClain for Anacostia River Church; Trip Lee to Cornerstone Church in Atlanta, Georgia; David Russell to Oakhurst Baptist Church in Charlotte, North Carolina; Nick Roark to Franconia Baptist Church in Alexandria, Virginia; Brad Wheeler to University Baptist Church in Fayetteville, Arkansas; and Zach Schlegel to First Baptist Church Upper Marlboro, Maryland.

are committed to the long-term growth and stability of the church. Finally, he reminded listeners to find their zeal and motivation in their forgiveness in Christ, recognizing that their sinfulness and need for forgiveness can fuel their love and passion for serving others. Dunlop concluded by encouraging members to place their ultimate hope in eternity: "Let's set our hearts toward heaven and let the transience of this church build in us an affection and a longing for the permanence of God's kingdom."[71]

For a congregation to not only endure but encourage that degree of pastoral turnover speaks not only to the church's maturity but also to its commitment to the Great Commission and hope in heaven. It is no wonder that many of CHBC's favorite hymns focus so much on heaven. Hymns like "Hark! I Hear the Harps Eternal" and "Jerusalem, My Happy Home" remind of those who have "crossed before us safely to that land of perfect rest"[72] and long hopefully for that home

where congregations ne'er break up,
and Sabbaths have no end.[73]

"Yes, we're 'hugging the parade,'" wrote Steve and Donna Boyer, as they reflected on their over twenty-five years as members of CHBC. "But that parade is marching towards heaven where we'll all be together again for all eternity with our Lord and Savior Jesus Christ."[74]

Such a deliberate focus on being a healthy church and training and sending out leaders is crucial, urgent, costly, and hopeful. It is crucial because of the Great Commission. It is urgent because people are lost

71 Jamie Dunlop, "Life in a Transient Church" (sermon, Capitol Hill Baptist Church, October 14, 2012), https://www.capitolhillbaptist.org/sermon/elders-talk-life-in-a-transient-church/.
72 Frederic Rowland Marvin, "Hark! I Hear the Harps Eternal," 1867.
73 Joseph Bromehead, "Jerusalem My Happy Home," in *Psalms and Hymns for Public or Private Devotion* (Sheffield, UK: Brittania, 1795).
74 Steve and Donna Boyer, email message.

and in need of a Savior. It is costly because of the pain of parting. But it is most fundamentally hopeful because of the reality of spending eternity together in the new heavens and the new earth.

———

How can a church steward success without losing its soul? How can a healthy church grow numerically without becoming unhealthy? In 2010 Mark Driscoll and James MacDonald expressed incredulity that Mark Dever would intentionally refrain from building as large a church as possible. They bordered on questioning his intelligence in wondering aloud why he would insist on a single service, much less a single site when CHBC could have easily expanded its local footprint into a regional megachurch. But rather than becoming as large or as influential as possible, CHBC focused on raising up pastors through its pastoral internship program and planting and revitalizing area churches.

Of course, giving teaching opportunities and raising up leaders is just one aspect of a broader vision of the church as cooperative rather than competitive. CHBC's weekender pastors' conferences, internship program, approach to church staffing, regular prayers for other churches during its services, practice of encouraging attendees to join another gospel-preaching church if it's closer to where they live—all these efforts are part of a broader push to encourage a spirit of gospel catholicity across churches. "If you can't see that the goal is bigger than your church and your ministry," Dever regularly tells pastors gathered for CHBC weekender conferences, "you are disqualified from the pastorate. You should not be the pastor of your church if you do not have a concern for other churches."

The focus at CHBC of diffusing teaching authority and planting churches has lessened the emphasis on a single individual. In other words, the church has intentionally *not* sought to make CHBC dependent on Mark Dever or to make the witness of the gospel in the Washington metro area dependent on CHBC. As Jamie Dunlop expressed it, reflecting on CHBC's future after Dever, "I look forward to being reassured of how much the Lord has done here is not dependent on Mark Dever. I don't look forward to it in the sense that I want Mark gone. But I'm quite confident it's not person dependent, and yet a lot of people think it is. And I look forward to that assumption being vindicated, and it being evident that the church really is built on Jesus and not on Mark Dever."[75]

At least part of the answer to the question of stewarding church growth lies in trusting God's sovereignty for his providential limitations (on a church and its leaders) and his providential instructions for how the church should gather and worship. Some of those providential limitations include the size of the building, the numerical size a church can be and still be faithfully shepherded, and the nature of the church's community. God's providential instructions include the Bible's teaching on the church as a single assembly that gathers corporately to celebrate the ordinances and listen to his word taught. Wisdom in Scripture consists in conforming our lives to the pattern of God's word. CHBC's decision in the mid-2000s was certainly costly. But as the church continued to preach the gospel, as pastors have been raised up and sent out, CHBC believed that embracing providential limitations and instructions was worth it.

75 Dunlop, interview.

Conclusion

The light we are privileged to send forth on Capitol Hill must not be permitted to flicker with any shadow of uncertainty but must be caused to shine more steadfastly than in any bygone day.[1]

WALTER A. PEGG, OCTOBER 2, 1956

DESPITE INTERNAL DISSENSIONS and the contextual challenges of being an urban church, Capitol Hill Baptist Church has remained centered on the gospel and rooted in its community for nearly 150 years. How did the church stay rooted both in the gospel and in this neighborhood all this time? How can this church—or any church—remain faithful for another 150 years if the Lord tarries?

The chief distinguishing mark of God's kindness toward Capitol Hill Baptist Church has been the preachers who have heralded the gospel from its pulpit. As Francis McLean stated in 1892, "If we've been spoiled with anything it has been by good preaching."[2] From Joseph W. Parker to Green Clay Smith to K. Owen White to Mark Dever, the church

---

1   Walter A. Pegg, "The Challenge Ahead," *Metropolitan Messenger*, October 2, 1956, MS 1744, p. 1, box 8a, folder 7, Capitol Hill Baptist Church Archives, Washington, DC (hereafter, CHBC Archives).
2   Francis McLean, "The Reunion," February 29, 1892, MS 1322, box 5, folder 22, CHBC Archives.

has been blessed by remarkably faithful and gifted preachers—in no small part due to the carefulness of members like Agnes Shankle! After concluding his forty-one-year ministry, John Compton Ball told the assembled congregation, "After you called me as your pastor, my greatest aim became to know no one save Jesus Christ and Him crucified, and I can say honestly to you and before God that I have tried to carry that out."[3] Churches will not remain faithful to the gospel for long apart from faithful preachers of God's word, so we should pray for the Lord of the harvest to continue to raise up and sustain pastors for the work of his harvest.

Another distinguishing sign of God's mercy has been the humble perseverance of saints like Celestia A. Ferris and Margaret Roy who lived hidden lives of quiet faithfulness. They never stood in the pulpit, but they knelt in the prayer closet, and the Lord Jesus Christ will reward them when he bestows eternal honors on his saints in glory. Heaven will testify to the cosmic impact of a quiet life centered around the local church.

Finally, any good that has come from the ministry of Capitol Hill Baptist Church can ultimately be traced back to the power of prayer. The church started as a prayer meeting. And the prayers of the saints have sustained the church during its darkest moments. In 1891 the church newsletter printed this testimony to the priority of prayer in the life of the church:

Nothing so well tests the spiritual pulse of a church as the interest the members manifest in and the number who attend the *regular* meetings, for in those sweet hours of prayer the brethren have their spiritual strength renewed and are thus better fitted for such duties and trials of life as, at times, very severely test Christian character.[4]

3   John Compton Ball, "What Think Ye of Christ" (sermon, Metropolitan Baptist Church, Washington, DC, March 11, 1945), box C, folder 2, CHBC Archives.
4   Benjamin F. Bingham, "Between Ourselves," *Metropolitan Baptist*, October 1891, 28, Kiplinger Research Library, Washington, DC (emphasis in original).

"The prayer meeting," wrote church treasurer Allen C. Clark in 1892, "is almost as essential to Christian activity as that organ of the human system which propels the vital current to life."[5] Apart from prayer, would the divided Baptists of Washington have come together during a financial crisis to plant a church on Capitol Hill? Apart from prayer, would the dwindled congregation have continued after the church split of 1884? Apart from prayer, would a godly successor to John Compton Ball's forty-one-year ministry have been secured? Apart from prayer, would the church have recovered after the fall of Mark Dever's predecessor? How much of what has happened during these past 150 years has been the direct result of the prayers of Celestia Ferris and her band of friends first uttered in November 1867? From the vantage point of heaven, the most significant factor in preserving the witness of Capitol Hill Baptist Church will undoubtedly be the prayers of the congregation.

Through the faithful preaching of the word, the selfless labors of godly members, and the prayers of God's people, God has preserved a brightly shining beacon for the gospel on Capitol Hill. Paul exhorted the Philippians to hold forth the word of life in order to "shine as lights in the world" (Phil. 2:15). Is the light of your church shining? What will it take to keep that light shining? Keep preaching the gospel, keep persevering in loving the church, and above all keep praying so that you may ignite a light set on a hill that cannot be hidden. May Capitol Hill Baptist Church continue to shine as a light on the Hill.

---

5   Allen C. Clark, "The Prayer Meeting," *Metropolitan Baptist*, June 1892, MS 1551, p. 10, box 6, folder 4, CHBC Archives.

Afterword

We might write a volume, but desist, for action
in the living present is all we want.

FRANCIS MCLEAN, DECEMBER 31, 1887[1]

THIS PROJECT originated during the COVID-19 pandemic. When local governments began considering issuing public health orders to close churches, I was working as Mark Dever's personal assistant. He asked me one day to find out how our church responded during the Spanish flu of 1918. Sifting my way through the dusty pages of minutes, stored in filing cabinets in a basement closet underneath the baptistry, I began to reconstruct the events of 1918 that led the church to cancel services for three weeks in response to the onset of the Spanish flu. When I published the story for 9Marks a few days later, the response was overwhelming.[2] The article went viral on social media and was picked up by the *Washington Post.*[3] I began to experience the firsthand impact narrative history can have on current events: to draw needed

---

1 Clerk's Annual Report, December 31, 1887, MS 1585, box 6, folder 5, Capitol Hill Baptist Church Archives, Washington, DC.

2 Caleb Morell, "How DC Churches Responded When the Government Banned Public Gatherings During the Spanish Flu of 1918," 9Marks, March 12, 2020, https://www.9marks.org/.

3 Michelle Boorstein, "For Millions Of Americans, No Church on Sunday Is Coronavirus's Cruelest Closure So Far," *Washington Post*, March 14, 2020, https://www.washingtonpost.com/.

light from the past to put present challenges in perspective. For the next months, I spent any spare time poring over newspaper clippings and members' meeting minutes.

When I made some of these recently gleaned lessons public while teaching a class on CHBC's history in 2020, two elders, Eric Beach and Justin Sok, hatched the idea of turning it into a book: "You wouldn't be interested in writing this by any chance?" Did they really need to ask? The project was a dream come true.

Thanks to the generosity of donors, I spent two years between 2021 and 2023 collecting materials, reading documents, and conducting interviews, mostly from the windowless closet underneath the church baptistry. There, and in various odd corners of the building, I discovered over thirty boxes of historical documents. I spent the first three months indexing, sorting, and digitizing these documents into the archival system referenced throughout the book. By digitizing the most important of these boxes (amounting to over 40,000 pages of documents), I hope to open up an avenue for research for future historians.

The most significant archival discovery was two folders of handwritten Carl F. H. Henry documents from a Sunday school class he taught in the 1960s, deposited at the church in the 1990s, and forgotten until this project. These original documents, available nowhere else, form a significant part of chapter 10.

The most significant historical discovery was the unpublished memoirs of CHBC's first full-time pastor, Joseph W. Parker.[4] This came to my attention through the meticulous research of famed Civil War historian James M. McPherson, who consulted it during his doctoral research on the abolitionist movement.[5] Deposited with the University of Virginia, Parker's memoirs shed previously unknown light on

4   Joseph Whiting Parker Memoirs, 1880, MS 14909, Special Collections, University of Virginia Library, Charlottesville.
5   James M. McPherson, *The Struggle for Equality: Abolitionists and the Negro in the Civil War and Reconstruction* (Princeton, NJ: Princeton University Press, 2014), 444.

the early history of the church and the otherwise unknown life of a remarkable man and pastor.

One of the special joys of this project was conducting dozens of interviews with current and former members. I'll never forget my visit on March 24, 2021, to John Compton Ball's great-granddaughter, Barbara Kelley, whom I found by scouring through obituaries and wedding announcements in search of a living descendant of CHBC's longest-serving pastor to date. Chapters 6 and 7 are only possible because of the meticulous documents kept in the Kelley family collection. At one point in our conversation as we pored over sermons and photographs, Barbara asked me, "So how is great-grandfather's church? Is it still around?"

As a work of historical nonfiction, all details recounted in this book are grounded in historical sources. The dialogues are reproduced from actual sources and not invented. Following the example of Gregory Wills's research on the history of the Southern Baptist Theological Seminary,[6] I endeavored to depend on written sources primarily for constructing the narrative. Interviews have been relied on sparingly to illuminate or expand what is always attested in primary sources.

May the Lord use this book to bless his church, and may the light continue to shine bright on Capitol Hill!

Caleb Morell

DECEMBER 2023

---

6   Gregory A. Wills, *Southern Baptist Theological Seminary, 1859–2009* (New York: Oxford University Press, 2009).

Acknowledgments

We are working partly for those who come after us,
while we enjoy the privilege and happiness of doing.

FRANCIS MCLEAN, DECEMBER 31, 1886[1]

THIS BOOK WOULD NOT EXIST if not for the amazing team at Crossway. I'm deeply grateful for Justin Taylor, who believed in this project and has been a generous sounding board throughout the research and writing process. Chris Cowan improved the manuscript in innumerable ways. I am astounded by Crossway's willingness to take a chance on a first-time author like me and am grateful for their partnership in the gospel.

This research would not have been possible apart from the generosity of the staff and curators of several institutions, including the staff of the Kiplinger Research Library; Mark Greek of the Washingtonia Collection at the MLK Library; Bridget Kamsler, the university archivist for George Washington University's Special Collections Research Center; and the Athenaeum of Philadelphia, whose curator, Bruce Laverty, generously provided access to and insight into the Thomas Ustick Walter papers. The Library of Congress graciously provided a researcher's shelf and hundreds of requested books and materials, and Amanda Zimmerman

---

1 Clerk's Annual Report, December 31, 1886, MS 1583b, box 6, folder 5, CHBC Archives, Washington, DC.

305

of the Rare Book and Special Collections Division at the Library of Congress provided generous assistance retrieving dozens of volumes.

Trisha Manarin at the DC Baptist Convention kindly allowed me to access the associational minutes. Other local churches generously opened up their archives, including Nathan Knight at Restoration Church (which I will always think of as E Street Baptist Church); John Burns at University Baptist Church (the original Second Baptist); Sarah Fairbrother at Riverside Baptist Church (originally Fifth Baptist Church); and Claudia Moore, Gretchen White, and Nancy Renfrow, the archivists at Calvary Baptist Church. Others made personal family collections available for research, including the generous Kelley family, which provided access to John Compton Ball's personal papers, and William Bates, who shared photographs and stories about his father-in-law Carl F. H. Henry. Thank you!

The dozens of current and former members who were willing to be interviewed brought life to the story. Countless members, former members, and relatives provided pictures, notes, and other research materials that filled in critical missing details. I will never forget the privilege of hearing your stories.

CHBC's own Kevin Fair, Christopher Dunlop, and Lucas Dunlop provided invaluable research and administrative assistance. So many friends and mentors provided critical advice and direction throughout the project. Special thanks to Thomas Kidd, Greg Wills, Geoff Chang, John Wilsey, Phillip Troutman, and Shawn Wright for their advice and encouragement along the way. Jamie Dunlop offered so much insightful feedback and invaluable advice that I doubt this book could have been completed without him. At various critical moments in the project, others like Thomas Terry and Mike Cosper provided timely advice in crafting the narrative and much-needed encouragement.

Friends and family members read early chapters and sections and provided feedback. Thank you, Elisabeth, Rachel, Alex, Elizabeth, Dave, Ryan, and many others.

Special thanks also to Eric Beach and Justin Sok who first dreamed up this research project, the elders at Capitol Hill Baptist Church who gave their support, and Mark Dever, who believed in the project and believed in me. My dear wife, Clare, encouraged me throughout in the way only a wife can encourage. And none of this would have been possible without the generosity of the donors who funded this project. You are unknown to me but known to the Lord. May he bless you richly, and may this book be a blessing to many.

Illustration Credits

Figures

1.1. Photo from the Thomas Ustick Walter Collection, the Athenaeum of Philadelphia. Used with permission.

1.2. Photo from the Willard R. Ross Postcard Collection, the People's Archive at DC Public Library. No copyright.

1.3. Photo used courtesy of Special Collections, Fine Arts Library, Harvard University. Public domain.

1.4. Photo from the Capitol Hill Baptist Church (hereafter, CHBC) Archives, Washington, DC. Used with permission.

1.5. Sketch by C. D. Gedney, Library of Congress. Public domain.

1.6. Photo from the CHBC Archives, Washington, DC. Used with permission.

1.7. Photo from the CHBC Archives, Washington, DC. Used with permission.

1.8. Photo by Pat Forrester. Used with permission.

2.1. Photo from A. W. Pegues, *Our Baptist Ministers and Schools* (Springfield, MA: Willey, 1892). Public domain.

2.2. Photo by Chris Streip. Used with permission.

3.1. Photo by W. H. Jennings of Norwich, Connecticut. Buck Zaidel collection. Used with permission.

3.2. Image from the CHBC Archives, Washington, DC. Used with permission.

3.3. Image published in the *Evening Star*, May 2, 1891. Public domain.

4.1. Photo published in William H. Young, *How to Preach with Power* (1896). Public domain.

4.2. Sketch from the CHBC Archives, Washington, DC. Used with permission.

4.3. Photo from the CHBC Archives, Washington, DC. Used with permission.

5.1. Photo from the Brady-Handy photograph collection, Library of Congress, Prints and Photographs Division. LC-DIG-cwpbh-04518. Public Domain.

5.2. Image from the CHBC Archives, Washington, DC. Used with permission.

5.3. Photo from the CHBC Archives, Washington, DC. Used with permission.

5.4. Image from the CHBC Archives, Washington, DC. Used with permission.

5.6. Photo from the CHBC Archives, Washington, DC. Used with permission.

5.7. Image from the CHBC Archives, Washington, DC. Used with permission.

6.1. Sketch from the *Washington Times*, March 8, 1908. Public domain.

6.2. Photo from the CHBC Archives, Washington, DC. Used with permission.

6.3. Image from the Kelley Family Private Collection. Used with permission.

6.4. Photo from the CHBC Archives, Washington, DC. Used with permission.

6.5. Photo from the CHBC Archives, Washington, DC. Used with Permission.

7.1. Photo from the Harris and Ewing Collection, Library of Congress. Public domain.

7.2. Photo from the CHBC Archives, Washington, DC. Used with permission.

7.3. Photo from the CHBC Archives, Washington, DC. Used with permission.

7.4. Photo from the Harris and Ewing Collection, Library of Congress. Public domain.

7.5. Photo from the CHBC Archives, Washington, DC. Used with permission.

8.1. Image from the *Saskatoon Daily Star*, December 4, 1920. Public domain.

8.2. Image from the *Evening Star*, May 22, 1926. Public domain.

8.3. Photo from the CHBC Archives, Washington, DC. Used with permission.

8.4. Photo from the CHBC Archives, Washington, DC. Used with permission.

8.5. Photo from the CHBC Archives, Washington, DC. Used with permission.

8.6. Photo from the CHBC Archives, Washington, DC. Used with permission.

8.7. Photo from the CHBC Archives, Washington, DC. Used with permission.

9.1. Photo courtesy of Billy Graham Evangelistic Associations. Used with permission. All rights reserved.

9.2. Photo from the CHBC Archives, Washington, DC. Used with permission.

9.3. Photo from the CHBC Archives, Washington, DC. Used with permission.

9.4. Photo from the CHBC Archives, Washington, DC. Used with permission.

9.5. Photo from the CHBC Archives, Washington, DC. Used with permission.

9.6. Photo from the CHBC Archives, Washington, DC. Used with permission.

9.7. Photo from the CHBC Archives, Washington, DC. Used with permission.

9.8. Photo from the CHBC Archives, Washington, DC. Used with permission.

9.9. Newspaper image, January 11, 1952, the People's Archive at DC Public Library. Used with permission.

9.10. Photo courtesy of Billy Graham Evangelistic Associations. Used with permission. All rights reserved.

9.11. Image from the CHBC Archives, Washington, DC. Used with permission.

9.12. Photo from the CHBC Archives, Washington, DC. Used with permission.

10.1. Image from the CHBC Archives, Washington, DC. Used with permission.

10.2. Photo by William Bates. Used with permission.

10.3. Image from the CHBC Archives, Washington, DC. Used with permission.

11.1. Image from the *Evening Star*, August 8, 1972, the People's Archive at DC Public Library. Used with permission.

11.2. Photo from the Prints and Photographs Division, Library of Congress. Public domain.

11.3. Photo from the CHBC Archives, Washington, DC. Used with permission.

11.4. Image from the CHBC Archives, Washington, DC. Used with permission.

11.5. Photo from the CHBC Archives, Washington, DC. Used with permission.

11.6. Image from the CHBC Archives, Washington, DC. Used with permission.

11.7. Image from the CHBC Archives, Washington, DC. Used with permission.

11.8. Photo from the CHBC Archives, Washington, DC. Used with permission.

11.9. Photo from the CHBC Archives, Washington, DC. Used with permission.

11.10. Photo from the CHBC Archives, Washington, DC. Used with permission.

12.1. Photo from the CHBC Archives, Washington, DC. Used with permission.

12.2. Photo from the CHBC Archives, Washington, DC. Used with permission.

12.3. Photo from the CHBC Archives, Washington, DC. Used with permission.

12.4. Photo from the CHBC Archives, Washington, DC. Used with permission.

13.1. Photo from Dever family personal collection. Used with permission.

13.2. Photo from Dever family personal collection. Used with permission.

14.1. Image from the CHBC Archives, Washington, DC. Used with permission.

14.3. Photo from Dever family personal collection. Used with permission.

General Index

abolitionism, 1, 10–11
abuse, 292
adultery, 95
African American churches, 35
African Americans, 82, 99–100, 173, 208, 220–22, 292
age distribution, 219, 220
age-of-consent laws, 109
alcohol, 95, 194
Allen, Asa Leonard, 139–40, 165n21
"Alley Dwellings," 23
"All Hail the Power of Jesus' Name," 177
American flag, 125
amillennialism, 153
Anacostia, 197, 200, 201, 205–7, 225
Anacostia River Church, 287, 288, 293n70
Anna Johenning Baptist Church, 211, 225
Anti-Saloon League of the District of Columbia, 95–96
Anyabwile, Thabiti, 285, 287, 290, 293n70
architecture, 8, 10, 11, 65, 74, 117, 196
Arlington Cemetery, 30, 31
Arthur, Chester A., 97
Ask-Seek-Knock Sunday school, 158
atonement, 149

Ballbach, John M., 150
Ball, Jeanette, 115, 122
Ball, John Compton, 105, 106, 110–16, 121–25, 133, 140, 144, 147, 148–52, 154, 159, 161–63, 164, 191, 223, 298, 299

bankruptcy, 58
baptism, 19–20, 44, 76, 93, 103, 140, 143, 147, 165, 168, 189, 220, 224
Baptist and Reflector, 145
Baptist Bible Union of North America, 140, 141, 142, 145, 146
Baptist Faith and Message, 143
Baptist Fundamentals, 140
Baptist polity, 43, 251
Baptist Young People's Union, 120
Barrows, Cliff, 173
Bass, Liston D., 107–8
Battle of Antietam, 55
Battle of Port Waltham Junction, 55
Battle of the Argonne, 121
Bauder, Kevin, 145n27
Beeson Divinity School, 253
Behrens, Bill, 282
believer's baptism, 140
Bellevue Baptist Church, 183
Bender, William, 228
Berean Baptist Church, 35, 51
Bible Baptist Union, 145
Billy Sunday Tabernacle, 126, 127
Bingham, Benjamin F., 57, 58, 60, 90, 91
Black Republicans, 10
Blackwelder, Oscar, 151
Blanchette, Andrea, 235n34
"Blest Be the Tie That Binds," 30
Bliss, Philip, 27
Boice, James Montgomery, 238
Boyer, Donna, 294

Boyer, Steve, 282, 283, 288, 294
Boylan, Anne M., 24n46, 91n27
Brandywine Valley Baptist Church, 246
Briggs, John E., 151
Briggs v. Elliott, 173
Brooks, Walter H., 95n37, 126–27, 150–52
Brown, Bill, 205
Brown, Frances, 205
Brown, J. Newton, 42
Brown, John, 9
Brown v. Board of Education, 173, 197
Bruce, Chris, 264, 274
Brundage, Alice P., 91
Brundage, Warren C., 91–92, 93
Bucknell University, 34n2
building plans, 54–57, 116, 234
Bureau of Civil Service Instruction, 107
Burge, Ryan, 3
Burnley, Raymond, 222
Burton, Robert, 47
Byrd, Brad, 265

Calvary Baptist Church, 14, 15, 18, 27, 29, 116, 117, 137, 182, 203
Calvary Baptist Church (New York City), 146
Calvinism, 251
Cambridge University, 5
Canipe, Lee, 145n27
Capitol Hill, 21, 22, 82
Capitol Hill Baptist Church, 2, 5, 225, 259, 299
Capitol Hill Baptist Sunday School, 23
Capitol Hill Metropolitan Baptist Church, 5, 193, 225
Carey, William, 99
Carlson, Herb, 239n45, 245, 252
Carneal, Pearl, 177
Carpenter, J. Walter, 155, 158, 172–74, 177, 178, 183, 191, 202, 204
Carson, D. A., 251, 256
Catherwood, Fred, 267
centennial celebration, 224
Center for Church Reform (CCR), 289
Chandler, Matt, 290, 291

character, 249, 256
charity, 64
childcare, 23
child development center (CDC), 232
Chinese Exclusion Act, 97–98
choir, 165
Christian day school, 203
Christianity Today, 5, 157, 181–82, 184, 185, 186, 271
Christian Life Commission, 208
church
    health of, 3, 76, 261, 270, 271, 284, 289, 295
    mission of, 167, 211
    nursery of, 89–91, 92
    reputation of, 219
church constitution, 16, 263–64, 267
church covenant, 42–43, 51, 52, 188, 261, 262, 267
church discipline, 44, 45–51, 91–92, 234–35, 255, 261
church finances, 14, 15, 26, 27, 34, 53, 57, 58, 70, 241, 279, 280
Church Growth Movement, 231n20
Church Manual of the Metropolitan Baptist Church, 42, 44
church membership, 14, 20, 45–46, 93, 103, 147, 166–67, 188, 255, 258, 260
church officers, 43
church planting, 283, 284–88
church polity, 51
church splits, 4, 5, 14, 28, 65, 72, 79, 80, 235n34, 236, 299
church visitation, 223, 260
civility, 64
Civil Rights Movement, 192
Civil War, 5, 8, 9, 12, 20, 30, 80, 81, 84, 87, 123
Clark, Allen C., 97, 117, 299
Clark, Appleton P., 117
Clay, Cassius M., 84
Clay, Henry, 103
coal shortage, 125–28
Cobb, Barbara, 232–33
Cobb, Mary Lou, 229

Columbia Association of Baptist
    Churches, 42, 47, 48, 49, 72–73,
    77, 79, 116, 128–29
Columbia Bible College, 172
Columbian College, 14
communism, 175, 182
community needs, 220, 231
complementarians, 153
Condon Terrace, 206
Confederacy, 9, 12, 107
confessionalism, 143
conflicts, 4, 53
conservatives, 113, 139
consumerism, 212
conversion, 44, 76, 91, 255, 262
Conwell, Russell, 112, 113, 114
Cornell University, 69
Cornerstone Church (Atlanta, GA),
    293n70
"Cottage Prayer Meetings," 173
covenant, 28–29, 30
Covenant Life Church (Gaithersburg,
    MD), 282–83
COVID-19, 134–35
Cox, Marvis, 200
creeds, 19
Croft, Scott, 272–73, 282
Crozer Theological Seminary, 69–70, 112,
    113
Culbreth, R. B., 198, 199, 203–4, 208,
    209, 210, 211, 212–13, 214

Daniel, Bert, 273, 275, 276, 288
Davis, Jefferson, 12
Davis, Jim, 3
deaconesses, 100–101, 187
deacons, 43, 45, 100–101, 162, 187,
    234–35, 244
Dean, John Marvin, 139
debt, 53, 57, 63, 110
Declaration of Independence, 97
decline, 212–15, 220, 224, 227
Delnay, Robert, 145n27
Del Ray Baptist Church, 287, 288
democracy, 71
Depressing Thirties, 138

Detterer, Harriet, 29n66
Dever, Mark, 1, 5, 251–67, 269–78,
    280–96, 297, 299
Devlin, Jeannette, 261
DeYoung, Kevin, 291
Dicks, Luella, 222
disability coverage, 230, 232
discipleship, 255
discouragement, 265
disengagement, 212
District of Columbia Association of Bap-
    tist Churches (DCBC), 144–45, 170
Diver, Lucy H., 29n65
divisions, 53, 64
divorce, 82, 95
Douglas, Lucretia E., 45
Driscoll, Mark, 269, 270, 295
Duke, Lena, 84
Duncan, Ligon, 290, 291, 292
Dunlop, Jamie, 274, 284, 293–94, 296
Dunmire, Madeline, 241

Earle, A. B., 20n35
Early, Ethelyn Callaway, 134
Early, Felix, 134
Early, Stephen Tyree, 119–21, 134
Early, Thomas Joseph, Jr., 133
East Capitol Street, 55, 57, 193
East Capitol Street Baptist Church, 62,
    63, 65, 66, 70, 72, 74
Easter services, 170–71, 216
Eckhart, William, 150
Eden Baptist Church, 253
Edmunds, Nicholas Sterling, 36–38
egalitarians, 153
Eisenhower, Dwight D., 182
ekklesia, 283
elders, 43, 66, 255, 263–67, 279–81
elders retreat, 282–84
Eliot, George, 31
Elliot, Jim, 6
eschatology, 168
E Street Baptist Church, 8, 11, 13, 20,
    22, 27, 29, 39
Ethics and Religious Liberty Commis-
    sion, 208

ethnic minorities, 98
Evangelical Christian Church of Dubai
    (ECCD), 287
evangelicals, 157, 169, 179, 181–82, 185,
    192, 211, 251, 271, 289–90, 292
evangelism, 37, 70, 79, 113, 219, 231,
    255
Evening Star, 12, 131, 141, 195
evolution, 202, 219
expositional preaching, 163–64, 191, 255

Faber, Doris, 176
factionalism, 65–66
Faith Baptist Church, 65
female deaconesses, 100–101, 187
female preachers, 139, 145, 153, 160, 264
Ferdinand, Franz, 121
Ferris, Abraham, 2, 7, 21–22, 30–31, 55
Ferris, Celestia A., 2, 5, 7, 8, 9, 11, 14,
    21–23, 25, 30–32, 51, 55, 99, 118,
    206, 225, 298, 299
Fifth Baptist Church, 116, 133–34, 306
finances, 14, 15, 26, 27, 34, 53, 57, 58,
    70, 241, 279, 280
First Baptist Church (Cambridge, MA), 34
First Baptist Church (Camden, NJ), 34n2
First Baptist Church (Charleston, SC),
    202, 203
First Baptist Church (Frankfort, KY), 86
First Baptist Church (Huntington Park,
    CA), 183
First Baptist Church (Lambertville, NJ),
    111
First Baptist Church (Minneapolis, MN),
    142
First Baptist Church (Pontiac, MI), 138
First Baptist Church (Upper Marlboro,
    MD), 293n70
First Baptist Church (Washington, DC), 29
First Great Awakening, 3
Folmar, John, 285, 287
Foreign Mission Board (FMB), 228,
    229–30, 232
forgiveness, 46, 63
Fosdick, Harry Emerson, 140, 141
Foster, Gaines M., 88n21

Fourth Presbyterian, 184
Fowler, W. C., 129, 131, 132
Franconia Baptist Church, 293n70
Franklin, Benjamin, 57
Franklin, Philip, 105
Fransisco, Clyde, 214
Freeman, C. Wade, 222–24, 230
friendships, 293–94
fruit, 77–79
fuel crisis, 125–28
Fuller Theological Seminary, 186
fundamentalist movement, 138, 139–47,
    152, 159, 181–82
fundraising campaign, 74, 110

gambling, 95
Gaskins, Madison, 49–50
Geddings, Nora, 261
George, Timothy, 256, 259
George Washington University, 285
Germany, 123
giftedness, 249
Gillon, J. W., 146
God
    goodness of, 134
    judgment of, 149
    providence of, 273, 296
    sovereignty of, 89, 134, 275, 277, 296
"God Bless and Guard Our Men," 125
godliness, 108, 249
Good, James, 110
Gordon-Conwell Theological Seminary, 112
gospel, 67, 86, 107, 148, 153, 255, 297,
    299
Gospel Coalition (TGC), 269
Gothic structure, 74
governing documents, 42, 51–52
Grace Baptist Church, 64, 65
Grace Condominiums, 64
Graham, Billy, 3, 5, 155–58, 171–78,
    182, 224
Graham, Michael, 3
Great Commission, 294
Great Depression, 120
Greater Washington Evangelistic Crusade,
    155

Griffin, Michael, 282
growth, 240, 255, 277–84, 296
Guilford Fellowship, 285–86

Habakkuk, 274
Halverson, Richard, 184
Hamlin, Hannibal, 85n8
Hamrick, John, 203
"Hark! I Hear the Harps Eternal," 294
Harper's Ferry, 9
Harvest Bible Chapel, 269
Hawley, Josh, 273
Heidelberg Reformed Church, 110–11
Henry, Carl F. H., 1, 5, 158, 181,
    182–86, 190, 192, 210, 215, 237,
    238, 240, 251, 252, 253, 259
Hernandez, Fredy, 286
Hilltoppers, 185
Hinson Memorial Baptist Church, 139
Hiscox, Edward T., 43n42
Holcomb, Carol Crawford, 95n34
Hollenbach, Jim, 282, 284
Holy Spirit, work of, 80, 277
Homewood, 36
homogenous unit principle, 231n20
housing shortage, 200
Huber, Paul, 245, 252
human progress, 123
human trafficking, 109
Hybels, Bill, 235
hymns, 23, 27, 30, 106, 149, 220–21,
    265, 294

idolatry, 158
Iglesia Bautista Hispana Guilford, 286
image of God, 98
immigrants, 82
immigration, 97–98
immorality, 46, 91, 241, 243, 245
inclusivism, 143
inexperience, 264–65
infighting, 28
influence, 270
Ingersoll, Wilbur M., 53, 55, 56, 59, 60,
    61, 62, 65, 66, 70, 73, 75
integration, 202, 203–4, 209

International Mission Board, 228
InterVarsity Fellowship, 285
invitation, 224
irreconcilable differences, 233

Jackson, Andrew, 14
Jensen, Philip, 273
"Jerusalem, My Happy Home," 294
Jesus Christ, return of, 2, 153–54
Job, 273
Johenning, Anna, 205–6, 225
Johenning Center, 205–12
Johnson, Andrew, 84
Johnson, Andy, 264, 265, 282
Jones, Wayman, 217
judgment day, 38
Judson, Adoniram, 99

Keisling, Bruce, 262, 263
Kell, Garrett, 287
Kendall, Amos, 14–16, 17, 18–20, 117
Kendall, R. T., 238, 249
Kennard, Joseph Spencer, 12, 14
Kennedy, John F., 161
Kentucky Baptist General Association, 85
Kerygma, 238
Kilbride, Harry, 237–43
King, Martin Luther, Jr., 209–10, 215–16
Knapp, Jacob, 56
Koons, C. Vinton, 223
Korea, 175
Korean War, 192

Lamson, Caroline J., 214
Landon, Charles R., 185
Lansdowne Baptist Church, 238, 240
Larson, Reed, 185
Lawrence, Michael, 282
leadership, 276–77, 288
Lee, Robert E., 17, 21
Lee, Robert G., 183
Lee, Thomas S., 126n22
Lee, Tripp, 293n70
Leslie, Preston H., 86
letter of resignation, 60–62
Lewis, C. S., 249

Lewisburg College, 34n2
liberalism, 88, 122, 123, 139, 140, 178
life insurance policy, 92
light on the Hill, 4, 67, 299
Lincoln, Abraham, 8, 9, 10, 35, 84, 85, 87
Lloyd-Jones, Martyn, 238, 240–41
Loder, Jenetta A., 111
Longan, Martha, 29n66
Longan, Oliver, 29n66
"Long Depression," 26
Lord's Supper, 140, 147, 218
Lowell, Camilla, 29n65
Lowell, Thurston, 29n65
Luther, Martin, 281

MacArthur, John, 291
Magnolia Avenue Baptist Church, 190
Mahaney, C. J., 282, 290, 291, 292
Mahan, Henry B., 114
marital infidelity, 91–92
Marsden, George, 83n4, 95
Marshall, John, 84
Mars Hill Church, 269
Martyn, Henry, 99
martyrdom, 123
Mary's Blue Room, 195, 197
Mason-Dixon line, 9
materialism, 88
Matthews, Shailer, 123
Maupin, John, 109
Maupin, Socrates, 109
Maupin, William Carey, 107, 109
Mbewe, Conrad, 273
McClain, Jeremy, 287, 293n70
McCloughlin, William G., 122n10
McDonald, James, 269, 270, 295
McKim, Randolph H., 132
McKinley, Mike, 285, 286
McLean, Francis, 2, 3, 24, 45, 58, 59, 60, 63, 65, 73, 77, 78, 84, 116, 118, 297
McPherson, James M., 34n4
membership decline, 212–15, 220, 224, 227
membership interview, 278
membership rolls, 161, 166–67, 188–89
Menikoff, Aaron, 264, 265, 266

Metropolitan Baptist, 102
Metropolitan Baptist Association, 24, 26
Metropolitan Baptist Church, 5, 29, 33, 40, 69, 82, 83, 103, 115
Metropolitan Messenger, 101, 187, 202, 212, 213, 221–22
Mexican-American War, 84
military service, 121, 123
Mirick, Stephen H., 34, 48
missionaries, 99, 228
modernism, 139, 145, 152–53, 159
Mohler, R. Albert, Jr., 251, 253, 255, 259, 290, 291
Moody, D. L., 113
Moon, Lottie, 34n2
Moore, Joanna P., 100
Moore, Susan F., 29n66
moral regress, 82
Morse, Samuel, 14
Mount, Mary J., 29n66
Muir, Edward, 134
Muir, J. J., 134
multiple services, 282
multisite churches, 269–72, 282
murder, 82, 88
Murray, Bentley, 8
Murray, Francis, 8
Murray, Iain, 240, 273

name change, 193, 259
National Association of Evangelicals (NAE), 182, 184, 185
National Council of Churches, 182
National Day of Prayer, 175
national revival, 167, 169
National Right to Work, 185
naturalism, 88
"Nearer My God to Thee," 106
Nero, 125
New Bethlehem Baptist Church, 113–14
New Bethlehem Vindicator, 114
New Deal era, 120
New England Freedmen's Aid Society, 17, 34, 39
New Hampshire Confession of Faith (1833), 42, 143

new members class, 165–66
Newsweek, 181
Newton Theological Institution, 39
New York Avenue Presbyterian Church, 130
New York Times, 13–14
Nicole, Roger, 256, 259
"Nine Marks of the Healthy Church," 254–55, 261, 271, 288–92
Nineteenth Street Baptist Church, 95n37, 127, 151
Nixon, Richard, 219
nonattendance, 45, 78, 223, 261
non-giving, 78
nonmembers, 16
"non-residential" members, 214
Nordan, Robert, 216
Norris, J. Frank, 138, 141
Northern Baptist Convention, 140–41, 142, 143, 144–45
Northern Baptist Theological Seminary, 139
Northerners, 106
Northwestern Bible Institute, 183
Noyes, Theodore, 131
numerical growth, 77–79
nursery, 89–91, 92

Oakey, Emily S., 27
Oakhurst Baptist Church, 293n70
O'Connor, James, 82
Olford, Stephen, 233, 238
Oluwafemi, Titus, 228
"Only Trust Him," 265
open membership, 140
ordinances, 43
ordinary means, 2, 80, 191, 257
orthodoxy, 144, 178

Packer, J. I., 240
Palm Sunday, 124
pandemic, 128–34
"Panic of 1873," 26
parable of the sower, 27
Park Avenue Baptist Church, 140–41
Parker Hall, 36

Parker, Joseph W., 1, 17–20, 32, 34–40, 47, 50–51, 54, 211
Parker, Virginia, 34n4
parking lot, 196, 198–99
Parks, Keith, 230, 232
pastoral visitation, 260
pastors, 43
Pastors Federation of Washington, 130, 131
Patten, Charles L., 45
Patten, Emma, 29n65
Paul, 115
Pearce, Mary A., 29n66
Pearce, Sarah, 29n66
Pearce, W. H., 46
Pearl Harbor, 119
Pegg, Walter A., 183, 184, 185, 187, 189, 191, 192, 198
Pegues, Albert Witherspoon, 35n8
Pelletier, Eric, 263, 264, 265
Pew, J. Howard, 182
Philadelphia Baptist Confession of Faith (1742), 10
Pierce, Earl V., 142–43
Piper, John, 285, 290, 291
Platt, David, 290, 291
plurality of elders, 43, 66, 255, 263
police brutality, 209
postmillennialism, 122
Post Office Department, 108
poverty, 95
Pratt, Martin L., 206, 208n47
prayer, 40, 298–99
prayer meeting, 2, 5, 7n1, 19, 22, 25, 26, 55, 76, 173, 198, 225, 298, 299
preaching, 10, 41, 70, 87, 139, 148, 163–64, 191, 240, 255, 257, 258, 299
premillennial eschatology, 153
Priest, Percy, 175
professions of faith, 14
prohibition, 95
Prohibition Reform Party, 87, 88
prostitution, 109, 194
Protestants, 126, 130
protestors, 193–96, 209

protracted meetings, 76–77, 78
Prout, Robert, 24n49
Prout, William, 24n49
Pruden, Edwin H., 151
public gatherings, 129–30
public schools, 202
Pullman, Annie, 91, 93
Purdy, Harold J., 259

race relations, 45–51, 150, 192, 205,
    216–17, 225
racial segregation, 150, 172–73, 202, 209
racism, 211, 212, 215
radio ministry, 164, 177
Rathbun, Pete, 263
Rayburn, Sam, 174
Reagan, Ronald, 230
recession, 26–27
reconciliation, 44, 66, 107
Redevelopment Land Agency, 201
Reedy, Ethan, 263
Reedy, Wendi, 245
Reformation, 281
reformed theology, 255, 292
regeneration, 79
Reichard, Jessie, 222
religion, and politics, 88
religious liberty, 126, 127, 131
renovation, 282
renovation project, 280
resignation, 54, 59–62, 79
"reverse-membership interviews," 260
revitalization, 240
revivals, 56, 75, 76–77, 79, 113, 156,
    158, 167, 169, 214
Richmond Times-Dispatch, 230
Riley, W. B., 141, 142, 143, 183
rioting, 216–17
riots of 1968, 65
Rise and Fall of Mars Hill, 271
rival church, 62
Roaring Twenties, 138
Roark, Nick, 293n70
Robertson, A. T., 185
Roman Catholics, 126
Roosevelt, Franklin Delano, 119, 159

Rosell, Merv, 214
Rothwell, Andrew, 27
Roy, Margaret S., 220–21, 222, 298
rules of church order and discipline, 42,
    44, 51
Russell, David, 293n70
Ryan, Raymond, 214

Sabbath breaking, 95
Sabbath laws, 96–97
"Sabbath school," 23
Saddleback Church, 283
St. Peter's Catholic Church, 203
salary, 79
Samson, George Whitefield, 14
Sangster, Libby, 195
Sankey, Ira, 27, 113
Savage, Henry H., 138
schism, 69. *See also* church splits
Schlegel, Zach, 293n70
Schmucker, Elizabeth, 241
Schmucker, Matt, 3, 241–43, 248, 254,
    258, 261, 263, 264, 265, 271–72,
    287, 288
Scripture
    authority of, 71, 139, 153
    exposition of, 10, 163
    inspiration of, 153
    wisdom of, 296
Second Baptist Church in Navy Yard, 8,
    27, 29, 48, 49–50, 134
Second Great Awakening, 3
Second London Baptist Confession, 10
segregation, 150, 172–73, 202, 205–12
self-sacrifice, 226
sentimentalism, 164
September 11 terrorist attacks, 272–78
sewage system, 33
sexual immorality, 241, 243, 245
sexual revolution, 192
Shankle, Agnes, 158–60, 163, 178, 298
Shawmut Avenue Baptist Church, 17, 34
Shaw, Rodney, 194
Shields, T. T., 141
Shiloh Baptist Church, 48–49, 132, 210
Sibbes, Richard, 252

sidewalk, 33
Simeon, Charles, 252
simplicity, 10
Sims, Jim, 236
sin
    and church splits, 65
    continuing in, 44
    conviction of, 79
    judgment of, 149
    as secret, 248
Skirving, Anna W., 29n65
Skirving, Carrie F., 29n65
Skirving, Fannie, 8, 29n65
Skirving, John, 8, 13, 29n65
Slater, Jonathan, 24n49
slave rebellion, 37
slavery, 14, 16, 24n49, 35–39
Smith, Alma C., 45
Smith, Green Clay, 1, 83–89, 93, 94, 96,
    103, 106, 107, 109, 118, 297
Smith, Jim, 282
social decay, 82
social reform, 94–98
Sorrels, Barbara, 236, 244, 247, 262
Sorrels, Bob, 227–30, 232, 236, 247, 262
Southard, Samuel, 209
Southeast DC, 200
Southern Baptist Convention, 1, 87, 106,
    143, 145, 161, 208, 230
Southern Baptist Theological Seminary
    (Southern Seminary), 107, 159, 205,
    209, 251, 253, 254, 255, 273
Southwestern Baptist Theological Semi-
    nary, 231, 233
Sovereign Grace Ministries, 291, 292
Spanish flu, 5, 128–34, 151
splits, 4, 28, 80
Spofford, Forrest, 8, 29n65, 54–57, 59,
    62
Spofford, Sarah M., 29n65
Sproul, R. C., 240, 291
Spurgeon, Charles H., 74
statement of faith, 42, 51, 144, 261, 267
Steer, John, 237
Steinle Ice Cream Parlor, 194
Sterling Park Baptist Church, 286, 288

Stiles, Mack, 287
Stockton, Amy Lee, 137–39, 145, 146
Stott, John, 252
Straton, John Roach, 137, 143, 145–46
streetcars, 198
Stuckey, John R., 216–17, 218–19,
    221–22, 231n20
substitutionary atonement, 149
suburbanization, 187–91, 196–205,
    212–15, 282
suffering, 115, 135
suicide, 244
Sumner, Charles, 10
Sunday, Billy, 113, 122n10, 125–28
Sunday school, 14, 23–25, 90–94, 99,
    124, 158, 171, 177, 185
Sunday services, 25

tax exemption, 211
taxing liquor, 87
Taylor, B. B., 87
Taylor, Clyde W., 184, 185
Taylor, Mary A. P., 29n66
temperance movement, 86–88, 95, 98
Temple of Praise, 225
testimonies, 76
theological liberalism, 88, 122, 123, 139,
    140, 178
"There Is a Fountain Filled with Blood,"
    149
Thurmond, Strom, 185
Thursz, Daniel, 201n28
Time, 181
Titanic disaster, 105–6
Together for the Gospel (T4G), 271,
    289–94
Tomme, Walt, Jr., 230–36, 238
Trainum, Charlie, 236
treasurer, 43, 55, 74
trials, 135
Trollinger, William Vance, Jr., 143n19
Trotman, Dawson E., 176
True Reformer, 87
Truman, Harry S., 169
Trumble, Carrie E., 66
Trump, Donald, 292

trustees, 43

Turner, Nat, 37

Tysons Community Church, 236

Uneasy Conscience of Modern Fundamentalism (Henry), 181

Union Army, 9, 81

Unitarianism, 10–11

United Arab Emirates, 287

United States Civil Service Commission, 107, 108

United States of America, 89, 167

unity, 51, 143

universal church, 2, 291, 293, 295

University Baptist Church (Fayetteville, AR), 293n70

University of Chicago, 107, 123, 139

University of Edinburgh, 290

urbanization, 82

urban renewal, 113

US Capitol, 117, 156, 174, 175, 254

US Capitol dome, 8, 10, 16–17, 20

Utley, Uldine, 145n27

Vail, Hattie M., 102–3

Van Osdel, Oliver Willis, 138, 145

video feed, 282

Vietnam War, 192

violence, 95, 203–5, 206

Virginia Union University, 36

visitation plan, 223, 260

Waldron, J. Milton, 132

Walker, Jane Maxine, 176–78, 198

Walker, Ralph, 159–60

Walter, Thomas Ustick, Jr., 8, 9–11, 13, 14, 16, 20, 175

Walker, William J., 49

Wanamaker, John, 111, 113

war, 275

Washington, Booker T., 35

Washington, George, 24n49, 89

Washington Post, 84, 173, 195, 196, 219

Washington Times, 100, 106, 130

Watchman, 107

Watchman-Examiner, 142

Watson, Paul C., 185

Wayland Seminary, 35, 36

Weaver, John L., 126, 128

Webster, Kenneth Dean, 147

Western Seminary, 139

Weston, Henry Griggs, 113

"What Shall the Harvest Be?," 27

Wheeler, Brad, 293n70

white flight, 196–205

White, K. Owen, 1, 144–45, 147, 157, 158–71, 183, 190, 191, 297

Williams, Granville S., 106, 107, 110

will of the majority, 59

Willow Creek Community Church, 235, 283

Winchester Baptist Church, 286

women preachers, 139, 145, 153, 160, 264

Women's Christian Temperance Union, 98

Women's Missionary Baptist Association, 205

Women's Missionary Union, 98–99

women's work, 98–103

World War I, 5, 120–25

World War II, 5, 120, 149, 154, 157, 158, 169, 192, 196–97, 200

Wright, Bland, 234–35

WWDC (radio station), 164, 177

Wyne, Roy, 200

Wyne, Susan, 200, 205

Yale University, 69

Young, Edward, 69

Young People's Society of Christian Endeavor, 109

Young, Peter H., 81–82, 102, 103

Young, William Henry, 69–73, 75, 78–79, 82

youth, 264–65

Zopf, Maxine, 261

Scripture Index

Psalms
37:5 245
127:1 239–40

Habakkuk
1:5–11 274
1:12–17 274
2:3–4 274
3 275
3:1–19 275

Matthew
7:24–27 80
16:18 2

Mark
10:45 103

Acts
6:2–4 70

1 Corinthians
14:34 146

2 Corinthians
1:3–7 135
1:14 66

Philippians
2:15 299

1 Timothy
3:1–7 .... 249, 264

2 Timothy
4:2 191

Titus
1:5–9 .... 249, 264

Hebrews
13:20–21 43

1 Peter
2:5 25

Revelation
2:5 226
22:2 225–26
22:4 226